*Radical*

# Radical Feminism

## Feminist Activism in Movement

*Finn Mackay*
University of the West of England, UK

First published 2015 by
PALGRAVE MACMILLAN

Palgrave Macmillan in the UK is an imprint of Macmillan Publishers Limited,
registered in England, company number 785998, of Houndmills, Basingstoke,
Hampshire RG21 6XS.

Palgrave Macmillan in the US is a division of St Martin's Press LLC,
175 Fifth Avenue, New York, NY 10010.

Palgrave Macmillan is the global academic imprint of the above companies
and has companies and representatives throughout the world.

Palgrave® and Macmillan® are registered trademarks in the United States,
the United Kingdom, Europe and other countries.

ISBN 978–1–137–36357–2

This book is printed on paper suitable for recycling and made from fully
managed and sustained forest sources. Logging, pulping and manufacturing
processes are expected to conform to the environmental regulations of the
country of origin.

A catalogue record for this book is available from the British Library.

A catalog record for this book is available from the Library of Congress.

This book is dedicated to:

My precious grandma, Margaret Walker (1924–2005),
to whom I owe everything

My friend and academic colleague
Jo Scamell MSc (1960–2011), a woman who walked
the walk as well as talked the talk

# Contents

# Acknowledgements

I would like to thank my editor Andrew James at Palgrave for always being enthusiastic and honest; the team have been really helpful through the process of writing this book. All the people I have met at feminist conferences and events, as well as the students I have taught, have helped me by asking questions and by presenting challenges for feminist theory; I have tried to answer some of them here. I owe thanks and gratitude to all the activists who took time to be interviewed in my research. I would also like to thank Eaves Housing for Women and Isobel, who said 'go for it' in 2004. Becca Morden and all the women on the Reclaim the Night Organising Committees past and present are due great thanks for their tireless activism and abilities to get things done. I thank all those Amazon women who I have marched alongside in the London Feminist Network and the London Reclaim the Night (RTN). Some of those women are no longer with us and are sadly missed; in particular, I take this opportunity to remember the work of warrior woman and genuine Amazon, Claudia Da Silva (1948–2012), founder of the London Centre for Personal Safety who provided feminist self-defence at our Feminism in London Conferences. Thanks are due to the inspiring activists named in this book, founders of the original UK RTN – Al Garthwaite and Sandra McNeill. I am blessed and proud to call them friends, sisters and comrades. Greenham Women and Peace Women everywhere have also been part of my feminist journey, and in particular, I owe a debt to one of the founders of Greenham Common, Helen John, who has always been an inspiration. The University of the West of England provided me with an office while I completed the book and thanks are due to all my colleagues in the sociology department. Last, but not least, thanks are due to my wife, Rosie Buckland, who read several drafts and gave invaluable suggestions, and also my cat Isambard, who regularly sat on the manuscript and provided a welcome distraction.

Finally, thanks to the women who provided endorsements and reviews of the book. I am truly humbled and honoured.

The latter section of this book on how to organise an RTN march started life originally as a blog. Sections of Chapter 8 are also reproduced from a blog for the Feminist & Women's Studies Association, first published online in June 2013. Some sections of Chapter 4 were developed from an article originally published in the *Women's Studies International Forum* (2014), 44, pp. 46–54. ISSN 0277-5395 and are reproduced with permission from Elsevier.

# Chapter 1

# Introduction: Why march through this book?

*The beginning*

In the midst of the Cold War, in a divided country, feminists were about to start a global movement that for decades to come would unite women in symbolic protest against male violence against women. Shortly before midnight on 30 April 1977, small groups of women began gathering in the centre of towns and cities across West Germany: Bochum, Frankfurt, Cologne, Hanau. They were dressed as witches, carried flaming torches and had painted women's symbols on their faces. The date of their synchronised protest was no accident. They were assembling on that night to mark what is still known across Germany as Walpurgis Night, a superstitious tradition to mark the coming of May; a time when witches and tricksters are believed to roam.

But that year, it was women who took back their streets on that dark night; on the stroke of the witching hour, women roamed freely in riotous processions down avenues and through parks where, on their own, they would have felt unsafe. They danced and laughed in city squares, and they pelted men who got in their way with flour bombs and with water pistols loaded with dye. They sang songs and chanted: we are not pieces of meat; we are not here to be leered at, grabbed at and abused; we are not cattle to be looked over by male eyes. They were protesting against sexual harassment, loudly voicing their anger against rape and all forms of sexual violence against women; they reclaimed the night to highlight how rarely they could. Men beware, they chorused, now the night belongs to women.

Those women started a movement that night; with the light of their flaming torches they passed on a tradition that has marched all over the world and which is still inspiring and empowering women everywhere to this day. The protest they popularised is called Reclaim the Night (RTN) across Europe and Asia and Take Back the Night in Canada and America. This is a book about the path that protest has taken, about how it has changed from that day to this and what that process means for the contemporary Women's Liberation Movement (WLM). It is a book about feminist activism, specifically feminist activism against male violence against women. It will speak to activists who are involved in the Women's Movement today; indeed, it will speak to anyone who believes in the urgency of change for women and who wants to think about how we might make that happen.

## *What is feminism?*

This book is in part about history; but it is also a book about our future. Not just a future for women, but also a future for all of us; a future that is more just and equitable, a future full of hope. It is my contention that feminist theory and politics contain answers that can help us get to that destination; I will try to prove this in the chapters to come. In particular, I will be exploring the politics and theory from the time known as the Second Wave of feminism and particularly from influential

American and British theorists. This is the period, from the late 1960s through to the 1980s, when feminism is last considered to have been at its height in the West. It was named the Second Wave because it was seen to follow on from a First Wave of feminism, the previous recognised upsurge of feminist activity during the 1800s and 1900s, most renowned for the activism of the Suffragettes.

It is impossible to begin a book about feminism and feminist activism though without first outlining what feminism even is, what it means and what it means to me. Feminism as a social movement can be defined in a very broad sense as a global, political movement for the liberation of women and society based on equality for all people. However, as any activist reading this will know, perhaps too well, there are probably as many unique definitions of feminism as there are people who identify as feminists. The term means different things to different people, it also freights meaning and it is charged with symbolism, not all of it positive. There is no one, agreed, unifying definition of feminism that I can outline neatly and clearly once and for all. To complicate matters further still, there are several different recognised types, tendencies or schools of feminism within this broad movement itself; each of them are overarching types which themselves contain additional diversification and disagreement. To name just a few of the recognised schools of feminism, there is liberal feminism, socialist feminism, anarcho-feminism, black feminism, womanism, eco-feminism, radical feminism, lesbian feminism, separatist feminism, pro-feminism and revolutionary feminism. I will attempt further explanation later, but throughout this book, I will be focussing mainly on just one of these schools: radical feminism. This is the school of feminism to which I subscribe. It is also the school of feminism that has arguably contributed most feminist theory on male violence against women, its causes, consequences and what we can do about it. The Reclaim the Night or RTN protest was just one of the ways that feminists did something about it, and, as I will show, it was radical feminists who played an influential role in making this happen and in bringing this protest to the UK.

The above typology of different schools and labels of feminism might not mean much to contemporary feminists or to women's rights activists who are reading this book today. It might seem like so much divisive division of what should be an all too simple matter; the matter of pursuing equality for women in all spheres, from the workplace, to the streets, to the home. Such a goal should surely be one that nobody could disagree with, much less fight over or create conflicts around. I understand the frustrations with such divisions, and throughout this book, I will explore some of them and uncover what theory and ideas lie behind them. Firstly, on a more positive note and in the spirit of charting our proud history, I will be spending the next chapter taking a look back at where the current UK WLM heralds from and in whose footsteps we are marching today. This history can inform and enrich our present work today and enable us to learn from mistakes and successes. Looking back like this helps us to see how far we have come, but for many in this movement, although much has changed for the better in terms of women's rights, the struggle will not be finished until patriarchy is overthrown.

## *What is patriarchy?*

So what is patriarchy? In its form as a social movement, which we can call the WLM, the purpose of feminism is to, as the feminist scholar bell hooks summarised so succinctly in 2004: 'challenge, change and ultimately end patriarchy' (2004:108). The term 'patriarchy' itself is one you will probably read and hear often in feminist circles, on and offline, in academia, in journalism and in blogs. I will use it frequently throughout this book. The term originally comes from the Greek language, and strictly speaking, it means the rule of the father. It is used mainly to describe a male head of household or a father or grandfather who headed up a family. But the term is now more widely and generally used to mean male rule or male dominance; for example, male dominance or male superiority in a whole community, a whole society or a whole world. Feminists use The P Word to refer to male supremacy, to societies where men as a group dominate mainstream positions of power in culture, politics, business, law, military and policing, for example – societies like ours.

Historians, such as Gerda Lerner in her 1986 book on the history of patriarchy, argue persuasively that male supremacy has marked social governance across the globe for a long, long time – for thousands and thousands of years. Lerner mainly argues this on the grounds that no evidence can be found for anything contrary. She contends that no evidence exists of any society or nation characterised by female supremacy; where women as a group have had power and control over men in every sphere of life, including their personal affairs such as reproduction and sexuality. Such a society, marked by female supremacy and male inferiority, would be termed a matriarchy; it would be a mirror image of patriarchy, just as unequal, but with women in charge instead of men. It is unlikely such a situation has ever existed and hopefully it never will. It is important to understand that this is not the destination that feminism is aiming for, contrary to many of the popular myths about feminism.

Feminism is a movement for change, not a changing of the guard. By this, I mean that we are not working for a world unchanged apart from the leadership. Ours is a revolutionary movement, thus it is about a different type of world altogether, one not marked by extremes of poverty and wealth, or by war and exploitation. Neither has our movement been struggling for centuries simply for equality with unequal men. In this book, I will address such myths and misunderstandings that surround feminism and its aims. This is an important task, because setting the record straight will give contemporary activists the opportunity to make up their own mind about one of the oldest and most powerful social justice movements the world has ever known – their own.

Too often, the lies that are told about feminism alienate people from this movement, particularly younger women. Some contemporary forms of activism also seek to define themselves against an imagined feminist past and in doing so they sometimes write off Second Wave politics as outdated, redundant, tired and second-hand. This perspective continues to flourish and thrive, even in the face of much evidence to the contrary. But when most of this evidence is offline, in archives and collections which are hardly easy access, it is not surprising that misconceptions about feminism are allowed to gather pace, growing stronger whenever the movement peaks again. If we are to avoid recycling lies, circulating incorrect received wisdom, reinventing wheels and spiralling down familiar debates then we have to escape a tradition of historical amnesia and reclaim what our retro feminist theory and activism has to offer us.

This feminism of the Second Wave is often called history, yet it is as relevant today as it ever was. It contains much of value to current feminist activists and to all people concerned with social justice. Many progressive women and men today are hungry for their history, or herstory, are curious to know where the contemporary manifestation of feminism began, what shaped its journey and how it differs from forms of activism today. This interest is partly because feminism is enjoying another peak today. Here in the UK a resurgence of feminism has been sweeping our shores since the early 2000s, and despite much efforts, it seems unstoppable. Whether we term this a new wave of feminism or not, whether we give it a number or whatever we call this new observable upsurge of feminist voices and feminist activism, it has the potential to leave a changed world in its wake; indeed, it is already doing so.

This new generation of feminist activists are stirring up a new women's movement; they are also active in struggles for social justice more generally. They can be found organising, supporting and leading in movements against cuts to welfare rights and in organisations against war and imperialism for example. This is admirable and urgent because it is not an easy time to be pursuing social justice, not for feminists or any other activists; we are facing a seemingly relentless rising tide of neo-liberalism. By this, I mean the not-so-new approach to the world that applies market rule to every area of life, not just in finance and business, but also in healthcare, education and welfare for example. These are all essential services, yet increasingly around the world, including in the UK, they are being privatised and treated as profit-making opportunities rather than as human rights. With this move comes decreasing access to such essentials, especially for poor and marginalised people. As competition generally increases, wealthy countries step up their military and economic might and wrestle for control over natural resources they can exploit for profit. The scholar Lisa Duggan has written about this process in her excellent book *The Twilight of Equality* (2004), which also provides a good history and background to just what this concept, neo-liberalism, actually means and where it comes from.

Alongside this shift, and not unrelated to it, individualism has increased and collective social movements have taken a battering. The new generation of activists, the likes of whom I have met and introduce in this book, is also a generation that has grown up being taught that they can be whoever and whatever they wish to be and that the only thing standing in their way is themselves and their own will and ambition. This myth of meritocracy and equal opportunities encourages individualism over collective action, because when people believe this myth, they obviously see no need for protest movements around particular classes or identities, such as the Women's Movement or the Civil Rights Movement. If things do not go well for people in the workplace, education or in their personal lives, they are more likely to blame themselves, rather than sexism, racism, class oppression or homophobia; concepts which in current society are often seen as out of date. This type of blame even applies to experiences of actual violence or harassment, with too many people believing that it is their fault if they are sexually harassed in the workplace or at school, abused by a partner or are a victim to sexual violence. Our society encourages this view, and in turn that keeps people isolated and alone, rather than providing them the opportunity to get involved in collective struggles against such common experiences. These are common experiences which are symptoms of an unequal, sexist world; they are not symptoms of what clothes someone chose to wear, who they dated, where they worked, what time of night they were walking home or what alcohol they had been drinking; nor are they caused by a lack of independence or willpower. This symptomatic violence is just one issue that feminism has long been tackling, and is one area where today's feminism is making a difference: on the life and death issue of male violence against women.

## What is male violence against women?

The current resurgence of feminism is taking on in new ways some of the oldest and most pressing injustices against women, and male violence is a unifying concern. This is also of course the key focus of global RTN marches. But what exactly do feminists mean when they refer to 'male violence against women', and how can this term make sense when violence is sometimes committed by women, including against other women, and when men are victims of violence too? The term applies to rape, domestic abuse, forced marriage, sexual assault, child sexual abuse, stalking, sexual exploitation in prostitution and trafficking for prostitution, female genital mutilation and so-called 'honour crimes'. It is estimated that up to three million women every year in the UK are affected by these crimes and male violence against women remains one of the biggest human rights challenges across the globe. The crimes listed above constitute, though by no means exhaustively, what I mean by the term 'male violence against women'. More formal, official definitions can be found in policy documents such as those from the United Nations, where it is often referred to, just to confuse my efforts at clarity, as 'gender-based violence'. For example, in the snappily titled 1993 UN *Declaration on the Elimination of Violence Against Women* and in the 1979 UN *Convention on the*

*Elimination of All Forms of Discrimination Against Women* (CEDAW), violence against women is defined as physical, sexual or psychological violence against women because of their sex alone or where such violence affects women disproportionately.

The precursor term 'male', which I am using here and throughout this book, is often missing from these policy and legal documents on violence against women. They often refer euphemistically to just 'violence against women' or to the supposedly neutral 'gender-based violence'. Such phrasing is significant – I suggest that it is not accidental either; and it is profoundly political. Language matters, and this type of language suggests parity, it suggests gender neutrality; because the terminology is not sexed, it is therefore both and neither male nor female. By referring to gender-based violence, the sexed facts and reality of sexual violence and intimate partner and family violence for example, are hidden and obscured in plain sight. The focus is stealthily shifted away from the brutal fact that men are overwhelmingly the perpetrators of such crimes and that women are overwhelmingly the victims.

But why does it matter what we call it, as long as there is concerted action to respond to and prevent such crimes? It matters because if we really want to fix something that is broken, if we want to heal these fractures in our society, then we need to understand their causes. If we do not, then we will forever continue to place giant sticking plasters over the wounds left by this violence, trying to bandage over losses that can never be replaced. As long as this violence continues, it is obviously the case that we do have to address the symptoms, but my argument is that we must also address the causes if we want a long-term reduction or even, perhaps, the eventual eradication of male violence against women. To this end, it is important to acknowledge that this type of violence is not a natural phenomenon, like bad weather. It does not just happen, it is not a fact of life; it is a fact of inequality. It has a perpetrator and a victim, it has a cause and likewise, it has a cure. The most important and relevant lesson feminism has taught us is that male violence against women is not biological, it is political. And if it is made, then it can be un-made; if it is learnt, it can be un-learnt. This is just one of the positive and inspiring messages from feminism that I will be covering in this book.

Feminism is not afraid to name the perpetrators of violence against women or gender-based violence by referring to these crimes specifically as male violence against women. This terminology is emphasised in many explicitly feminist approaches, but is particularly present in the theory found in radical feminism. This school of feminism defines male violence against women as both a cause and a consequence of male supremacy and female inferiority; and as a symptom of patriarchy. What this definition means is that while male violence is indeed a blunt and bloody symptom of patriarchy, it is also, at the same time, a foundation which props up patriarchy. If this definition is accepted, then it is vital to address and challenge patriarchy as part of the struggle to end all forms of male violence against women. Contrary to anti-feminist myths, feminism has promised that this is possible; feminism promotes the belief that all of us can change, that men are not naturally violent or abusive. This is an important facet of feminist theory to grasp, because it goes against that most well-known lie about feminism, the lie that our movement hates men and defines and reduces all men to rapists and abusers. Feminism actually does not let men off the hook in this way.

The theory and politics from feminism is far removed from what is called biological determinism or essentialism. This means that feminism does not believe that there is anything in men's biology that makes them violent, nor does feminism believe that there is some essential truth or essence to men that makes them inherently violent. It is in nobody's interests to write our futures in stone like this, or rather, to write off our futures. We understand that most men do not rape or abuse the women and children they know and love; we posit that this means there is no excuse for the men who choose to do so. Radical feminist theory in particular, identifies male violence against women as a form of social control. This perspective highlights that when they do happen, these widespread and targeted acts of violence affect all women, whether we personally are lucky enough to have avoided them or not. They affect all women by restricting women's freedom, liberty and personhood. All women, in all our diversity, know what it is to live with the fear or reality of male violence. I will be discussing this perspective in much more detail later in this book, and exploring further the reasons behind such epidemic levels of male violence against women and what we might do to end it.

*Feminist activism against male violence against women*

Although I am focussing on quite recent feminist activism and theory against male violence against women, this activism is by no means new. There has likely been resistance to such violence for as long as it has existed, and there has been organised feminist resistance across the world for centuries. RTN is just one such way that people have organised this resistance. The march is still a common and powerful response today. It was how communities responded to the tragic rape and murder of Jill Meagher, walking home one night in Melbourne, Australia, in September 2012. It was also how people protested in towns and cities across India, reacting to the news of the horrific gang rape and murder of a 23-year-old student in Delhi, attacked by a group of men while she was travelling home by bus.

The thousands of people who take part in these protests all over the world are marching in the foot-steps of the brave and pioneering women who founded such methods of activism decades before. Those women set in place these tactics of direct action, and they also established support services and provisions for women affected by male violence. In the UK, these activists built women's refuges, they founded the Women's Aid Federation in 1974, they set up Rape Crisis Centres in 1976; they brought the crimes of male violence into the public domain, into the light of day. In so doing, they changed laws, policies, hearts and minds, and they saved lives. The legacy of the services they created is still benefitting women, children and, indeed, men to this day, albeit under almost continual funding threats which endanger decades of specialist work. This is especially the case now, as ideological welfare cutbacks are attempting to push women back into the home where they are expected to do caring work for no pay, caring work they may have previously done outside the home for low pay. Facts of unequal life, facts such as domestic abuse and sexual violence, are seen in this neo-liberal climate as private, individual matters. Those affected are expected to fund their own support or to find it themselves within the nuclear family. Despite all the work feminists have done, such services are still considered far from essential, and in times of recession, they are often the first to be dropped.

Much has been written on the legal and policy work to reduce male violence against women, so it is the specific activist response that I focus on here in this book. While researching such activism in the form of RTN, it has become clear that not much history of this protest has been written down. There is a great deal of theorising, reflection and analysis of other street protests, for example the anti-capitalist Reclaim the Streets Movement across the UK and Europe in the 1990s, or the environmentalist anti-roads protests in Britain in the same period. While many arty coffee table books of photojournalism document the colourful, creative and angry methods of such protests, nothing similar exists on RTN. This is despite this movement being a global protest and being just as colourful, creative and angry. Perhaps because it has traditionally, and often still is currently, women-only, this method of protest has been considered too controversial or niche for scholars who often too readily settle on examples of male, perhaps macho, political heroes. Whatever the reasons may be, RTN is often absent from histories of social movements, from academic studies of street marching and protest and from herstories of the WLM. Given its global reach, and continuing relevance and resonance with a new generation of feminists, I hope to demonstrate in this book that this is a serious omission.

To remedy this omission, I will provide a background to the emergence of RTN in Europe and to how it was born in the UK in 1977. For the first time I will put on record the herstory of this important protest. I will also go back further still, to explain some of the background to the WLM of the Second Wave, looking at how the term 'women's liberation' came into being and how the Second Wave began in the US and the UK in the late 1960s. While marching through the chapters of this book, as well as learning about the history and present of feminist activism, you will also travel through some of the most controversial issues affecting feminism today. Just as in the past, there are still many different definitions and understandings about what feminism is and what it means; there are still also feminists aligned to certain schools or types of feminism rather than others. There are also still several areas on which feminists disagree, and some arguments which have been going on for decades; our movement is by no means one unified family. These disagreements are being discussed both within and outside the movement, on and offline.

These disagreements concern issues such as the role of men in feminism; the inclusion of transgender, transexual or self-identified gender-queer people in feminism; and also the long-running divisions between feminists positive about the so-called sex industry – namely, prostitution and pornography – and those feminists who include these institutions in their definitions of male violence against women. Adopting a phrase from the well-known feminist activist and policy theorist, Professor Liz Kelly, I refer to these divisions as 'feminist fault lines'. This is not to suggest however that these are the only controversial areas of feminist debate; our movement has more than its fair share of disagreement. However, these are the main disagreements which impact on the organisation of RTN marches and which affect the activist organisers who are trying to make those marches successful. I will therefore explore these particular disagreements in this book. I will try to show that it is only from carefully considering such conflicts that theory and practice can move forward. Although it can seem off-putting to new feminists or those interested in women's rights, discussion, debate, conflict and difference is an essential part of feminism, as it is of any social movement that continues to live, grow and learn.

## *Difference and intersectionality*

Many of these disagreements between feminists obviously come down to personal political standpoints, but many of them also emerge from power relationships between women. It should go without saying that not all women are the same; there are differences between women, powerful differences of power. These have always been, and remain, potential areas of division and exclusion in the WLM. For example, along the social fractures of ethnicity, social class, sexuality, age, caring responsibilities, immigration status, economic position, health and language to name but a few. All of us, women and men, inhabit all of these identities, by which I mean that all of us have an ethnic background, a first language, an age, a sexuality, a social class background, a sexed identity, a gender identity, a body with differing degrees of health and an economic position which may or may not be strong.

These identities also change for all of us; they are not fixed, they do not stay the same. For example, we may become parents or we may become carers of elderly or sick relatives, we may become disabled ourselves or get ill, we may change our religion or our sexual identity or we may change our sex or gender identity. Our concerns and priorities will react as these identities flux and alter. The changes and intersection of these identities affect how we experience our world, and the barriers we may face, based on the differing levels of power and privilege that society attaches to certain identities rather than others. Ours is unfortunately a racist, sexist, homophobic and prejudiced society; these structural inequalities affect all of us and they have not gone away, despite the claims of neo-liberal narratives and despite the assertions of some queer politics or third wave feminism. These inequalities affect feminists too and they also play out within the WLM. Women are not immune to such prejudices of course, but neither are they immune to enacting prejudice against others.

There is a special term used in feminism to describe the fact of multiple and intersecting identities and the structural power relationships between them; that term is 'intersectionality'. The term was first coined by feminist legal scholar Professor Kimberle Crenshaw in 1989. She used the term in an article about how Black women are failed in employment discrimination cases, by a legal system that can only respond to them as either Black, or as women, but not as both. Crenshaw pointed out that Black women often faced discrimination precisely because they were Black and women. In the legal cases she documented, women testified that they saw White female employees being treated differently to them and Black male employees being treated differently to them too. So it was not as simple as identifying the prejudice they experienced against them as just racism or just sexism, it was both of those mixed together.

Crenshaw used a metaphor to explain this position; she said it was like someone standing at a crossroads or intersection, with traffic rushing towards them from all different directions. They were going to be knocked over and hurt by that speeding traffic, and it would not be an easy job to say precisely which lane of traffic or which car had hurt them the most, it was a combination of forces that hit them and harmed them. The same is true with the intersection of personal identities; these cross over, they run into one another and form a unique blend, so identities such as race and sex cannot be separated, they in fact intersect. The term 'intersectionality' has become widely used, especially in feminist activist circles, to refer to how power relationships intersect within certain groups, as well as between groups. It draws our attention to fractures of race, social class and sexuality between women themselves; for example, it usefully highlights the point I emphasised above, that women are not a homogenous group.

We can use the idea of intersectionality to consider our own identity. Being aware of our own identities, and acknowledging and understanding how these bring us varying levels of privilege compared to others is an important political reflection. It helps us to understand our personal biographies, our life history and how the society around us has shaped those and continues to shape our futures. When we consider ways that certain elements of our identity have brought us access, or resulted in us being excluded, we can extend this awareness to analyse whether and in what ways we may be part of excluding others. We can aspire in our language and in our actions to be inclusive, rather than exclusive, to remember that we cannot speak for everybody; not even everybody who belongs to the same group that we do, for example, all women, all lesbian, bisexual or gay people or all Black people. This awareness is called having an intersectional approach and it has become central to contemporary feminist activism, sometimes perhaps in ways that were never intended when the term was first coined, and perhaps in some ways that ironically hold the movement back rather than helping it to grow. Later in this book, I shall delve further into these often-fraught debates, presenting the views of contemporary feminist activists on just what this terminology means to them and their activism.

## *Positionality: Where does the writer speak from?*

For now, because it is important to be transparent about our identities and understand how they act upon our lives and the lives of others, I shall outline my own identity and the position from which I speak. This is what is called 'positionality', and all writers, commentators, academics, journalists and bloggers speak from a certain position or standpoint. No researcher or writer lives in a vacuum, nobody is neutral. Our opinions on social issues are shaped and informed by our own life experiences and in turn, those life experiences are shaped by the very social issues that we comment upon; I am no exception.

Different elements of my identity have shaped my own biography and trajectory in life, contrastingly benefitting or hindering my journey. I am White, Scottish and I come from a very rural, working-class area of Scotland, largely dominated by farming and forestry. I identify as a radical feminist. I am also an out lesbian. I am lucky enough to have no serious disabilities and I have benefited from a university education. Although my family were far from rich, I was enriched by many books in the house and by the left-wing political opinions of my parents and my parents' friends, which instilled in me a passion for politics and particularly for protest politics about matters that affected daily life. I was never interested in how a bill becomes law or in the difference between a white or a green paper. I was interested in how ordinary people could get issues onto the public agenda and make things happen. From a very early age, I wanted to be one of those people.

In 2004, I founded the London Feminist Network, a network aimed at bringing together feminist groups and individuals in action. As part of this group, I also revived the London RTN in the same year. I had been somewhat disappointed by the lack of feminist activity in the capital at that time, having moved there in 2002 to work in a small charity offering advice and guidance to Scots in London. My own political background is rooted in the Women's Peace Movement, where I cut my political teeth in my late teens. I was looking for similar, lively, angry and practical feminist activism when I moved to London; instead, I found little activism around and most of it online only.

My interest in the Women's Peace Movement goes back a long way. As a child, I was obsessed with the women's peace camp at Greenham Common in Newbury, Berkshire in the South of England, which was active during the 1980s. Lasting approximately 12 years, this protest remains one of the largest women's peace camps the world has ever known, sometimes attracting 50,000 women to particular demonstrations, including what were called Embrace the Base actions. This was where rings of women held hands and encircled the nine and half mile perimeter fence of the US military base blockading entry to military and civilian personnel. The women were protesting against nuclear cruise missiles being stationed at Greenham, and they established many creative and humorous methods of campaigning, which we now call non-violent direct action or NVDA. They blockaded the gates to the military base to stop convoys of trucks carrying missiles from leaving on manoeuvres for example, they organised mass trespasses into the base, often in fancy dress, they utilised criminal damage to sabotage military machinery and they also made their oppositional presence felt by camping directly outside the gates of the base, living outdoors in all weathers. They bore witness to the military machinations of those protecting weapons of mass destruction, and, in their novel approach, they drew the eyes of the world onto what was supposed to be a top-secret military establishment.

Growing up in isolated rural Scotland, I was many miles and far removed from this type of revolutionary women-only protest. Fortunately, I saw coverage on the news and my parents were also friends with two women who spent their holidays camping at Greenham; from the age of seven, I was hooked. I listened to vinyl records of Greenham women's peace songs, I designed my own Greenham supporter tee shirts and waited for the day I could be part of it myself. Alas, I was born too late, and by the time I was a teenager, the Greenham protestors had been in place long enough to watch the last American soldier leave by the gates they had built and the base was being cleaned up and used by NATO for exercises. It was eventually given back to the local council in Newbury though, and much of it turned back into common land for local people and businesses. This did not spell the general demise of the patriarchal, military industrial complex in the UK, however; that was unfortunately far from dormant.

I was thus able to become part of another, more recent women's peace camp instead, protesting outside the largest US listening base in the world, a place called Menwith Hill in Yorkshire, run by the National Security Agency or NSA of America. Following the Snowden revelations of 2013 and allegations of economic, political and military spying by the US, which have emerged from Wikileaks, for example, the NSA is an organisation now far more well known than it was when local CND, Greenham and peace activists in Yorkshire began to organise resistance outside Menwith Hill in the 1980s. Many Greenham women were part of this protest, including a woman called Helen John, who was one of the original founders of the Greenham Common Women's Peace Camp in 1981 and who then became involved in building a permanent women's peace camp outside the base at Menwith.

I was 17 when I first got involved in the protest at Menwith Hill, or Wo-Menwith Hill as we called it. I then moved to live at the peace camp when I was 18, and lived there permanently for about a year. I took part in all elements of the campaign. I wrote newsletters, conducted media interviews, organised protests, took part in NVDA, defended myself in court and fundraised for the peace camp. Our camp ran as a collective as much as possible, we had circle meetings to discuss most things, from the serious to the mundane. We shared tasks and somehow, without rotas or too much arguing, everything that needed doing seemed to get done, whether it be chopping firewood or washing muddy plates. It was this sense of collective, real-time rather than online, women-only, dynamic and direct protest that I was looking for in the WLM of the early 2000s. When I couldn't find it, I decided to try to build it myself.

## Reviving Reclaim the Night

In the summer of 2004, I floated the idea of an activist network for London on the few feminist online lists and egroups that I knew of. I sent out an email asking any interested women to meet in the café space of the Royal Festival Hall in central London on the South Bank of the River Thames. Around six women turned up to that first meeting; they were all energised and enthusiastic about a face-face, activist network in London to co-ordinate activities and plan possible events. We arranged another meeting and similarly advertised it around the few online groups that we knew of; at that time, the online presence of feminism was nothing like it is now. It was really only in its early stages. The advert obviously travelled around though, virtually and by word of mouth, because at the next meeting around a dozen women participated. Women wanted to plan campaigns we could run, events we could set up and actual, physical, real things that we could do, rather than just talking about things online. So the meetings continued to grow and word continued to spread, so much so that in that November of 2004, the London Feminist Network, as I named it, held the first revived London RTN march, following a break of that type of protest in the capital for several years.

I had long wondered why RTN had appeared to decline across the UK, seemingly since the 1990s, albeit still being kept alive by some women's sector organisations and by creative university women's officers in the National Union of Students. I had learnt about the history of this protest from women I had met through the Women's Peace Movement; in particular, from a feminist activist named Al Garthwaite from Leeds in Yorkshire, who founded the first RTN marches in the UK in 1977. I had listened intently to stories of women marching through city streets with flaming torches. I knew all the words of the folk singer Peggy Seeger's 'Reclaim the Night' song and I wondered why, with a rape conviction rate estimated at only around 6 per cent, this urgent protest had so declined.

When Sylvia Walby and Jonathan Allen's report on the British Crime Survey in 2004 suggested that one in four women were living with domestic violence and that

around 60,000 women every year were affected by rape,
I remember discussing with other feminists why we were
not taking to the streets any more. It seemed to me that
demonstrations like RTN were needed more, not less,
than they had been in the 1970s. It transpired that a few
others thought the same and that some of them were
even willing to help make it happen. So, with the help of
women at the Lilith Project, part of Eaves Housing for
Women, who offered assistance with photocopying fliers
and setting up a website, the London Feminist Network
organised a small RTN march in November of 2004.
We had no idea how many women would attend, but a
small group of 50 assembled at Euston station to march
through parts of Camden and into Cambridge Circus
near an area called Soho in central London. At that
point, the local police had no idea who we were or what
our protest would look like. We did not get roads closed
down for us and we had to march down the pavements
all the way, with some women carrying candles in jars
and veterans teaching us old chants and songs from the
original marches. We could not afford to hire a venue
to hold a rally at the end of our march, as we do now,
so we just gathered in Cambridge Circus, outside a the-
atre there, and sang our songs and waved our banners,
before retiring to one of the many nearby pubs.

From those small beginnings, the revived London
RTN grew and grew. It expanded into a central event
on the feminist and women's sector calendar. It now has
the support of most major Trade Unions, of women's
sector organisations and of many organisations working
for peace, human rights and justice. It regularly attracts
over 2000 women from all over the UK and beyond, and
for one night it closes down the streets of central London
so women can march for the right to live free from the
fear of male violence. The idea has caught on, and many

other towns and cities have been inspired to revive their own tradition of RTN, with several places holding their first ever marches.

RTN is not the only organised protest against male violence against women to have emerged in recent years though, indeed, this issue has become a key feature of the growing feminist resurgence. Million Women Rise (MWR), founded in 2008, for example, is an annual march through London against all forms of male violence against women; it is held to mark International Women's Day, which is held annually on 8 March. Attracting attention more recently, the so-called SlutWalks against violence against women, emerged firstly in Canada and then in the UK in 2011. These usually mixed marches were a response to what is known as victim-blaming; this is the term used to describe the phenomenon whereby society appears to blame the victims of male sexual violence for crimes against them, rather than the perpetrators themselves. You can see this phenomenon sometimes in media reports of rape, where great attention is paid to whether a female victim was walking alone, or to what she was wearing, whether she had been drinking alcohol and whether the attack took place late at night for example. The SlutWalk grew out of such victim-blaming, the march being provoked by advice to women from a male police officer in Toronto, Canada, who warned women not to dress like 'sluts' if they wanted to avoid rape and sexual assault. These marches drew a lot of attention globally. This attention was arguably partly due to their title and the fact that some participants attempted to protest victim-blaming by marching in clothes they believed society would view as 'slutty', meaning sexually 'provocative' or overtly sexual. RTN is not the same as SlutWalk. It covers similar issues, but it does it with clothes on. Unlike SlutWalk, RTN also has a long history going back to the 1970s and it is truly global. My own interest in the history of RTN and my own involvement in its resurgence are what motivated me to research this area.

## *Background to the book*

The activist voices that you will hear in this book come from individuals involved in RTN and in many other social justice protests and movements. The research I carried out, however, was specifically on views and experiences of RTN, the UK WLM and feminism more broadly. I conducted 25 face-to-face interviews with feminist activists and surveyed 108 using an online survey. All participants had either marched or organised on RTN, they came from all over the UK, from a variety of backgrounds and they had been active feminists for between one to over 40 years. I carried out the research in early 2012 and it was part of my PhD fieldwork for my thesis on changes in the British WLM, which I completed at the University of Bristol in 2013.

Much of the data I gathered on my field trips around the UK is presented in this book, in the form of activist accounts and direct quotes from activists themselves in their own voice. To research the beginnings of RTN and of the Second Wave in the UK, I also turned to feminist archives such as those in Bristol and Leeds run by the charity the Feminist Archive, where many original fliers, posters, badges and photographs of the early RTN marches can be found. I used collections of feminist magazines from the Second Wave, such as *Spare Rib*, probably one of the most well known of the British feminist magazines in the 1970s and 1980s, which was published until 1993. I also used periodicals that will be less well known, such as the *Rev/Rad Newsletter*, the Revolutionary and Radical Feminist Newsletter, which looks a bit like what we now call zines. It was printed on old print presses, stapled by hand and mailed out to activists around the country. Similar amounts of hard work, late nights and repetitive strain injury went into the higher circulation *WIRES*, the Women's Information Referral and Enquiry Service, which was the official newsletter of the British WLM from 1975 until 1985. These periodicals trace the history of RTN in the UK, through letters, adverts and articles, right from when it first started.

Searching through these archive materials and interrogating the memories of those who marched on the original UK RTN, I hope to show you how the protest has changed over the last 40 years. I will consider whether these changes are positive or negative and what we can learn from them. Rather than dismissing the Second Wave period of feminism out of hand or simply describing only the current feminist resurgence, I hope to analyse both together, and consider what original feminist theory can offer to the struggles we are facing today; some of which are remarkably similar to those addressed by the feminists before us. To do this I will translate, or perhaps re-translate, classic radical feminist texts, in particular the 1969 publication from Kate Millett, *Sexual Politics*, which still stands as one of the most enlightening and surgical analyses of patriarchy ever written. Forget the myths you have heard about radical feminism, for only some of them are true. Instead, prepare to think about why so many lies are told about this particular brand of feminism, how it acts as a scapegoat for all that is most threatening about our social movement and how any revolutionary movement for change could

really ever be anything but threatening. These are the
women you were warned about; you can be too.


## The route

The next chapter will provide a brief introduction to
the emergence of Second Wave feminism in the UK
and the influences from America and from the many
social movements active at the time. The New Left, civil
rights, Black Power, gay liberation and anti-war organising all influenced this recent upsurge of feminism.
In the UK, things really got started in 1970 with the
famous women's rights conference at Ruskin College
in Oxford. Following that, National Women's Liberation Conferences began to be held regularly and many
magazines and journals were produced. Throughout it
all, male violence against women was a key concern,
becoming addressed in one of the Seven Demands of the
UK WLM.

In Chapter 3, I will look at some of the differences
I mentioned between feminists and between different
types or schools of feminism. I will introduce some basic
defining features of these different schools and note
some of the main sites of divergence. One of the big
disagreements which complicated and enriched much of
the activism and theory on male violence against women
was that between socialist feminists and radical feminists.
These two schools of feminism disagreed over the causes
of male violence against women and consequently, over
what should be done about it and what methods of
protest should be used. These conflicts played out in
RTN, not least in some of the criticisms of the original
marches which still influence perceptions today.

The herstory of RTN will be put on record in
Chapter 4, from its European roots to its fiery progress

across the globe. In this chapter, I will also shed light on the beginnings of RTN in the UK in the city of Leeds in the North of England. I will present some of the possible influences behind the protest march emerging when and where it did, because the location of Leeds was far from random. High-profile crimes against women during the mid-1970s and the slow, sexist and disorganised police response were all motivators for the march, as was the sophisticated sharing of international news throughout the Women's Movement and the UK coverage of the German RTN. This period was a time when new feminist theory on male violence against women was in development and in contestation; issues such as rape were just being taken up in the new Rape Crisis Movement and in local action groups. Socialist and radical feminists clashed, as did the autonomous anti-rape groups with the organised actions of a group called Wages for Housework. As well as delving into these theoretical disagreements, this chapter will also consider some of the early but long-lasting controversy around RTN; namely, the charges of racism made against the UK marches.

Continuing the theme of disagreement and conflict, Chapter 5 will look at how the modern RTN has fared in a climate influenced by queer theory and by new liberation movements. Queer theory is not just a strand of scholarship, investigation and academia; it also refers to a politics and to methods of activism. The term 'queer' is also a label that many of the new generation of feminist activists use to describe themselves. It has become a label particularly for those who do not wish to be boxed in by the conventional, narrow categories for sex, gender and sexual orientation. For those who feel their sexuality is more fluid than the standard tick boxes of LGB – lesbian, gay or bisexual – and for those who feel their gender identity is not typically masculine or feminine, for example, 'queer' can be a useful and inclusive descriptor.

In this climate, challenges to feminism have questioned to what extent a movement can really speak or act for such a diverse group as women. Here I will state some of the main differences between radical feminist theory and queer theory on such questions – questions of sex, gender and structural inequality for example. However, in this chapter, I will also consider some of the similarities and the debt that much queer theory owes to feminism, particularly early radical feminist thought.

In Chapter 6, the voices of contemporary feminist activists can be found, with the ideas and motivations of marchers today being compared with the views of original marchers from the past. This chapter looks at how the practicalities of the march have evolved, in policing and in direct action for example. Activists provide different reasons for observed changes in RTN, including the influence of neo-liberal narratives and also the influence of third wave feminism. I explore their views of this particular brand of feminism, many of which were negative. This chapter also introduces one of the biggest and most controversial changes in RTN – the shift to including men on marches.

Chapter 7 focusses in more depth on the shift from women-only to mixed marches, which has happened over the course of RTN from the 1970s to the present day. This chapter outlines and explores the main key arguments made in favour of male inclusion and the counter arguments against. The activists I met were mainly pragmatic about expanding the borders of the march and building a successful and well-attended event. Alongside that however, there was often a tension between unease about excluding anyone and an emotional connection to women's leadership.

Chapter 8 continues to look at the shifting borders around the march and explores wider issues of exclusion and inclusion on RTN. Not just in terms of men's presence on the marches, but considering the role of self-defined transgender or queer activists and also the competing arguments over the approaches marches take towards the sex industry. In this book, I use the term 'transgender' to refer to those people who identify as non-gender normative or as non-binary; that means anyone who does not consider their presentation or their identity to be feminine or masculine in a mainstream way – they cross the lines of gender. I use the term 'transexual' to refer to those people who have chosen to legally, socially and perhaps medically cross the lines of sex – that is, they define as the opposite sex to that which they were labelled at birth. As a shorthand, I will sometimes use the term 'trans' rather than the two terms 'transexual' and 'transgender'; though there are in fact important differences between these two identity categories, as I cover in more detail in Chapter 5. When I refer to trans women, I mean transexual women, and when I refer to trans men, I mean transexual men. Issues around the inclusion and exclusion of groups such as trans women and also men and queer activists shape the form that RTN marches take; they also affect those organisers who are trying to build large and successful marches. This chapter explores some of the common critiques and arguments that these activist organisers face, critiques which are based on quite abstract gender and queer theory but which have very real and practical ramifications.

Feminism is not all about controversy and disagreement though, and in Chapter 9, I will look at the many aims and motivations which feminists of all different tendencies shared. I asked all the activists I met about what sort of feminist world they were working towards and what short-term goals or indicators of feminist success we might be able to focus on now. This chapter then compares those aspirations to the previous goals of the Second Wave in the Seven Demands and invites contemporary activists to update and add more to this wo-manifesto.

The last chapter, Chapter 10, forms a brief conclusion and summarises the history, theory and activism which I have explored in this book. I have only touched on many issues here and there is much more to find out, not least from returning to the feminist classics from the Second Wave. While it is not the case that all the answers we are looking for will be found there in the archives and in old journals, it is certainly the case that such material contains useful information. Amongst all the mistakes of the past, there were many, many successes. It is important that we learn from both the rights and the wrongs of our movement, as well as from what lies in between, in those unsure areas from which grand theory springs. We have no shortage of such uncertainty today, as a new generation of activists try to navigate a changed terrain, where stubborn inequalities nevertheless remain the same. What we do not have so much of today is safe spaces where that journey can take place.

During the Second Wave, these places were created; their importance was understood and recognised as they gave birth to classic feminist theory, and to exciting and original methods of direct action and protest. Our WLM came from the ground up, it started with women's everyday experiences and it sought to change those for the better, for all women. In the next chapter then, I will look back at some of this herstory, at the beginnings of the Second Wave in the UK.

# Chapter 2

# Surf's up: Surfing the Second Wave

RTN is a product of the Second Wave WLM. For any modern feminist activist today, or any young person interested in women's rights, this period of time is our most recent history. It is from this peak of feminism that we have inherited many of the laws, policies, ideas and support services which we take for granted today. It was this period of feminism which most recently changed our world. Yet many activists today do not really know much about this upsurge of feminism and often what they do hear about it is biased and incorrect. To try and correct this situation, it is worth going back to the beginning and outlining just how the Second Wave began here in the UK and look at some of its main features. In this chapter then, I will firstly explain the wave narrative, I will then chart how the Second Wave began across the Western world firstly in the US and what influences lay behind that emergence. This chapter will introduce some of the classic feminist texts of this period, such as Juliet Mitchell's 1966 article 'Women: The Longest Revolution', and Betty Friedan's 1963 book *The Feminine Mystique*. Early protests will also be covered such as the dramatic demonstrations at the Miss World Pageant in London in 1969 and the foundational conference held in 1970 at Ruskin College in Oxford. The tradition of consciousness raising or CR will be explained and contextualised and the birth of famous feminist magazines and periodicals noted, such as *Spare Rib*.

## *Back to the beginnings*

RTN emerged in the UK at the height of the Second Wave WLM. The protest is just one of the many and lasting fruits of that phase of feminism. That phase was an upsurge that actually built on a much older history of course, dating back to the First Wave of feminism, to the work of the well-known Suffragettes. Most people have learnt about the Suffragette campaigns and their valiant direct action to secure the right to vote, which they eventually won in Britain for women on equal terms with men in 1928. The Suffragettes were also involved in other important campaigns though, which are far less known or publicised. They campaigned against rape within marriage for example, for fair divorce and custody laws, to raise the age of consent – which was eventually raised from 13 years old to 16 years old in 1885 – for equal education for women and also against prostitution and the prostitution of children. Many of these same campaigns were taken up again by feminists during the Second Wave from the late 1960s.

This does not mean however that this kind of feminist activism died out between these waves; indeed, many scholars have pointed out that the metaphor of a wave is perhaps misleading precisely because it obscures all the activism that was going on prior to, between and after these so-called waves. We can think of the wave descriptor as a handy and popular shorthand to refer to recognised peaks in the movement, but we must also acknowledge that this is a distinctly Western chronological measurement and that feminism certainly did not die out and rise up again in such a simplistic and linear way. Also, in other parts of the world, the progress of feminism followed a different timeline, with the 1980s for example being seen as a peak time, while here in the UK this was a decade often bemoaned by activists who felt feminism was beginning to decline. However we measure that past, in waves or peaks and troughs, all of the work that activists are doing today is influenced by what went prior and the same was true for our sisters before us, just as what we do now will, for better or worse, inspire the feminism that comes after us.

To chart where our own current resurgence comes from then, it is necessary to return to the roots of the Second Wave in the late 1960s. This was a period marked by uprisings; the WLM was just one in many of what were called New Left movements. Across Europe, in France, Italy and Germany during the 1960s, revolutionary movements, often led by students, were enjoying huge popularity. Further away, in China, Cuba and with the resistance in Vietnam, Communism was also providing inspiration to activists interested in alternatives to Western capitalism and was adding to the general revolutionary fervour that exploded across industrialised democracies following the post-war 1950s. Out of this political melting pot came the Black Power movements from the US for example, and the Civil Rights Movement and global, organised peace movements mobilised against the US war in Vietnam. This bloody war lasted from 1955 to 1975, and it was waged between the Communist North Vietnam and anti-Communist South Vietnam, the latter being supported by anti-Communist states including America. There was a huge resistance to American involvement in this war; many anti-war and pacifist organisations grew out of that resistance and many women were involved in such movements, not just in the US but across Europe too, including the UK. In fact, it was American women who had been active against the Vietnam War who were involved in founding some of the first women's liberation groups in London

during the beginnings of the UK Second Wave – as
I shall explain later.

## Sisters across the pond

It is generally recognised that the Second Wave in
the UK was influenced by the slightly earlier emergence of the WLM in America. The women who were
part of those beginnings in the US did not come from
nowhere, many of them already had political experience and a track record of activist involvement in the
New Left movements of the time, which inspired and
equipped them with the practical and theoretical knowledge needed to organise politically. Several histories
of the Second Wave, such as David Bouchier's 1983
comparison of British and American feminism, identify
anti-racism and anti-war activism for example as fertile grounds for the new manifestation of the Women's
Movement to emerge. Specifically, it was often women's
experiences of sexism in such New Left movements that
led to them identifying a need for their own spaces,
indeed, for a movement of their own. Records show
that women in the new social movements of the time
were sometimes blocked, even ridiculed and harassed
by predominantly male leaderships when they tried to
raise women's issues. Legend has it that this was why
women then had to demand their own liberation within
the liberation movements they were part of, hence the
development of the term 'women's liberation'.

Bouchier (1983) reports that the first usage of
the term itself, 'women's liberation', actually came
from women in an influential 1960s, interracial student organisation called the Student Non-violent Co-
ordinating Committee or SNCC. This was a movement

known for campaigning against racial segregation in the Southern states of America. As early as 1964, women in the SNCC in Chicago were meeting together separately to discuss their unease at the way that they and women's issues generally were being sidelined. Throughout the male-led New Left in fact, it was all too common for women activists to be expected to take on subordinate roles. In a 1968 memoir, two American activists called Beverley Jones and Judith Brown actually refer to the women activist's role at that time as a 'secretarial tour of duty for the movement' ([1968]2000:44).

Jones and Brown also recall women in another group, an international student group called Students for a Democratic Society or SDS, being shouted off stages by male colleagues when trying to speak about women's issues, and being told by male activists that they were not suited to leadership positions. These problems eventually came to a head in 1967 at the US National Conference on New Politics in Chicago, where women again found themselves silenced by a male leadership blocking women's issues from the agenda. Historian of the US WLM, Jo Freeman, herself a feminist activist, reported that at this conference, one woman delegate who protested at the situation was told by a male chairman to 'cool down little girl, we have more important things to talk about than women's liberation' (Freeman, 1975:60). He clearly did not know who he was dealing with, this nameless male chair, as the delegate in question was Shulamith Firestone, an activist who was to go on to write one of the key radical feminist texts of the Second Wave with her 1970 publication *The Dialectic of Sex: The Case for Feminist Revolution*.

Against this backdrop of sexism and marginalisation, women in the New Left movements of the US gradually began organising politically themselves, separately

from men, from around the mid-1960s onwards. Also
by this point, quite early on, a liberal feminist organisation called NOW, the National Organisation for Women,
had already been founded by author Betty Friedan. This
organisation grew out of women's dissatisfaction with
slow progress at the Third National Conference of Com-
missions on the Status of Women, where Friedan and
other delegates met to decide what could be done to
move faster on women's rights. Freidan was already well
known; she had published her groundbreaking best-
seller *The Feminine Mystique* in 1963. Her book spoke to
the disenchantment of the female half of middle-class,
White America in the 1950s, a period which saw many
women benefitting from higher education, only to be
expected to spend their lives as wives and mothers supporting their husbands to progress in their own careers.
While nobody, let alone Friedan, was suggesting that this
was in any way a lesser or demeaning option for women,
feminists *were* arguing that all women should have the
choice between the home and a career, and, perhaps
more importantly, should also be facilitated financially
and culturally to do both if they so wished. This message resonated at the time with educated women who
had found themselves isolated in the home, women who
often blamed themselves for any boredom, loneliness,
illness or insecurity that they experienced, with many
turning to individual therapy and medication as a cure.
Friedan shed light on the minutiae of their lives, noting poignantly that as these women were busy making
peanut butter and jam sandwiches, dropping their children off at school and ironing their husband's shirts,
they were all asking themselves the same question – is
this all? The book is credited with paving the way for a
broader, mainstream and sympathetic reception for the
emerging Women's Movement of the period.

NOW was not the only group to form at this time. Several women's liberation groups emerged with radical aims and less hierarchical, less formal organised structures than NOW; most were also women-only, which NOW was not. While NOW was formally mixed, men were apparently largely members on paper only and they never took leadership positions in the organisation. The new feminist groups that emerged however were explicitly women-only, and they also began to develop theories of political autonomy, separatism, political lesbianism and self-organisation for the Women's Movement; ideas which would go on to be hugely influential and be picked up by feminists in the UK too. These were pioneering groups such as The Feminists in New York founded in 1968, The Furies in Washington DC, the Redstockings also in New York and the New York Radical Women, which had been founded by Shulamith Firestone and another activist called Pat Allen in 1967. Later I will look in further detail at some of the feminist theory around separatism, so it is important at this stage to clear up right away a common misunderstanding between separatism and political autonomy. For readers less familiar with the history of Second Wave feminism, I will also discuss exactly what political lesbianism was and what it means – and no, it did not mean that everybody had to be a lesbian in order to be a feminist or in order to be a good or proper feminist (whatever that is).

Firstly, to clear up the misunderstandings about separatism then, it is important to note a clear distinction between political autonomy and separatism. The former – political autonomy – refers to political self-organisation for any oppressed group, on their own in their own spaces, be it women, Black people, disabled people or lesbian and gay people for example.

Self-organisation is widely considered by most social justice movements as a political right and it is an important, powerful and tested political tactic. So, in the case of feminism, political autonomy or self-organisation refers to women-only political organising. Separatism on the other hand, refers to a full-time political choice to live and build a domestic, activist, cultural and social life in and with women-only communities, avoiding wherever possible any interactions with men.

Autonomous, women-only political organising is not the same as separatism. Autonomous organising usually refers to temporary political or cultural spaces, which are not necessarily created in exclusion of participation in mixed spaces, domestically, politically or socially. In other words, women-only groups might be just one of many groups that feminists belong to. Feminist activists are usually involved in numerous political causes, most of which will be mixed, which means that feminists will, and do, work alongside men; including in the Feminist Movement, which today is by no means a women-only movement overall. Being part of a women's group today, for some cause or another, feminist or otherwise, does not mean that all those women live full-time lives apart from men – the great majority do not. If they did consciously, and politically, live full-time lives apart from men, then they would be separatists, and that tactic has a proud and significant history in the WLM too, a fact which should not be overlooked.

In contrast to the often-mixed Feminist Movement today, the movement of the past, as mentioned, was generally consciously and explicitly women-only and some groups were indeed separatist. This decision was partly influenced by the sort of sexism I noted earlier, which women activists often experienced in the New Left movements in the early days of the emergence of the Second Wave. It was also influenced by emerging political feminist theory around the importance and significance of self-organisation, the empowering potential of women-only spaces and the need for women to design, build and lead their own liberation movement. I shall return to all these ideas in more depth later in this book.

Returning to the timeline of the history of the Second Wave, it was in 1968, in the US, that the young movement held its first major public demonstration; a demonstration which has gone on to shape the global perception of women's liberation ever since. Led by the author and activist Robin Morgan, the group the New York Radical Women organised a picket of the Miss America Pageant in Atlantic City, New Jersey, in September 1968. The women were protesting against the objectification of women, against the valuing of women based purely on their looks and on how much they matched up to a male-defined ideal of what feminine beauty looked like. Their picket was highly publicised by the mass media and picked up by news worldwide. At their protest, as well as ironically crowning a live sheep (apparently, no animals were harmed in the making of the protest) as a token Miss America, women also threw representations of femininity into what they called a 'freedom trash can'. They binned make-up and bras, high heels and corsets; they demanded the right to define their own appearance, their own meanings of human beauty and worth. They did not burn the contents of this trash can. However, this action was reported in the media as 'bra-burning' and has become a symbol of women's liberation which has entered into global consciousness and which is still used to denigrate the movement today.

## *Second Wave hits the shores of the UK*

It was through news coverage of American events such as the infamous Miss World picket and also through influential publications such as those from Freidan and Firestone that the uprisings of women's liberation in the UK began to stir. American authors were signifi-cant, with Kate Millett's *Sexual Politics* being published in the UK in 1971, for example, and Susan Brownmiller's *Against Our Will* reaching the UK in 1976. Through pub-lications such as these and news of the organised and active women's groups emerging in the US, the seeds of this new phase of the Women's Movement hit the shores of the UK and began to roll. Not all roots lead back to America, however; British theorists were influ-ential too in these early days. Juliet Mitchell for example wrote a motivating article in 1966 called 'Women: The Longest Revolution' which was published in the British *New Left Review*. Reflecting a similar male-dominated sit-uation to that of the New Left in the US, Mitchell was at that time the only woman on the editorial board of the publication. Her article was hugely important, and helped to spark the interest of socialist groups in the UK, and in 1969, the International Marxist Group or IMG formed women's groups and began to publish a journal called *Socialist Woman*. In the same year, cottoning on to the upsurge of interest in women's rights, another radi-cal UK publication, the anarchist-socialist journal *Black Dwarf*, had also published a special issue on women's rights, which was largely written by the famous socialist feminist and historian Sheila Rowbotham.

Rowbotham is probably the most prolific historian of the UK WLM. She identifies one of the first women's liberation groups in the UK as beginning in Hull in the North of England in 1968, growing out of a campaign by working-class women for better safety and conditions on the fishing trawler boats that their husbands worked on. This, and also the famous strike by women workers at the Ford motorcar factory in Dagenham, Essex, in the same year, are frequently cited in most histories of the movement as influencing the beginnings of the Second Wave in the UK. The Dagenham strike involved women sewing machinists who pieced together the interior upholstery for the cars, such as seat covers and door trims, which they argued should be recognised as skilled work. The workers demanded equal pay to that of their male colleagues assembling other parts of the cars on the factory assembly lines. Their strike garnered political support and smoothed the way for the passing of the Equal Pay Act in 1970. The strike also influenced trade unionists, who, in May of 1969, formed the National Joint Action Committee for Women's Equal Rights. Indeed, trade unions were also very important in these early founding days of the UK Second Wave; their role built on a long and established history, with the Trades Union Congress (TUC) having organised a women's conference since as early as 1926 for example.

There were other important motivators too though, which can also be found playing an inspirational role behind the formation of the UK WLM in the late 1960s. For example, women's long-standing role in the Peace Movement and particularly women's activism in the British organisation CND, the Campaign for Nuclear Disarmament, which was launched in 1958. The International Vietnam Solidarity Campaign proved another fertile arena from which new feminist activists emerged, as did the IMG as mentioned earlier, along with another group, the International Socialists – which later became the Socialist Workers Party or SWP, still active today.

Communism in China was also influential to the new feminist movement. Communist politics generally were receiving popular attention from many of the New Left movements at that time, not least due to the great anti-colonial struggles and national liberation victories which marked the Cold War period. In China, Mao's Cultural Revolution of the 1960s also provided a new focus for left-wing groups globally. Many of these groups were disillusioned with the model of Communism from the USSR, particularly due to their violent suppression of reform movements in Czechoslovakia, for example in the 'Prague Spring' of 1968.

Regardless of one's political stance, Communist China had an undeniable influence on the early WLM. Chairman Mao, who was Chairman of the Communist Party of China from 1949 to 1976, made several proclamations about women's equality, or as he termed it, the fact that women held up half the sky. Comments and slick slogans such as this, being shared and popularised throughout the New Left globally, reached and resonated with women in the early movement. The idea of a cultural revolution was also a powerful one, and it underlined the feminist focus on the need for cultural as well as economic revolution. In 1969, Kate Millett wrote that in any revolution, 'the real test would be in changing attitudes' ([1969]1972:170). The global focus on China by the New Left also highlighted specifically feminist critiques of the earlier Russian Revolution; namely, the perceived failure of valid Soviet Union experiments with alternatives to the patriarchal, nuclear family. Feminists in the West had learnt of Russian women's multiple burdens, as their freedom to work and to serve the state had seemingly just been added to their presumed primary domestic duties, while promised provisions of state childcare and other collective facilities rarely materialised.

The influence of China can also be seen in one of the primary and powerful organisational methods of the Second Wave WLM, that is, CR. CR was reportedly first inaugurated in the movement, firstly in America by the group the Redstockings in New York. Both Rowbotham (1992) and Brownmiller (1999) in histories of the early movement, credit the term itself to an activist called Kathy Sarachild. But, allegedly, the roots of the term go back much further, to late 1940s and 1950s Communist China and the tool of 'speaking bitterness' or 'speaking pains to recall pains'. This method was employed by women and men to raise class consciousness of class oppression, and that included women who were raising their consciousness to denounce not only feudal landlords but the culture of oppression they faced in all areas of their lives, including in the domestic sphere. This process became an inspiration to feminists in the West, as they began to uncover their own history under patriarchy and their shared resistance to it. Through sharing and collectivising their own struggles, they realised those daily struggles were not unique to them, and that so many of their problems were not in fact individual, but were faced by many other women. In talking about their personal experiences, of work, childcare, parenting, marriage, sexuality, violence, discrimination and poverty, they put these personal experiences in a political context. They realised that such issues targeted them and affected them not because of their own personal choices or life courses, but simply because they were women in a society where that meant second class. This powerful and life-changing realisation is summed up in the now well-known feminist slogan 'the personal is political', a term popularised in an essay of the same name by the American feminist activist Carol Hanisch.

Early CR groups were formed in London in the late 1960s, for example in a small women's group in Tufnell Park in North London. Rowbotham highlights the importance of global networks here, when in a short 1972 history she identifies that many of the women who formed that early women's group in Tufnell Park were American women, living in London, who had first been active together in a group in the London borough of Camden against the Vietnam War. Being a micro-cosm then of how the early movement formed overall, these women gained political experience in the Anti-War Movement, worked together and then began to organ-ise together as women on women's issues. Rowbotham records that in 1969 the Tufnell Park group joined with four other small women's groups in London: Peckham Rye, Islington, Belsize Lane and Notting Hill. Together they formed the London Women's Liberation Work-shop, which went on to publish the feminist journal *Shrew* from 1969 to 1978.

In 1969, these fledging London groups organised their first public demonstrations at the Miss World Beauty Pageant and the Ideal Home Exhibition. The groups were protesting against narrow beauty stan-dards for women, like their American sisters at the Miss America contest. Activists wore sashes with differ-ent, subverted pageant-style names such as Miss Judged and Miss Fit. Also, slogans such as Miss Fortune, who demanded equal pay for all women, and Miss Concep-tion, who demanded safe, free access to abortion for all women. Miss Treated meanwhile, demanded an end to unequal household labour, and this same message was deployed at the protest at the Ideal Home Show.

Activists picketed the show, critiquing what they saw as the oppression of women within the nuclear family, where women were expected to do most of the unpaid household labour, often on top of paid employment outside the home. Writer Sue O'Sullivan was at both events. In a reflection published in 1982, she recalls that activists targeted consumerism and capitalism, giving out flyers to women attending the Ideal Home Show asking if they would trade places with their husband if they could, and if buying goods for the home really could make them happy as advertisers promised.

Both of these events were covered in the British media and they raised awareness of the growing Women's Movement in the UK. Fuelled by this growing awareness, in the autumn of 1969, a left-wing history group, called History Workshop, founded by historian Raphael Samuel in 1966, decided to hold a conference on women's liberation. The successful conference went ahead at Ruskin College in Oxford in the South of England from the 27th February to the 1st March 1970. Exceeding expectations, it drew over 500 delegates, mostly women. Many historical collections cite this conference as the most discernible beginning of a national WLM, with Rowbotham herself stating that it is from this moment on that it becomes possible to talk about a UK Women's Movement.

## Forward Ruskin

While men manned the crèche at Ruskin and made piles of sandwiches for lunch, children evaded supervision and ran amok, swapping sugar for salt on the refreshment tables and greatly enjoying their experience of the first feminist conference of the Second Wave. The women delegates meanwhile, managed to discuss what exactly their new movement should be asking for and where it should be headed. Together they identified four key demands which they thought were paramount for the pursuit of women's rights. They also decided that such a conference should happen again the next year and annually to form a consistent and coherent anchor, a national conference for the UK WLM.

Inspired by the turnout, obvious interest and energy, women organised another conference for the following year. It was held in Skegness, in the North of England from the 15th to the 17th of October 1971. At this conference, the four demands that had been discussed and put forward at Ruskin were formally adopted for the movement. These were equal pay now, equal education and job opportunities, free contraception and abortion on demand and free 24-hour nurseries. It was not all just about conferences and standing orders and organising committees though; direct action protests continued and in February 1970, in a repeat of actions by their American sisters, women also organised another, much bigger demonstration against the Miss World Pageant that year being held at the Albert Hall in London. Utilising direct action tactics, thanks to carefully placed plants within the Albert Hall itself, activists flour bombed the stage, presenters and contestants, resulting in the arrests of five women. Media attention on events such as this, although it was often negative, highlighted the existence of the movement to the public and led to an exponential rise in women's groups across the country. For example, membership of the London Women's Liberation Workshop reportedly rose from around 16 to 66 groups, in just a few months following the International Women's Day march in London in 1971.

This cold and snowy protest march was held on Saturday the 6th of March 1971, to mark International Women's Day, which is annually on the 8th of March. It was a mixed march of around 4000 people, mainly women, but including men and children. It started at Speaker's Corner of Hyde Park in central London and marched down Oxford Street, the main shopping street of the city. Feminist activist Al Garthwaite attended the march. She told me about her memories of waltzing through the city streets, chanting along in trend-setting irony to the 1930s song 'Keep Young and Beautiful, If You Wanna Be Loved'. Singing, chanting and waving washing lines and banners emblazoned with the four demands, the march then detoured to Downing Street to deliver a petition to the Conservative Prime Minister of the time, Edward Heath. The petition called for the government to meet the four demands that had been raised at Ruskin and agreed at Skegness. After that brief detour to the parliamentary seat of power, the march finally ended at a huge rally a short distance up Whitehall with speakers in Trafalgar Square. This march had been coordinated by the National Women's Co-ordinating Committee, which had been established at Ruskin in 1970. However, this committee was not to last long and it was actually disbanded in 1971 in Skegness due to fears of infiltration by factionist left groups pursuing their own agenda, such as the Maoist Women's Liberation Front. From that point on, there was no central, single co-ordinating body for the UK WLM. This is a structurelessness that has been seen as both a strength and a weakness of the movement. It has been the source of much commentary and complaint, both at the time and in accounts and reflections on the movement right up until the present day.

---

**The Seven Demands**

Equal pay

Equal education and job opportunities

Free contraception and abortion on demand

Free 24-h nurseries

Financial and legal independence

An end to all discrimination against lesbians and a woman's right to define her own sexuality

Freedom from intimidation by threat or use of violence or sexual coercion, regardless of marital status; and an end to all laws, assumptions and practices which perpetuate male dominance and men's aggression towards women

---

This is not to say that the movement of that time was not organised however, as the national conferences carried on from 1971 right up until the (as yet) last National Women's Liberation Conference in Birmingham in 1978. Over the course of these conferences, women added another three demands to the previously agreed four, resulting in what still stands as a manifesto, or womanifesto, for the UK WLM today, known as the Seven Demands. The three additional demands are financial and legal independence; an end to all discrimination against lesbians and a woman's right to define her own sexuality; freedom from intimidation by threat or use of violence or sexual coercion, regardless of marital status; and an end to all laws, assumptions and practices which perpetuate male dominance and men's aggression towards women. This last seventh demand is indicative of a focus in the movement at that time on male violence against women. It was a focus which was fraught with much controversy then, particularly between feminists identifying as radical or revolutionary feminists and those identifying as socialist feminists. The former two schools of feminism – radical and revolutionary – insisted on conceptualising male violence against women as a keystone of women's oppression and a tool of male supremacy, whereas socialist feminists, often reluctant to problematise men as a homogenous group in this way, focussed instead on the role of capitalism in the oppression of not only women, but men too. This is a much-simplified summary of just some of the many theoretical disagreements that rocked the WLM at the time, some of which are still going on today; I shall discuss these in more detail later in this book in Chapter 3.

Although significant in any chronology of the UK Second Wave, and providing some degree of strategic direction in the form of the Seven Demands, these national conferences were by no means the only large-scale events of the period. There were also national conferences all over the country on many different themes and topics, for example on rape, women's health, parenting and many more. There were national lesbian feminist conferences from at least 1974, with the first Black lesbian group being formed in London in 1982. There were Black feminist conferences from at least 1979, organised by, for example, the Organisation of Women of Asian and African Descent or OWAAD, which founded in 1978. In 1979, Southall Black Sisters was formed, responding to and campaigning against male violence against Black women, an organisation that is still very active today. In the same year, the Brixton Black Women's Group, founded earlier in 1973 by an activist called Olive Morris, opened the first London Black Women's Centre. There were feminist groups of younger women, older women, disabled women, religious women, mothers and carers. There were also many specifically socialist feminist, revolutionary feminist, lesbian feminist and Black feminist groups, journals and conferences organised, and all of this was going on between the annual national conferences. Such was the extent and diversity of feminist events of that time, it would be a difficult task to provide an exhaustive list, though the wonderful Feminist Archive at their Leeds site has produced a valiant attempt, which can be easily accessed online.

If you revisit original journals, flyers and other publications, many of which can be viewed in summary on websites such as that from the Feminist Archive, you will see the vast array of topics that the Second Wave WLM addressed, from childrearing and poverty to housing and immigration, as well as male violence, which is my focus here. RTN was one response to male violence, a direct action, public, highly visible and creative mass demonstration against rape and all forms of male violence, but it was not the only response. Practically, feminists of the Second Wave also established service provisions and support services around all forms of violence against women. They set up the first refuges for example for women fleeing domestic abuse, they founded the first Rape Crisis helplines and the first projects in schools on safe relationships. These women brought previously taboo crimes into the public domain, and they influenced laws and shaped opinion on rape, domestic abuse and prostitution. They secured the Domestic Violence Matrimonial Proceedings Act for example in 1976, which introduced civil protection orders, or injunctions, for those at risk of violence from their partners. They secured changes in the Sexual Offences Act 1976, which proclaimed to improve the treatment of rape victims at trial. Feminists of many different schools and tendencies were involved in this practical work, including radical and socialist feminists, even though they did not always see eye to eye on the complex issue of theorising the causes and meanings of male violence against women. I shall now uncover some of the reasons behind such disagreements and look in more detail at the tendencies or schools of feminism which were prominent during the Second Wave.

# Chapter 3

## Feminist tendencies

Today many feminists describe their feminism as a certain type of feminism; they feel a certain allegiance to say socialist feminism or anarcho-feminism if they support anarchist politics for example, or eco-feminism if they are involved in environmentalism. Back in the Second Wave, these sorts of types of feminism were more important than they are today though and whole journals, groups, campaigns, newsletters, conferences and protests were held around one particular type of feminism or another. Often the types critiqued one another and pointed out the benefits of their type of feminism and their specific feminist analysis, theory or activist methods. In this chapter, I shall explore these types in more detail and consider some of the disagreements between them, particularly in terms of the area of focus in this book, the area of theory and activism against male violence against women.

In 1979, *Spare Rib* journalist Amanda Sebestyen drew up her infamous 'tendencies chart'. It was a typology of feminists, a map of all the many different schools of feminism and feminist theory that were influential at the time. It was meant to be taken humorously, but some did not see it as such, and some outside the movement took it literally as a sort of spotter's guide to the wildlife of common or garden feminists! Today there are still lots of different schools of feminism, some are similar to how they were in the 1970s and there are also some new ones just to make things interesting and even more complex. Things are so complex in fact, that many activists today might feel glad of a modern spotter's guide to all the different types of feminists. Even if such a guide were created however, feminists would no doubt argue over definitions and borders, just as they did during the Second Wave itself. For some activists today though, the label of just 'feminist' alone is quite enough. It is often seen as a label that is radical enough yet broad enough to contain a myriad of views and standpoints. Meanwhile, for other activists, the very idea of boxes or labels of any kind is anathema, and that may particularly be the case for self-defined queer activists for example, as I shall go on to discuss in later chapters.

At the time when RTN was born in the mid-1970s, certain schools of feminism were leading the way in producing pioneering, original and daring theory on male violence against women. It was radical feminism which arguably wrote the book on what male violence against women is, why it happens and what we can do to end it. Revolutionary feminism as well was influential, becoming known for theory on male violence as a form of social control, and also for work on the importance of separatism and political lesbianism within feminist organising. This feminist theory on male violence, which was emerging and being debated at the time, directly influenced the emergence of RTN and the form that the protest took. Let us look in more detail then at some of the theory behind the action.

To recap the herstory then, many different schools of feminism emerged in the West during the Second Wave, each with their own groups, conferences and publications. Many of these were influenced by the trends in American feminism, which took off earlier than in the UK and thus proved an example and inspiration. As mentioned in the introduction, just a few of the recognised schools are liberal feminism, socialist feminism, anarcho-feminism, Black feminism, womanism, eco-feminism, radical feminism, lesbian feminism, separatist feminism, pro-feminism and revolutionary feminism. Referring to these complex historical, political and cultural theories as schools, types or branches of feminism can falsely suggest that there are clear-cut lines of demarcation between all such variances of feminism. Alas, things are not that simple. All of the types of feminism visible and loud enough to be given names and be recognised overlap with each other. Within all of these schools are still emerging ideas and theories, which borrow from one another and indeed from examples of feminism around the globe. Each school also contains individuals who may pick and mix theories and approaches from different strands of feminism in order to make a feminism of their own, while perhaps feeling allegiance enough to one or the other strand to sometimes take on that label.

Socialist feminism is usually recognised by its focus on the role of capitalism in the oppression of women and all people. Sometimes it is asserted that capitalism should be viewed as the primary oppression in the world, and therefore that it pre-dates patriarchy – a significant divergence from radical feminism. Taking theory from the important work of Marx, Engels and Babel for example, socialist feminism (like radical feminism) often identifies the family as a primary site of women's oppression, viewing women as labourers to the labourer. Through their caring and reproductive work, women maintain the current labour force, reproduce the workers of the future and are also a reserve army of labour themselves, to be called into the formal wage economy as and when required. The assertion sometimes then appears to be that if capitalism were overthrown, women's oppression would cease to exist. It is this assertion, sometimes made explicitly by some socialist groups, which contributes to just one of the many divisions familiar to those feminists who are immersed in the movement and its various scenes. The concern is that the prioritising of capitalism as the cause of women's oppression leads to a prioritisation of the class struggle, over and above women's liberation. In turn, this leads to the perception, by no means universally correct, that women's rights are sometimes sidelined in some socialist explanations, campaigns and groups.

Liberal feminism is also called equal-rights feminism. It is often scorned in unison by feminists of many hues; it can be distinguished by its focus on reform rather than explicit revolution. This lends to activities within the system, so to speak, such as lobbying government, monitoring equal pay, or the lack of it, working on improvements to maternity rights or campaigning for more women on the boards of major companies. As feminist historian and activist Jo Freeman pointed out though in 1975, scorn against liberals is perhaps misplaced, as their goals are often general feminist goals and, if they were won, would actually have quite revolutionary consequences. 'Some groups often called "reformist" have a platform that would so completely change our society it would be unrecognisable' (1975:50). One of the main areas of conflict with liberal feminists however is around women's participation in a system that many feel is beyond repair. The idea of tinkering around the edges of a patriarchal, capitalist system is unattractive to those feminists who believe their movement is revolutionary rather than reformist.

While feminism in general has been, and still is, subjected to stereotyping, it is radical feminism, and sometimes the lesser-known revolutionary feminism, which are often the targets of much vitriol. They have been accused of many things, for example, splitting the WLM at the (as yet) last National WLM Conference in Birmingham in 1978. This rather grand charge perhaps grew out of the fierce debates that took place at that conference over the wording of the seventh demand, particularly disagreements with revolutionary feminists.

These disagreements centred on whether the wording of the demand should acknowledge male violence against women as a tool of male supremacy benefitting all men, or whether this downplayed the role of capitalism and socio-economic factors, analyses most commonly associated with socialist feminism. This was not the only disagreement however; this last conference seems somewhat marked by controversy, although we should note that the archives suggest that this was not exactly unusual, with plenty of debate and disagreement an expected factor given such serious political formulation. There was equally fierce debate in Birmingham over whether the sixth demand, on lesbian rights and women's freedom to define their own sexuality, should be split or moved to make up a preamble at the start of all the demands. Some revolutionary feminists had also controversially suggested that perhaps it was time to scrap all the demands altogether, instead making a statement on ending male supremacy, arguing that it was nonsensical to make demands of a patriarchal state.

As well as splitting the entire movement and closing down the national conferences forever, the radical and revolutionary schools of feminism are also accused of splitting the London Women's Liberation Workshop (Campbell, 1980); alienating activists through an insistence on lesbianism and separatism; essentialising women and men; demanding a shift from political autonomy to sexual segregation (Byrne, 1996); and of being solely responsible for the movement's reputation as 'man-hating' (Gelb, 1986). In 2000, in her history of the London Women's Liberation Workshop, Setch defines revolutionary feminists as 'vehement separatists who declared war on men' (2002:187). Lynne Segal referred to revolutionary feminism as 'fundamentalist feminism' in 2013, echoing Patrick Califia's earlier description of radical feminism as 'feminist fundamentalism' (1997:86). These critiques are not entirely history, as any activist will know, and indeed a lot of these same issues arose in my research with contemporary feminist activists, as I shall explore later in this book. For now, it is time to properly investigate the contentious and infamous schools of feminism, and their sets of so many theories and ideas which have been, and still are, so frequently attacked: radical and revolutionary feminism. I will attempt to disentangle their theory and their body of work, particularly their work on male violence against women, from the highly critical received wisdom on these two influential schools of feminism.

## *Revisiting radical feminism*

Just like with the tendencies chart, any definitive summaries or clear definitions of any type of feminism are fraught with difficulty. Everyone has their own unique understanding of their own feminism and everyone sees merits in the theory which resonates with them personally. I am no exception. Just as I am keen to present the merits of those feminist theories I find most persuasive, so have been other authors and historians; and unfortunately, there has not been much support for radical or revolutionary feminism thus far. This situation is not helped by the fact that much of the radical/revolutionary work historically was not even written down, and when it was, it was signed anonymously or simply by 'a group of feminists', as activists at the time did not believe in taking individual credit for work which is never produced in a vacuum by one individual. So far, so worthy, but this has unfortunately allowed others, who never identified with those schools of feminism, to define that theory for them and write its herstory.

As part of rectifying this situation then, I will attempt some brief summaries of these two schools of feminism, fraught as such an exercise is. I will outline some of the identifiable, basic identifying features of radical and revolutionary feminism. These are the features which emerge from the literature, the classic American radical feminist texts for example, and the British conference papers and archive periodicals such as the *Rev/Rad Newsletter* and *WIRES*. Perhaps it will become clear that these often-demonised schools of feminism are actually not so bad after all, that they share much in common with other feminist perspectives, have indeed contributed to those other perspectives and that they have a great deal to commend them.

Radical feminism usually identifies patriarchy as predating capitalism and recognises women and men as two distinct political classes – ruled and ruling, respectively. Radical feminism is generally considered to have emerged first in the US in the late 1960s. I suggest that there are four main defining features of radical feminism which make it distinguishable from other schools. It is important to note that these are not the only features of this expansive and sophisticated school of feminism; they are simply the points at which it can be set apart from others. If you want a simple spotter's guide then, to tell a rad from a rev and a soc from a rad, then this is how you could identify radical feminism. Firstly, radical feminism believes in the existence of patriarchy and seeks to end it. Secondly, it promotes women-only space and women-only political organising as paramount. Thirdly, it views male violence against women as a keystone of women's oppression. Fourthly, it expands the understanding of male violence against women to analyse the institutions of pornography and prostitution.

By prioritising male violence against women in their analysis, radical feminism departed from socialist feminism in particular, which generally maintained a class-based analysis of societal oppression, focussed on socio-economic conditions. This latter view, however, could not explain the growing evidence and loud personal testimony of women during the Second Wave. At that time, women's experiences, shared in CR groups, was busily publicly exposing widespread male violence, affecting women from all socio-economic, ethnic, religious and other backgrounds, being perpetrated by men of all classes and all backgrounds. Into this heightened awareness and growing collective, politicised anger, and indeed, as a direct result of it, radical feminism began to develop theory which framed male violence as a symptom of patriarchy, rather than a symptom of capitalism.

Meanwhile, a little bit later and informed by the development of radical feminism, the uniquely British school of revolutionary feminism emerged. This was the school of feminism which fired up the organisers in Leeds who founded the original UK RTN. The school was first instigated at the April 1977 National Women's Liberation Conference in London by the feminist activist and academic Sheila Jeffreys, in a workshop paper titled 'The Need for Revolutionary Feminism – Against the Liberal Takeover of the Women's Liberation Movement'.

This school appears to share much in common with radical feminism. It is unafraid to identify men as a group and as a social class as 'the problem' and the cause of women's oppression. It perhaps goes slightly further in this sense than radical feminism. Feminist policy activist and academic Marianne Hester summarised the features of revolutionary feminism in 1992. She highlighted that 'it is men who are primarily responsible for women's oppression, and it is men, rather than "capitalism" or "society", who benefit from the system of male–female social relations where women as a group are kept subordinate to men' (1992:33). Like radical feminism, revolutionary feminism also identified male violence against women as a keystone of women's oppression, perhaps *the* keystone, a symptom and a tool of patriarchy, which affects all women directly or indirectly.

As these two schools seem to share so much in common, unfamiliar readers may be wondering why there are two schools in the first place. Why and when did the label radical feminist stop being enough for those feminists who then took on the new label of revolutionary feminist? Veteran readers, however, will perhaps be recalling all the many sites of division and debate, the calls to unity, the song published in the second issue of the *Rev/Rad* Newsletter in 1978, 'The Raddies and the Revvies Can Be Friends', the many articles and letters penned on this topic. There are indeed differences between these two similar schools of feminism. The main difference between the two seems to be in the critique from revolutionary feminism accusing radical feminism of turning into what feminist author and playwright Bea Campbell in 1980 called 'a cult of woman'. By this she meant a form of cultural or lifestyle feminism, involving for example the reclamation of Goddess worship and the promotion of environmentalism, veganism,

New Age beliefs or animal rights as intrinsically connected to this particular strand of feminism. Incidentally, it is this notion of cultural feminism that is often still invoked, incorrectly, in criticisms of radical feminism in general. Supposedly then, radical feminism is guilty of conjuring up the 'different spheres' debates common in 1800s Europe, by pronouncing the natural, romantic and spiritual superiority of women and femininity. The accusation then follows that radical feminism is essentialist; that it naturalises the differences between women and men and simplistically and naively places women on an angelic pedestal, while blaming all the ills of the world on men as a group and, in fact, also on men as individuals. To put it even more simply then, the critique is that radical feminism essentialises all men and posits that all men are inherently or essentially 'bad' or violent due to their biology alone, while all women are inherently or essentially 'good'. Indeed this would be simplistic and naïve, which is probably why this has never been the main, or mainstream at least, argument of radical feminism. It would certainly not be an argument that I would find persuasive.

In reality though, during the Second Wave, activists themselves were not altogether confident on the differences between these two or any other schools of feminism. Many feminists pointed out that actually the differences between liberals, radicals, revvies and socialists were not that clear and that there was much overlap between them. Many radical feminists described themselves as anti-capitalist for example, and many socialist feminists did not subsume patriarchy under capitalism. Nor was it only radical or revolutionary feminists who organised or attended the early RTN marches or made up the groups of activists who established provisions for women affected by male violence. As the activist and academic Professor Liz Kelly points out, such practical work to address the effects of violence against women and children united many feminists, even while their theories often differed. 'Violence against women was a faultline in the many acrimonious debates between socialist and radical feminists in the 1970s, yet at the local level the reality was always more complex. Feminists of all shades established refuges and rape crisis centres in small towns and cities' (2013:134).

Although a focus on male violence against women unites both radical and revolutionary feminism, Kelly's quote above highlights that this was also a major site of departure with other schools of feminism, in particular with socialist feminism. As introduced above, the radical analysis was often seen by some as just anti-male, as just simplistically claiming that all men always oppress all women, on an individual, one-to-one basis, as if men never face any form of oppression themselves. To make such a claim is to simplify radical feminism inexcusably, is to miss entirely the point of theory we should instead be learning from. It can and must be possible of course, to view masculine cultures and practices as harmful, not just to women, but to all life, without subjecting the categories of woman and man to some sort of icy cryonic treatment and essentialising them in stasis.

While it has been misread, misunderstood, simplified and criticised, it was nevertheless radical and revolutionary feminism that contributed most to the Western feminist theory on male violence, filling a gap that demonstrably was not being filled by any other school of feminism at the time. In 1984, Weir and Wilson stated in an article for *New Left Review* that radical feminism had determined contemporary theory not only on violence and pornography, but also on race and peace.

In his history on the WLM, Bouchier (1983) for example, alleges that socialist feminism could not 'compete' with the theory being produced by radical and revolutionary feminists, as the former's analysis of patriarchy and male violence was lacking or sometimes even absent altogether. As stated earlier, the feminist theory on male violence against women was emerging at the time as a direct result of the explosion of CR groups across the UK. In these groups, women collectivised their intimate knowledge of male violence, and through that process, were able to understand their experiences not as individual problems or personal failings, but as a consequence of structural male supremacy and female subordination. Out of these experiences grew urgent explanations for male violence against women, explanations which were rarely biological, despite the critique of radical feminism as essentialist.

Both radical and revolutionary feminism emphasised patriarchy as responsible for women's oppression and male violence as the most brutal manifestation of male supremacy, as well as a cause of it. From this perspective, male violence was then able to be understood as a form of social control. As some rad and rev feminists wrote in the introduction to a classic text on male violence, this violence can be understood as a tool in 'the maintenance of men's domination over women' (Jeffreys et al., 1985:6). Male violence was not seen in isolation, but as the extreme end of a continuum, which included girlhood sexual abuse, workplace harassment, exposure to pornography and degrading sexist advertisements for example. This continuum of male violence ranged from 'the insistence on crippling fashions through to incidents of rape and murder' (ibid.). All these facets of oppression were seen to instil fear in women, whether women had been directly affected by male violence or not. All of these examples on the continuum were considered to underline men's power and restrict women's lives, operating as 'threats to our lives and well-being, and blocks to our freedom, our creativity and our self-respect' (ibid.). In turn, the fear of male violence was seen to then encourage women into dependence on male partners and family members. The irony of men being portrayed as women's natural protectors from other men was not lost on feminists who knew then what the statistics still bear out today – that women are in fact most at risk from known men in their own homes.

Apart from their important focus on male violence, another unifying feature between radical and revolutionary feminism was their emphasis on women-only political organising, and their radical and pioneering investigation of political lesbianism and separatism, following earlier feminist activity in the US. Like their focus on male violence, these ideas were also controversial within the WLM at the time, and indeed still are, and they set these two schools of feminism apart from others. Two incidents in particular serve to highlight these conflicts. Firstly, the part publication of the American Radical Feminist 'CLIT Statement' in the London Women's Liberation Workshop newsletter in 1974 on lesbian separatism, which engendered such a hostile response, the group chose not to print the remaining chapters after only the third instalment. Secondly, the debates initiated by the Leeds Revolutionary Feminist Group with their paper on 'Political Lesbianism', initially a conference paper for a radical and revolutionary feminist conference, and then published in *WIRES* in 1979.

This paper, later reproduced in a small booklet from OnlyWomen Press in 1981, sought to question the role of heterosexual women within the movement, and indeed

the desirability of heterosexuality at all, in a revolutionary movement requiring all of women's energy
and passion. The paper suggested that women should
withdraw their energies from men through separatism.
As explained earlier, this is therefore going much further than autonomous women-only organising or spaces,
which are temporary and not in exclusion of mixed political, cultural or social activity. The argument was that
women should consider forging full-time women-only
communities and lives, giving their energy not to men,
but only to the WLM and their sisters within it. This did
not mean becoming a lesbian necessarily, though this is
how the idea has often been mistaken and misquoted.
Contrary to much rumour since, the paper was not
suggesting that women should simply pursue same-sex
sexual activity; it was really more about political activity.
It was about the political choice to dedicate one's life to
women. In fact, in the paper, the Leeds Revolutionary
Feminist Group clearly reassure heterosexuals that the
lesbian bit is not compulsory, and that celibacy is always
an option.

Now that some of the defining features of radical and
revolutionary feminism have been explored and some
of the differences between them outlined, let us turn
back to the critiques of these schools which were set out
earlier in this chapter. These schools of feminism are
accused of man-hating, of an alienating insistence on
lesbianism and of promoting an unrealistic, unnecessary
and sexist separation from men. It is true that both these
schools of feminism did indeed promote the benefits of
autonomous women-only organising and in some cases
separatism. They promoted these for political reasons,
valid reasons which should not be dismissed so lightly
under the tired catch-all charge of 'man-hating'. At the
time, separatism was considered an option, a possible

political strategy vital for movement success. On a less full-time level, autonomous women-only organising was also considered vital, and political self-organisation was considered a right for all oppressed groups; indeed, as I pointed out much earlier, it was a feature of many social justice movements at the time, not just the WLM. Unsurprisingly, many groups of the Second Wave were women-only, as were CR groups, because these were aspiring to be safe spaces where women could raise their feminist consciousness. The broad National WLM Conferences were also women-only after 1971, and self-organisation seems to have been a staple of the mainstream WLM in the UK, including for socialist and liberal feminist groups, even if this was through a caucus or small self-organised group within a larger mixed group, a tactic also used in trade unions and left organisations, a situation that is still the case today. It is important to note that autonomous organisation was not a new phenomenon however, it was not some radical US import, it had long been a part of trade unions for example, and there is a tradition of women-only organising in the many long-standing liberal or conservative women's guilds, societies and philanthropic trusts in the UK. The widespread and seemingly popular women-only feature of the Second Wave is in fact one of the key differences between the movement then and now, as well as between the RTN march of the past compared to the protest today. It is a feature which still arouses many passionate views amongst contemporary feminist activists, perhaps being more controversial than it was then, as I will discuss later in this book.

While there was a long tradition of women organising politically separately from men, what was new was the radical and revolutionary feminist analysis of women-only organising as essential to the project of women's liberation, and their definition of men as a group as a barrier to this project. Looking back through the archives and original texts it is clear that many feminists viewed it as counterintuitive to attempt to organise for liberation alongside members of the oppressing class – men. It was perhaps such an unapologetic analysis, alongside their promotion of separatism and their focus on male violence, which partly led to the familiar critiques of 'man-hating' and essentialism, critiques which are still popular today of course.

To conclude then, it is just worth reiterating that contrary to popular belief, original theory from both radical and revolutionary feminism was usually careful to underline that patriarchy, and the violence identified at its core, was not natural or biological. This is clearly emphasised in a classic text of edited collections from Women Against Violence Against Women or WAVAW campaigners. 'We have concluded that men's sexual behaviour has been socially constructed to be aggressive, exploitative, objectifying. It is not nature that has constructed this effective system for the exploitation of women' (Jeffreys et al., 1985:7). Despite such evidence, the accusation of essentialism is one that is frequently directed against feminism in general, and against radical feminism in particular. The belief still seems to be that certain types of feminism – read: radical feminism – have tried to argue that all men are rapists, or that all men, every single one of them, are violent and abusive simply because of their male sex. In the more academic arenas, there is also an assumption that certain types of feminism, usually meaning radical feminism, are guilty of essentialism by viewing men and women as distinct social classes and by promoting a movement of women as a class. In Chapter 5, I shall explore these and some of the other challenges that are rallied against radical

feminism in particular. I shall attempt to reclaim radical feminism as a valid, modern and relevant political
theory, one which is fully compatible with contemporary
understandings of gender. Before moving on to those
more theoretical debates, it is time to return to the
activism that did manage to unite so many feminists of
different schools during the Second Wave, the activism
against male violence against women and in particular
the birth of the RTN protest in the UK.

# Chapter 4

# From Brussels to Leeds, San Francisco, Delhi: The global march of Reclaim the Night

In this chapter, I will outline the herstory of the RTN protest and its European roots. I have gone back through the archives to navigate the path the protest has taken, from its inspiration in Brussels to West Germany and then to the UK in Leeds in 1977. This path is not without twists and turns and I shall also endeavour in this chapter to explore some of the controversies that surround the beginnings of RTN, namely the charge that the march is racist. I will also tackle the assumption that RTN began in Leeds influenced purely by the murderous actions of serial killer Peter Sutcliffe. There were many reasons why the march began where and when it did, and it followed the example of international feminist activism as well as feminist theorising and organising on rape in the UK which was burgeoning in the mid-1970s. I will now take a look back at that period and at the start of our most recent feminist activist past against rape and sexual violence.

*Where did Reclaim the Night begin?*

RTN is now a global movement; it has been growing under the current resurgence to the point where the marches are now bigger and more popular than they ever were before. But, like so many great things in activism, the protest seems to have had relatively humble beginnings. Those beginnings can be followed back to a conference held in Brussels, Belgium in March 1976. The conference itself was not humble; in fact, it was huge and very significant, but in the history of RTN, it was what happened after the close of the conference, on the last night that resonated with so many and put this method of protest into action. The conference was the International Tribunal on Crimes Against Women and it was held to mark International Women's Day 1976. Taking place from the 4th to the 6th of March, it was attended by over 2000 women from 40 different countries. Delegates provided testimonies of the extent, impact, nature and form of male violence against women which they were resisting in their own countries. This was essentially a catalogue of brutality, a global snapshot of the various bloody ways which patriarchal governance impacts on women's bodies. Outraged and united by what they had heard and shared, in candlelit procession the women delegates decided to take to the city streets on the evening of the last day of the conference to loudly and visibly demonstrate their anger and resistance to all forms of male violence.

Returning to their own localities after the conference, taking news of the gathering with them, the delegates also recounted their experiences of claiming the night-time city streets to make their protest heard, and the tactic inspired others to do the same. Only a few months later, in Rome, Italy, a similar night-time march was held; this was in protest against a reported rise in rapes in the city that year. This march appears to be the first time the title 'Reclaim the Night' was formally used for the protest. Early the following year, on the 1st of March

1977, women in Berlin held the first Take Back the Night march in Germany. The torch-lit march was in protest against the rape and murder of a 26-year-old local woman, named Susan Schmidtke. Soon after this event of course, Germany became home to the first-ever synchronised RTN march, taking back towns and cities across West Germany on the night of the 30th of April 1977. Since at least 1976 then, with the event in Belgium, women's night-time marches through cities have been an organised form of protest against male violence against women. Throughout the late 1970s, this protest tactic grew in popularity, being held around the world in America, Canada, India and beyond. The phenomenon marched onto the shores of the UK in November 1977.

The first-ever British RTN marches were held simultaneously across several cities on the night of the 12th of November 1977. Lancaster, Brighton, Bristol, York, Newcastle, London, Bradford, Guildford, Salisbury and Manchester all took part; but the marches were born in Leeds. This industrial metropolitan city in Yorkshire in the North of England was at that time in the 1970s a hotbed of political activism and home to many important developments in the herstory of the UK WLM. Leeds was where the first national Women's Liberation newsletter, *WIRES*, was founded and published for example, it was home to some of the first revolutionary feminist organising, as well as WAVAW and Angry Women direct action. Some of the first feminist and lesbian feminist communes sprung up here in housing cooperatives and the cheaper housing available in areas between the city centre and the suburbs. The city was therefore ideally placed to take up RTN as a new and dynamic tactic of feminist protest, but not just for the reasons above; another more sinister influence lurks behind the birth of RTN in that city and at that time.

## *Leeds: Birthplace of the British Reclaim the Night*

News of the coordinated RTN marches across West Germany in April 1977 had reached activists in the UK courtesy of journalists at the national WLM magazine *Spare Rib*, who had picked up on news coverage in the German magazine *Courage*. Founded in 1976, and running until 1984, along with another magazine called *Emma*, which is still published to this day, *Courage* was one of the key periodicals of the New Women's Movement, the WLM of West Germany from around the mid-1960s. With the headline 'Germany: Reclaiming the Night', a relatively small news item relays accounts of the various marches in West Germany in Issue 61 of *Spare Rib*, published on the 21st of August 1977. It was thanks to the language skills of the international reporters at *Spare Rib*, such as Amanda Sebestyen and Jill Nicholls, that this news item got picked up at all, and the team at the magazine at that time could not have known what much bigger news RTN was to become, in only a matter of months.

Hundreds of miles away from the *Spare Rib* HQ in London, activists up North in Leeds were working on news items for the *WIRES* newsletter. The Women's Information Referral and Enquiry Service ran for a decade, from 1975 to 1985. The newsletter was founded when Leeds feminists in an important local group in the city, the Chapeltown Women's Liberation Group, suggested the need for a national newsletter to share information around the movement. Chapeltown is an area in the North East of Leeds, around a mile from the city centre and it had a high concentration of feminists at the time; it was also one of the locations for the start of the city's first RTN march, and this will become important later on, as I shall explain. The Leeds women took their suggestion for a national newsletter to the National Women's Liberation Conference in Manchester in 1975; their idea was enthusiastically received and agreed, and activists in Leeds produced the first 45 issues of the national news and listings newsletter, before responsibility passed to women in York from January 1978.

The women in the *WIRES* Collective saw the news item in *Spare Rib* on the German RTN, and decided to copy the idea. A suggestion had actually already been made to bring a similar style of protest to the UK – slightly earlier this had been mooted by a then London-based feminist activist named Sandra McNeill. McNeill had been inspired by the same coverage of the German marches in *Spare Rib* herself and raised the idea of a replica protest while she was attending a conference on revolutionary feminism, held in Edinburgh, Scotland in July 1977. This discussion in Edinburgh had two significant consequences. One was that shortly after that conference, Scotland became home to the first-ever RTN march in the UK, apparently a fairly small protest held in the Meadows, parkland South of the city centre of Edinburgh. The second consequence was that the discussion sowed the seeds for the first organised, synchronised UK RTN marches, as Leeds-based activists, present at the Edinburgh conference, took news of Sandra's suggested protest tactic back to their women's groups locally. So it was that the news was carried back to the Chapeltown Women's Liberation Group, already enthused by reading of the success of the exciting marches across West Germany. The idea of going out at night, en masse, with flaming torches and banners and physically taking back the streets against male violence against women appealed to activists at the time. The appeal was not just because it was new and exciting, but because women in Leeds had a particular interest in taking back the streets of their city.

Leeds, Yorkshire, the North of England generally and indeed the whole of the country was at that time intently following the search for Britain's most notorious serial killer, Peter Sutcliffe. At that time still an unknown attacker, the 'Yorkshire Ripper', as the press dubbed him, murdered 13 women between 1975 and 1985, overshadowing the North of England. The response of the police included telling women to stay indoors if they wanted to be safe and encouraging women not to go out at night, especially not on their own without a man to escort them. This impractical advice was viewed as a curfew by feminist activists, and thus the notion of reclaiming the night and the streets held particular resonance. The chosen routes of the Leeds RTN were also influenced by Sutcliffe's crimes, passing places where victim's bodies had been found; I shall discuss this in more detail later, as the route of the Leeds RTN was to go on to become somewhat controversial following the event, influencing long-held assumptions about the protest march to this day.

Sutcliffe's crimes were not the only reason that male violence against women was in the public consciousness and in the news at that time however. Influential American feminist Susan Brownmiller's book *Against Our Will* on the history of rape was published in 1976 in the UK, and the year before, in 1975, saw the Morgan legal ruling set a precedent of 'honest' belief in consent, focussing legal attention on the mental motivations of those accused of rape, no matter how unreasonable their 'honest' belief may seem. The issue of male violence and feminist responses to it had also long been discussed in the movement, and was the subject of numerous items and articles in both *WIRES* and *Spare Rib* prior to 1977 when RTN was born. The first Rape Crisis Centre in the UK had been founded in London for example in 1976 and rape was a formal conference topic at the National WLM Conference in Islington, London in April 1977. This conference focus actually motivated several women's groups to set up action groups on the issue around the country, including in Bristol, London and Manchester. The crime of rape was not only being discussed by insiders in the movement at feminist conferences, however; in the late 1970s, the crime and legal responses to it became a major news item in the national press due to the case of a young soldier named Tom Holdsworth.

Holdsworth was convicted of a brutal sexual assault in March 1977 and initially sentenced to three years in prison for his attack on a young woman. During the attack, he penetrated the woman with his fists causing her severe internal injuries, partly due to the large sovereign rings he wore on his fingers. Later, in June, at his subsequent appeal, the three judges hearing his case noted that the young woman could have avoided such serious injuries if only she had 'accepted his advances'. Given such an attitude, it is perhaps unsurprising that these judges then reduced the initial three years custodial to a six month suspended sentence, on account of Holdsworth's previous good character and promising army career. The judgement was widely reported and denounced in the national press; it also caused outrage throughout the WLM. 'How can we organise against rape?' asked *Spare Rib* writer Jenny Hall, in a news item on the appeal verdict in Issue 61 of the magazine. In the days immediately following the verdict, women did organise. To demonstrate their outrage, graffiti was daubed on the streets outside the law courts in central London on Chancery Lane and also on military monuments along the Mall. Activists were arrested for demanding justice for women and defacing army careers offices throughout the country, including in Bristol and Manchester where anti-rape groups had earlier already been set up.

The Bristol Anti-Rape Group wrote a report of their actions and campaigns following the Holdsworth appeal, calling for more creative protest against rape; this was published in Issue 36 of *WIRES* in July 1977. It was actually in response to this article, just underneath it, in a small subtitle, that the idea of a national UK RTN was first aired to the movement. The idea was obviously informed by the earlier West German marches, and it was initially put forward by 'the *WIRES* Collective', as follows:

> Women in West Germany demonstrated for the right to walk unafraid and unhassled on the streets at night (See Spare Rib 61) ... Women in Britain are afraid to walk home at night, especially with the all the recent rape reports fresh in our minds. Couldn't we organise similar national demonstration, to help turn our fear into anger and action (sic).
>
> *WIRES* 36, July 1977:16

Those who blinked might have missed this small item, in its square block typeface, never quite in a straight line and complete with grammatical errors and a few more extra commas than necessary. But it was this short addendum to the preceding article which actually marked the beginning of an organised RTN Movement in Britain.

Women in the *WIRES* Collective and the Chapeltown Women's Liberation Group took on the organisation of RTN. Several of these women went on to become members of another important group, which would actually prove to be internationally significant: the Leeds Revolutionary Feminist Group. They were inspired by a then London-based feminist named Sheila Jeffreys, now a feminist academic and activist living in Australia. Jeffreys presented a paper at the 1977 National UK WLM Conference in London on what she saw as a liberal takeover of feminism; she called for a more revolutionary movement and, in so doing, founded a new school of feminism called revolutionary feminism. Rooting the UK RTN firmly in this fairly recent and UK-specific school of feminism, it was the Leeds Revolutionary Feminist Group who made the first official call for, and took on the coordination of, the first synchronised RTN marches, thus inaugurating this type of protest method in Britain. Their plan for a UK-wide RTN was formally announced in Issue 38 of *WIRES*, published on the 24th of September 1977:

> Torchlit demonstration: The Leeds Revolutionary Feminist Group wants to hold a womenonly midnight demonstration on the theme of 'every woman has the right to walk alone at night without fear' and 'fight rape'. We want to hold ours in the Chapeltown area of Leeds where a Jack the Ripper type character has murdered several women over the past two years, and to get as many women as possible on the march. We thought it would attract a lot more publicity and have more effect if women in as many different towns as possible all over Britain could demonstrate on the same night, which we have fixed for NOVEMBER 12th. We'll give more details next newsletter. In the meantime, please contact *WIRES* if you are interested in planning to put a demonstration in your area, so that when we tell the press we can

tell them exactly where the demos are going to take
place (sic).

*WIRES* 38, September 1977:9;
emphasis in original

More details then followed in Issue 40 of *WIRES*, and by
this time, the organising group had changed their name
to the more neutral 'Leeds Reclaim the Night Group', no
longer organising under 'The *WIRES* Collective' or 'The
Leeds Revolutionary Feminist Group'. In a short message, the organising group congratulated all the women
who had contacted them with plans for their own local
marches around the UK. The Leeds organisers had not
exactly been resting themselves, badges had been produced to fundraise for the Leeds march and thousands
of flyers printed to give out in the city, particularly in the
local areas where the march routes were to begin. Not
to be outdone by the German protest, prominent local
feminist activist Al Garthwaite had been busy scouring
local telephone and business directories to source suitable flaming torches, eventually placing a bulk order for
some outdoor garden-style candles. In the same issue of
*WIRES*, in the events listings section, the national march
was advertised again and several cities already confirmed
to be holding marches. RTN was only advertised once in
*Spare Rib*, shortly before the date of the protest, which
was the 12th of November, and the event is credited
here to the Leeds Revolutionary Feminist Group again.
In a listings section for upcoming events, the march is
advertised in Issue 64 of *Spare Rib* as follows:

> 12 November. Torchlit women only midnight demon-
> stration in the Chapeltown area of Leeds, organised
> by the local Revolutionary Feminist Group on the
> themes every woman has the right to walk alone at

night without fear, and fight rape. They hope women
in other towns will do the same on that night in order
to attract publicity.

*Spare Rib* 64, 1977:24

Following the event, the synchronised marches were
reviewed as a huge success, with at least ten cities taking part. In January 1978, RTN took up the whole
front cover of *Spare Rib*, emblazoned with a photo-
graph of marchers, faces painted with women's symbols,
carrying flaming torches and across the photo the headline: We Will Walk without Fear. The magazine carried
reviews from most of the cities involved, with reports
of up to 400 women marching on their city centres.
In that blaze of flaming torches, the UK RTN was born
and the protest tactic grew and continued regularly,
often being held several times a year in some cities and
being a common response to particular incidences of
male violence against women or perceived legal failures.
As highlighted, the first marches were held in many different cities, but Leeds is often wrongly seen as the site
of the first-ever marches and the routes of the protest
through that city have since become seen as controversial. In the next section, I will look more closely at these
Yorkshire routes of RTN.

## *Practical influences behind the emergence of Reclaim the Night*

It is important to look in more depth at some of the
practical influences behind the founding of the RTN
march, particularly the crimes of the Yorkshire Ripper
and the feminist activist response in Leeds. These crimes
were partly behind the decisions on which routes the

march would take through the city, but the choices over routes became controversial because one section of the march went through a predominantly BME or Black and minority ethnic area in Leeds. In the years following, several commentators have assumed that this was the only march in Leeds, and that it was the first UK march and concerns were raised that the birth of the UK RTN was rooted in racism, conscious or otherwise.

Just as RTN marches in Rome and Berlin were partly motivated in response to particular rape cases in those cities, this particular crime was also significant in the emergence of RTN in the UK. As already noted for example, the issue of rape was a specific theme at the 1977 National Women's Liberation Conference, held in Islington, London, the same year that RTN began. This national focus at the conference is credited with mobilising women's groups around the country to set up local theory and campaign groups on rape. For example, at the London Women's Liberation Workshop Women's Centre, called 'A Woman's Place', at that time situated on Earlham Street in Covent Garden in central London, a 'rape group' was set up.

> Following the workshops on Rape at the National Women's Liberation Conference we would like to see the debate on rape growing all around the country. One, for discussion at the next National Conference; two, for women to become active on the issue (sic).
>
> *WIRES* 36, 1977:13

Groups against rape were also formed in Manchester in the North of England, Nottingham in the Midlands and Bristol in the South West of England. These groups were then able to organise quickly in response to events such as the Holdsworth case as introduced above, as well as take part in revived campaigns for the criminalisation of rape within marriage for example; a long-running feminist campaign carrying on from the First Wave, which was not successful until as late as 1991 in England when rape within marriage was finally recognised as a crime. Bristol was to become particularly significant in the anti-rape campaigns due to the presence of two anti-rape groups in the city, one aligned with the non-partisan Women's Centre, which opened in 1973 in the home of activist and academic Dr Ellen Malos in the North of Bristol, and the second aligned with the national organisation Wages for Housework (W4H). Disagreements with the latter, aired in letters and articles in national WLM newsletters, usefully serve to highlight the main theories on rape and male violence generally, which were being explored and debated in the movement at that time. These were the debates which formed the backdrop to the founding and popularity of RTN in the UK; they also expose some of the stark theoretical differences within feminist theory on male violence, particularly differences between radical/revolutionary feminism and socialist feminism.

W4H was formed in July 1975 by writer and activist Selma James. She and another feminist, Mariarosa Dalla Costa, had written a paper three years earlier calling for wages for housework to be one of the formal demands of the UK WLM. This proposition was presented to the 1972 National Conference, where it was rejected, and continued to be so whenever it was raised. W4H spawned numerous sub-groups to tackle a huge variety of issues, from prostitution to lesbian oppression and immigration law. Many of these groups are still in existence today under several different names, such as Global Women's Strike, Wages Due Lesbians, English Collective of Prostitutes and All Women Count, and they are all run from the W4H premises at the Crossroads Women's Centre near Kings Cross in North London. Historically, W4H were also involved in the famous Greenham Common Women's Peace Camp in the 1980s, where they are accused by some scholars, such as the academic and Greenham woman Sasha Roseneil (1995), of attempted sabotage. Amongst their many campaigns, in 1976, W4H also formed Women Against Rape or WAR in Bristol, which was later launched as a national campaign with groups all over the UK. Although WAR was therefore already known to activists in Bristol, this group leapt onto the national stage and into the media spotlight too, through their controversial organised response to the Holdsworth case.

## *WAR resistance*

On the 28th of June 1977, several days after the Holdsworth appeal verdict, a picket was held outside the Court of Appeal on the Strand in central London, as Judge Eustace Roskill, who had presided over the Holdsworth appeal, was sitting there that day. Numerous feminist groups and individuals attended the picket, including the *Spare Rib* Collective for example, Camden Women's Aid and the newly formed London Rape Crisis Centre. WAR also attended the picket and afterwards they stormed Judge Roskill's courtroom, calling for him to be sacked. An article in *Spare Rib* asserts that shortly after this action, WAR got a great deal of press attention and allegedly claimed sole responsibility for organising the picket. Following this, WAR formally called a public demonstration in London to be held on Saturday the 16th of July 1977. This was to include a march from Lincoln's Inn Fields to Trafalgar Square in central

London where a 'speak out' was to be held. A speak
out has a history in the WLM, the first known one was
reportedly organised by the New York Radical Feminists in January 1971 in America. They are usually
women-only events where survivors of sexual violence
are supported to speak about their experiences, in defiance of a culture which silences, shames and blames
victims of male violence. The Bristol Anti-Rape Group
explained further at the time:

> Speak-Outs against rape have a certain herstory, they
> were originally women-only events in which we con-
> fronted the damage by rape, spoke of it, asserted our
> anger and decision to take action – by strategies for
> growth, in both the personal and political sense (sic).
>
> *Spare Rib* 62, 1977:28

The WAR demonstration caused some deal of controversy, elements of which can be followed in both *WIRES*
and *Spare Rib*. Complaints about the protest ranged from
the practical to the theoretical. One practical complaint
was that allegedly the demonstration was announced
only two to three weeks before the planned date, giving
other women's organisations little time to contribute or
arrange their involvement. *Spare Rib* journalist Amanda
Sebestyen reported on the WAR protest in an article
titled 'Rape Rally Wrangle'. She recounted that some
groups did attend the protest, but later left in anger,
including National Abortion Campaign supporters. This
actually highlights another very specific practical complaint, as apparently these particular supporters left in
protest at the participation on the demonstration of an
anti-choice group called 'Women for Life', whose banner is clearly visible in Sebestyen's photographs from
the event printed in her *Spare Rib* coverage. The North

Camden branch of the National Abortion Campaign
alleged that 'Women for Life' was allowed to carry their
anti-abortion banner on the march, and participate at
the rally, despite reports that WAR demanded there be
no political banners at the event at all, aside from their
own. On a more theoretical level, the Bristol Anti-Rape
Group meanwhile had earlier decided not to attend at
all, citing local problems with W4H over at least two
years and also opposition to the WAR analysis that rape
is a result of women's inferior economic status.

This WAR demonstration also crystallised apparent
concerns that were already arising in the movement
over the 'ownership' of campaigns and also over communications with the media. 'We hope that the issue of
rape does not become the partisan "property" of any
one group' explained the London Rape Group in 1977
for example (*Spare Rib* 62, 1977:28). It is important to
understand that this discussion was occurring at a time
when the UK Movement was really only just taking up
the issue of rape. It was a period when new analyses were
being formed on the causes and impact of this type of
sexual violence and its role in women's oppression more
broadly. It was also a period when the new Rape Crisis Movement was growing in the UK, with other cities
and towns following the example of London and opening their own centres. As mentioned earlier, due to the
focus at the 1977 National Conference, the local anti-
rape groups had also been spreading. Each were taking
their own kinds of action, from delivering school talks
to organising vigils for example. In short, rape was fast
becoming a key issue in the movement at this time and
it was also being taken up outside. Scottish women from
the Glasgow Women's Centre explained at the time that,
'[e]very woman knows that rape is becoming increasingly
fashionable' (*WIRES* 41, 1977:14). So fashionable was

the subject that a group of men in Glasgow had actually announced their plans to open a Rape Crisis Centre for women in the city. This plan was receiving widespread coverage in the Scottish media at the time, much to the consternation of established groups such as the Glasgow Women's Centre.

As the issue was becoming debated more widely both in and outside the movement, the theory around it also grew, emerging mainly from CR groups within the WLM itself and then being formulated, fought out and refined through conference papers, newsletter articles, letters and periodicals. The group who brought RTN to the UK, the Leeds Revolutionary Feminist Group, were just one of the many feminist groups, who, like the Bristol Anti-Rape Group, did not share WAR's theoretical stance on rape. This stance from WAR was as follows:

> Every woman must have the financial independence she needs in order to leave a situation where she feels in danger of rape. She must have the money and therefore the social standing to defend herself from a husband or individual man and from any judge, police officer or doctor biased against her.
>
> Jenny Hall, 1977:14

This was the demand on the WAR flyer which they distributed at their July protest in 1977. Women should not expect the police or courts to solve the problem of rape WAR maintained, condemning any calls for higher rape conviction rates or increased prison sentences. These were not the answer, stated WAR spokeswoman Ruth Hall, in an article for *The Guardian* shortly after the July demonstration. Although the state was identified as being responsible for preventing rape and also for financially compensating any woman reporting rape, the only real solution was through the 'organised refusal of rape by women ourselves' (Ruth Hall, 1977:14). No advice was offered as to how this could be achieved though, aside from increasing women's incomes.

Bristol Anti-Rape Group, in efforts to put clear theory between themselves and the Bristol-based WAR, emphasised that they did not support this analysis that 'if women had money they could not get raped' (*Spare Rib* 62, 1977:28). They branded the WAR stance 'misleading and naïve...the oppression of women cannot be fought by paying women in and for their oppression' (*WIRES* 42, 1977:19). An anti-rape group in the Midlands of England shared this view; the Nottingham Women's Liberation Group wrote in *WIRES* that no amount of money could rape-proof any woman and that being financially independent 'is no guaranteed defence against a rapist' (*WIRES* 41, 1977:12). Agreeing with this theoretical stance, the London Rape Group also formally disassociated themselves from the WAR analysis. All of these dissenting groups identified rape instead as part of a continuum of sexism and a product of male supremacist society. 'Sexism is how male power operates against women; rape is the inevitable brutal expression of that power' summarised the London group in 1977 (*WIRES* 36, 1977:14).

Taking a position that will be familiar from our previous explorations of feminist schools of thought, these groups identified strongly with the radical and revolutionary feminist perspective on male violence against women. The Leeds Revolutionary Feminist Group identified men, rather than lack of money, as the cause of rape: 'any man can be a rapist' they asserted in 1978 (*WIRES* 47, 1978:13). They were not arguing that all men are rapists though; they were pointing out that any man could be a rapist and that women cannot know who is and who is not a potential attacker. The threat of rape then affects all women, whether or not they have been directly affected. The threat was seen to have broad ramifications therefore on women as a group. 'Men keep us in fear of going out on our own – we all carry with us all the time the fear of male violence. All men gain by these things and all women are weakened and rendered easier to control' (Seven Revolutionary Feminists, 1981:7). Obviously, there was also a heightened consciousness around women's fear of using public space, particularly at night, due to the much-publicised crimes of Peter Sutcliffe and the inappropriate police response. Against this raised consciousness and the brutality of the crimes being reported, it is perhaps unsurprising that the reductionist claims of WAR, maintaining that rapists could be fended off with finances, appeared glaringly hollow to many. There was already then a certain level of contention and disagreement around activism against rape; this was then aggravated following the Leeds RTN when the march was accused of racism. It is important to note that such accusations and the discussion which follows them take place in a context. That context is one of structural racism, a racism which marked Britain in the 1970s and which still scars our society today. As I shall discuss in the next section, there are many valid reasons why Black feminists may have had concerns about this new type of protest in the birth of the early RTN marches.

### Routes of conflict: Reclaim the Night and racism

In the initial call for a UK RTN from the Leeds Revolutionary Feminist Group, first advertised in *WIRES* in 1977, the route of the march in Leeds was said to have been chosen due to the recent murders of several young women, suspected victims of the Yorkshire Ripper. The bodies of Wilma McCann in October 1975, Emily Jackson in January 1976, Irene Richardson in February 1977 and Jayne McDonald in June 1977 were all discovered in Chapeltown in North Leeds. It was for this reason that Chapeltown was chosen as one starting point for the Leeds RTN march, but there was also another second sister-assembly point in Hyde Park. The latter is a popular student residential area, close to the University of Leeds and also in the North of the city. Unfortunately, at the time, it was an area affected by high crime rates, including muggings and assaults, particularly on a large piece of parkland called Woodhouse Moor. RTN founder Al Garthwaite explained to me in an interview in January 2012 the decision to use the two starting points:

> We decided to have two marches in Leeds, one setting off from Chapeltown community centre and one setting off from Hyde Park going across Woodhouse Moor, because there was lots of harassment and rapes and attacks on students around Woodhouse Moor, it was a notorious place.

The two marches, of around 30 women assembling in Chapeltown and a further 85 women starting at Hyde Park, later converged to march together into a central pedestrianised square in the city centre called City Square. Several members of the RTN organising group lived in the Chapeltown area and were members of the Chapeltown Women's Liberation Group. There may therefore have been practical reasons to organise an assembly point in that locality, as well as the symbolic marking of the young women's lives lost there in the run up to the march being founded. In an interview for *Spare*

*Rib*, following the first successful RTN, the Leeds Revolutionary Feminist Group stated that they had also been influenced by discussions on the issue of male violence at the Edinburgh Conference on Revolutionary Feminism in July 1977 and were looking for 'a new area of action radical enough to really fire people' (70, 1978:23). They also stated that they were 'particularly concerned because there'd been a series of women murdered in West Yorkshire' (ibid.). However, following the march, the organising group faced criticism for choosing the Chapeltown route, and the Leeds RTN was publically accused of racism; a charge which has frequently been applied to RTN generally and which has become widely accepted as a truism ever since.

It is reported in a letter from the Leeds RTN Group to *WIRES* in March 1978 that charges of racism were first raised, to their knowledge, by women at a Socialist Feminist Conference in Manchester in January 1978. Their letter recounted that unnamed women had suggested that one RTN march 'unthinkingly went through a black area' (*WIRES* 47, 1978:13). The Leeds RTN Group assumed that this criticism was aimed at them, as Chapeltown was, and indeed still is, a 'multi-racial area' (ibid.). Specifically, the criticisms made against the RTN march were firstly that the march only focussed police attention on an already over-policed area; secondly, that it called for increased policing on that area; and thirdly, that it reinforced racist stereotypes linking Black people with crime, and Black men in particular with the threat of sexual violence. The RTN organisers refuted these charges, stating that their organisation of the march was far from unthinking. They emphasised the amount of time they put into liaising with local community groups and distributing over 1000 flyers outlining the aims of the march; they also pointed out that on the day itself many women took part in the march, including Black women and that it was not only White women on the protest. When I asked her about it for my research in early 2012, Leeds activist and founder of RTN Al Garthwaite continued to question the charges against the protest. She maintained that it was just practical to organise in those locations, as that was where so many of the active feminists in the city were living at the time:

> locations were chosen because that was probably the two biggest concentrations of active feminists in the area. We didn't choose it [Chapeltown] because it was a Black area. We chose it because we lived there; we all lived there, and you organise where you live.

It is also a fact that, despite the charges made against them since, increased policing was not a demand of the original RTN organisers and this demand did not feature on any of the flyers which were distributed before the march and on the night itself. This was actually reported by Polly Toynbee in *The Guardian* coverage of the first marches, shortly after their inauguration in an article two days after the march: 'They were not asking for a change in the law, or even for greater police protection. They were campaigning for a change in society's attitudes to women, no less' (1977:50). Indeed, the whole of the WLM at that time was largely working outside of the state, as founder of the original London RTN Sandra McNeill reiterated to me in an interview. She highlighted that the original marches did not seek or receive police permission

> God no, we didn't get police permission. I mean no, I mean that to us at the time would have been an anathema.

(21 January 2012)

This seems to be a feature in most of the reviews of local marches which were published in the January 1978 issue of *Spare Rib* celebrating the first RTN. Reviews actually highlight that women danced through their city streets and between traffic, that ineffectual police arrived and stood by not quite sure what to do, that women joyfully reclaimed space in what comes across as quite an anarchistic way; reviewers even comment on this atmosphere and the lack of police or formal stewards.

In their letter, the Leeds RTN organisers also stated again the significance of the routes chosen; namely, that victims of the Yorkshire Ripper had tragically been found in Chapeltown. 'We chose the Chapeltown route because of several brutal murders of women in the area over the last two years. This was understood by all the local people we talked to, informed of the march, gave leaflets to' (*WIRES* 47, 1978:13). The flyers which were printed and given out to passers-by on the night of RTN had only one simple statement: 'we are walking for all women – all women should be free to walk down any street night or day without fear'. Even in the original call out for the march, months before in July 1977 and all the subsequent adverts following, only two formal aims were ever publicised for RTN: 'fight rape', and 'every woman has the right to walk alone at night without fear'. A duplicate of the Leeds organiser's letter to *WIRES* was also re-published in *Spare Rib* in Issue 70 in May 1978.

If the organisers hoped at the time that this would be the end of the matter, they were wrong. The charge of racism is one that appears to have stuck to RTN and which surfaces fairly frequently. In 1986, scholars Bhavnani and Coulson wrote an article for the academic journal *Feminist Review*, re-printed in a special 25-year review edition in 2005, in which they assert that the racism of the UK WLM can be clearly seen in the example of RTN. Their particular reference to RTN has since been much quoted. They describe 'the failure of anti-rape campaigns to challenge racist stereotypes of the sexuality of black men' and critiqued the UK RTN of the 1970s and 1980s.

> Not only have these generally not taken up racism as an issue, nor seen how their campaigns against male violence are complicated in the context of racism, but by their actions they have affirmed racist ideas by marching through black areas and calling for greater policing.
>
> 2005:88

Several other academics have made similar charges, often referencing the Bhavnani and Coulson article from 1986, but never citing which RTN march/es in particular they are referring to. For example, this statement from Grover and Soothill in 1996:

> Although the bestial imagery of black male sexuality was at its height in the nineteenth century, it is an image which still exists. It is significant that the 'reclaim the night' marches in the mid to late 1970s focused on areas in which the communities had a high proportion of minority ethnic men.

These authors then refer readers to the original Bhavnani and Coulson article (Grover & Soothill, 1996:568).

In 1990, a similar statement is made by another academic, Cox, though this time the original claim in Bhavnani and Coulson's article is not cited, in fact there is no reference at all for the following claim.

The 'Reclaim the Night' marches in the late 1970s demanded, amongst other things, greater police protection for 'women' (read: white women). Many of these marches were routed through the hearts of black communities. Not only was this interpreted as an invitation to exert greater control over these areas, but it reinforced the association of Afro-Caribbean youth with crime. This played into racist notions of the 'coloured' male rapist and white female victim.

Cox, 1990:239

Again, not citing any other references or naming a particular RTN march, scholar Tang Nain made similar accusations in an article in another academic journal in 1991.

There have, however, been problems with 'reclaim the night' marches in Britain, for example, when some white feminists marched in areas of black concentration. This had the effect of suggesting a link between black people and violence and was justly criticised.

Tang Nain, 1991:12

Whether all such references could be traced back to 30 women marching through Chapeltown in Leeds in 1977 is unknown. It should be noted however, that although the organisers refuted these charges when they were made at the time, that does not mean that the march was not perceived as racist by fellow political activists; or that RTN through Chapeltown, being a predominantly BME area, or what some people may refer to as, using a statistically more accurate term, a Black and global majority ethnic area, was not read as racist by the general public through media coverage. There are always

such gaps between intent and reception and it is the job
of political organisers to attempt to predict and traverse
these, though that is no easy task.

Original RTN organisers claimed at the time that they
did indeed understand how the march could be perceived by the public and by the media, and that this
was partly why they conducted such a great deal of local
publicity and community awareness raising prior to the
event. It is possible that the critiques of racism made
against RTN are perhaps linked to much more general critiques of the UK WLM and feminism as a whole.
Whatever the background and history to these specific
accusations against RTN, there were many reasons at the
time why any concerns around racism were particularly
highly charged.

Concerns over policing and police attention for example, at the time when RTN emerged in the UK, were
understandable. Britain in the late 1970s and 1980s
was fraught with racial tensions and marked by explo-
sive clashes between the police and marginalised urban
communities. Reflecting years of racist and inadequate
housing and welfare policies, such communities were
often made up of a high number of Black citizens and
were areas 'defined by urban decay and official neglect'
(Hernon, 2006:201). The imposition of stop and search
powers, known colloquially as the 'sus laws', gave free
rein to the police to accost, harass and question anyone
they thought to be behaving suspiciously, a law which
was used disproportionately in UK cities against young
Black people, mainly young men. This discrimination
did not stop with harassment however, with the police
being implicated in numerous cases of racist violence,
some of it fatal.

Leeds in 1971 had actually seen the first, and to
this date, the only successful prosecution following a

death in police custody. In 1969, the body of a beaten Nigerian man, David Oluwale, was pulled from the River Aire which runs through the city. Witnesses had reported seeing him dashing through the streets screaming, being chased and attacked by two police officers. The two officers, Ken Kitching and Geoff Ellerker, had waged a long period of sustained racist violence against Oluwale, the brutal facts of which emerged later at their trial for manslaughter. Such incidents of racist discrimination at the hands of the police eventually resulted in violent resistance across England, for example in Bristol in the South West, Toxteth in Liverpool in the North and also in Brixton, London in the 'riots' of the spring and summer of 1981. The disturbances in Brixton were later the subject of the Scarman Report, published by the Government in November of that year and recommending urgent action on racial discrimination, although tellingly, refusing to accept the existence of institutional racism within the police or any other part of the state.

Police harassment and biased stop and search exercises continued however, disproportionately affecting Black people, particularly young Black men; cases of assault and further tragic deaths in police custody also continued. In such a climate, the police, for many people, especially Black people, were not seen as a source of protection, but as a threat. Many women, in particular Black women, but also poor or otherwise marginalised women, may therefore have had understandable reticence towards a Women's Movement or particular protest that they believed to be calling for increased policing. That is the structural context, a context of historic and continuing racism, which influences the critiques of the early RTN marches and the debate which followed.

Unfortunately, concerns over racist policing are far from history of course and remain key social justice issues today. Black males are still disproportionately represented in the statistics on deaths in police custody in the UK for example, and recent figures suggest that Black and Asian people in the UK, particularly young males, are *still* overwhelmingly the target of police stop and search exercises (Dodd, 2012). Men are by no means the only victims either, with some of the most infamous cases of police brutality over the years resulting in the deaths of women, for example Cynthia Jarrett and Cherry Groce in London in 1985, and Joy Gardner also in London in 1993; their families are still awaiting justice.

## Race, rape and racism

The context of brutally racist policing in the UK at the time of RTN's emergence could then possibly explain some of the suspicions around the march and its perceived aims. Another possible reason for those suspicions may lie in the history of racist stereotypes linking Black men with criminality and sexual aggression. This linkage was not a construct of feminists however, let alone those organising RTN in Leeds in 1977, and it dates back to at least the period of slavery in both the UK and the US. Bourke (2007) for example, in her thorough history of rape, highlights that in the US and the UK there has long been more frequent and more severe punishment for Black men accused of rape as compared to White males. This was particularly the case when the alleged victim was a White woman. Black women meanwhile, as Crenshaw (1991) argues, rarely saw justice, and were often constructed in US law as almost un-rapeable, being subject to both racist and sexist sexual stereotypes, regardless of the ethnicity of any alleged assailant. These stereotypes associated White women with passive purity in need of paternalistic protection from White males who were seen as their owners and protectors. In contrast, Black women were associated with animalistic insatiable sexuality and Black men with sexual violence and predation. Early works such as the infamous American film *The Birth of a Nation* directed by DW Griffiths (1915) for example clearly reflect such racist assumptions, suggesting that Black males are biological rapists due to their ethnicity.

Such racist and patriarchal stereotypes connecting sex, race and rape have arguably not lost their impact. For example, in Britain in late 2010, in a well-publicised case concerning the grooming and prostitution of girls and young women in Derby in the Midlands region of England, certain elements of the media, and some politicians such as the then Home Secretary Jack Straw, chose to focus on the Asian ethnicity of the men charged, rather than the generic issue of male sexual violence against women or the male demand for prostitution. The media often search for connections between the perpetrators in such cases, clutching at similarities such as race or religion, instead of the most obvious connection of them all, that being that they all share a sex in common – the male sex. In 2013, similar racism was clear in commentary over a case involving the grooming and prostitution of girls in Oxford, in the South of England, where the charged perpetrators were Asian and allegedly of Muslim faith. Such racist coverage continues in the UK, for example around the scandals in Rotherham in 2014, and this is despite the fact that official reports show the majority of those charged with sexual offences against children are White men.

These recent cases above highlight how easily issues of male violence against women can be hijacked by a racist media to fuel racism; while the all too real facts of sexual exploitation and abuse are sidelined in the process. This was certainly no less the case in 1977 when RTN was founded in the UK. Therefore, there were indeed arguably justifiable suspicions around the pioneering and evolving politicisation of the issue of male sexual violence at that time, in a racist context where Black communities had for a long time already been stereotyped as not only disproportionately affected by such crimes, but disproportionately the perpetrators of such crimes. Public views of RTN may well have been understandably influenced then by these sorts of concerns, along with more general critiques of Western feminism. The Second Wave in particular is often critiqued for lacking in intersectional analysis and for overlooking race and racism. These critiques were highlighted by feminist writer Hazel Carby in her influential 1982 essay addressing White women, when she summarised that '[m]any black women had been alienated by the non-recognition of their lives, experience, and herstories in the Women's Liberation Movement' (1982:211).

In the 1970s and 1980s, debates around who the WLM could speak for and concerns over the universality of sisterhood were key. Tensions around power relations between women, not only along the fractures of race, but also social class and sexuality for example, troubled the idea of a universal women's movement which could act for all women. In turn, this troubled the possibility of a meaningful identity that could comfortably contain all women, in all their diversity. These tensions were present from the early days of the Second Wave and they were acknowledged and wrestled with in CR groups and at conferences throughout the UK as feminists tried to avoid and interrogate essentialism. This history reveals itself in published accounts as well as in letters and articles in periodicals of the time (Kanter et al., 1984; FAC, 1981; Freeman, 1975; Morgan, 1970).

The factual evidence proving that debate took place on these issues in the movement of the 1970s when RTN first emerged does not mean that the power relationships between women, or prejudice between and amongst women, were all eradicated, solved or resolved positively. Clearly, this is not the case, as these remain ongoing concerns for feminism as a movement today, with racism and ethnocentrism still troubling notions of sisterhood and solidarity. When RTN first emerged in the UK, it was therefore just one element of a wider WLM which had already long been justly critiqued for historic and ongoing racism and ethnocentrism. It is perhaps then unsurprising that RTN, as one highly visible and well-publicised aspect of that movement, also became subject to these valid and still pressing critiques. However, the specific charges being investigated here made against the original RTN rely on claims that the early marches called explicitly for increased policing and that they cynically targeted their protests in predominantly Black and global majority ethnic communities. I have endeavoured to highlight in this chapter that these particular charges are unfounded; while acknowledging the context in which they were made. There were very well-founded reasons for apprehension and distrust in a racist culture which permeated institutions such as the police and also social movements such as the WLM.

The issue of inclusion and exclusion on RTN is no less an important issue today for modern marchers and organisers. Representation in terms of ethnicity remains key, but current activists, especially activist organisers, are perhaps most publically exercised today over the inclusion of men on RTN and also the inclusion of trans- or queer-identified people. In the next chapter, I shall begin to explore some of these current fault lines in feminism and the fierce ongoing rifts which have formed a chasm over recent years between some transgender/transexual and feminist activists. To provide a background to this particular fault line I will have to delve into queer theory and point out where this meets and diverges from radical feminist theory on sex and gender.

# Chapter 5

# Tending to borders

In this chapter, I shall look at definitions and terminology covering issues such as what the label 'queer' actually describes and how women in all their diversity can possibly be defined under one label or banner. I will also consider some of the critiques of feminism which have come from some sections of academic scholarship, such as queer politics and poststructuralist theory; critiques which usually rely on the charge that feminism is essentialist. I will introduce theory from famous scholars such as the philosopher Judith Butler, who has posed questions for feminism and introduced many contemporary activists to queer theory and queer politics. Queer theory is informed by postmodernism and is associated with the academic study of sex, gender and sexuality. Scholar Gayle Rubin (1984) suggests that whereas feminist theory is about the study of gender oppression, queer theory is the study of gender as a whole, including all the different kinds of gendered and sexed identities, identifications, possibilities, sexualities and sex and gender minorities. Queer politics is concerned with gender fluidity and with promoting the idea of fluid sexualities rather than using fixed labels which can constrain people; somewhat ironically then, it is a label for people who do not like to be labelled. It is a label that is also sometimes, by no means always, associated with promotion of the sex industry, pornography and prostitution, and with a rejection or troubling of notions of structural inequality, especially sexism. This is just one of the reasons I myself do not ascribe to the label. Queer politics often seem more likely to view human individuals as individuals who are affected by and in turn enact individual power and privilege over others in a myriad of different ways, rather than viewing them as members of fixed and narrow social classes such as women, Black people or gay or lesbian people. While it may appear passé or out of date to some, the bad old structural inequalities of sexism, racism, class oppression and homophobia have not disappeared. That is why I firmly believe that identity movements around those identities are important, until the day those identities are no longer oppressed; and that is why I am not drawn to fluid and individualistic queer politics. This background will be important later in the book when I move on to look at some of the particular conflicts between queer and transgender/transexual activists and feminist activists.

Although from the previous discussions in this book about feminist typologies and the history of feminism we can see that the term 'patriarchy' is used frequently without question in many of the journals, classic texts and periodicals from the Second Wave, it has gone on to become far from accepted. From at least the 1980s and from the 1990s in particular, this term increasingly came under the spotlight and has been subject to much criticism, particularly from queer theory and other academic approaches. These are not just academic arguments being debated within the proverbial ivory towers and hallowed halls of our fine universities however; they are also being hotly contested within activist circles, especially online. The main critiques of the term 'patriarchy' suggest that the concept is naïve, universalising and ethnocentric.

The concept is also critiqued for essentialising women and men. In translation, this means that the term 'patriarchy' allegedly assumes that there is some fixed biological essence to all women that makes them one way, and some equally fixed and fundamental essence in all men that makes them another, different way. Critics go on to argue that not only do feminists invoke and construct these essential differences between women and men, they then use them to separate out human beings by sex alone and unfairly turn one group into a dominator class and the other into a subordinate class. This is seen by critics as simplistic and generalising, because power relationships work in many different ways, and it is argued that not all men oppress all women and that creating a sexed dualism like this just hides more complex relationships between human individuals. In this chapter, I will explore these critiques of the concept of patriarchy. In addition, I will also consider a much broader challenge, a challenge which raises a critique for feminism more widely; indeed, it is a critique which threatens feminism as a whole movement. This challenge comes from the academic deconstruction of the term 'woman', and with it the deconstruction of the terrain upon which the Feminist Movement has been built and on which it perhaps still rests.

Judith Butler is arguably one of the most well-known philosophers to have raised these important challenges for the Feminist Movement. Linking to the critiques listed above, one of her arguments is that much feminist theory has been guilty of ethnocentrism, by assuming that patriarchy is universal and that the sex/gender relationships and embodiments in the West are duplicated in every human society. Butler is also known for troubling the category of 'woman', seeing this concept as a corollary to the concept of universal patriarchy. She asserts that the category of woman has become a totalising category, a label which falsely assumes a 'seamless category of women' (1990:4). Far from being seamless, Butler emphasises the limits of identity politics within the group 'women' and she questions what the category even means: what is a woman anyway?

This question may sound like a non-question to many readers, but to feminist activist organisers, it is no doubt one they have encountered numerous times. It is both an academic but also a practical question and it has a history, an important history. It contains challenges to racism within feminism for example, and to homophobia within feminism; it asks us to think about who our movement speaks out for, who we mean when we say 'women' and who we exclude and include. As we all see the world from our own perspective, standpoint or position, we can sometimes assume that the issues we face as women in our own personal lives will be similar for all other women. But too often, this 'we' in feminism is White, heterosexual, able-bodied, feminised, heterosexualised and highly educated for example. All these features are factors of identity, and they will affect one's experiences of sexism, as well as of advantage and disadvantage more broadly. This is summed up in the term explained earlier – intersectionality – a term which has recently moved out of academia and into fairly mainstream commentary on contemporary feminism and feminist activism. It is a term which many activists today will probably be overly familiar with. Even if you are not immersed in feminist activism though, but follow reviews or accounts of feminist campaigns and publications in the media, then you may also have come across this term before. Recent attention on the term does not mean that it is widely understood however.

## *Intersecting inequalities across borders*

To move on then from the earlier brief introduction to this term, intersectionality, we can use this term to describe how power relationships intersect and inter-relate, both within and between different identified social groups or identities. For example, there is a power relationship along the fault line of sexed identity between women and men, but there will also be power-ful differences between women and men along the lines of race and class. There are power differences between men, who share a sex but may not share a race or social class or sexuality. Women too are not all the same, or all equal. There are power relationships at work between women as well, along the lines of social class, sexual-ity, disability and race for example. Sometimes, in the Western context at least, when we think of terms like those in that list, like 'gender' or 'race', we tend to think about rights for women and rights for Black people. It seems like the term 'gender' has actually developed a sex, or maybe it always did have; and the term 'race' definitely has a race, and probably always did. It is not so common then to think of White people when we hear reference to race or to men when we hear reference to gender. An intersectional perspective draws our atten-tion to the fact that all human beings actually inhabit many identities all at once, that all of us have a race, a gender identity, a sex, a social class and a sexual identity for example.

An intersectional perspective highlights then that identities are never fixed and singular, but often many and varied; thus, power relationships between individu-als are rarely straightforward. There are power relation-ships between all of us, whether we like it or not. They surround us like camouflaged contours on the maps of

our lives and they play out in our relationships, our
careers and our education for example. Power relationships may seem simple enough; they are often hierarchical dualisms with which we are familiar: Black/White,
adult/child, gay/straight, man/woman. But we also know
too that of course, no individual is just one of these
labels or identities, nor do these identities necessarily
stay the same throughout our whole lives – our age
changes, our sexuality may change, our health may
change, our caring or parenting status may change. With
such changes, we move in and out of certain recognised
social groups; we also move in and out of power. This
power shift happens because certain elements of our
identity might bring us degrees of privilege in society,
and others may not.

We all then inhabit a complicated position at the eye
of the storm of power relationships which surrounds us,
our history and our trajectory. At different times, we may
be made by our society to be more aware of certain elements of our identity rather than others, and they may
not always be the features others might assume would be
paramount. For example, my experiences of homophobia throughout my life have been far more visible to me
than my experiences of sexism. This is an example of a
difference between myself and a heterosexual feminist
woman, who may be much more alert than I would be
to sexual harassment and everyday sexism.

The scholar Kimberle Crenshaw, who coined the
term 'intersectionality' in 1989, explored how a failure
to adequately recognise those standing at the intersection of various oppressed identities, such as Black
women, results in the ultimate failure of political social
movements for racial equality and for women's equality. Crenshaw argued that in relation to male violence
against women for example, adequate prevention and

response for BME or Black and global majority ethnic women who are affected by male violence is limited by racism and sexism, including from within anti-racist and feminist communities themselves. Crenshaw pointed out that some anti-racist groups were male-dominated, did not understand the needs of Black women and were sexist. Likewise, some feminist groups were White-dominated, racist and did not understand or pay attention to the experiences of Black women who face both racism and sexism together. The persistence of racism and sexism within movements aimed at overturning those very oppressions is perhaps an example of what feminist academic and activist Mieke Verloo (2005) calls the 'interfering inequalities', which trouble and complicate the passage of all equality movements.

While such interfering inequalities have always been a key concern in the WLM, issues of inclusion and exclusion have continued to become increasingly significant for contemporary feminist activism, with many activists today enthusiastically committed to opening up feminism to all allies, rather than imposing any borders around the movement. Many activists are committed to an intersectional feminism, to a social movement which actively tries to recognise the complexity of identity, as well as notice and include those previously and currently silenced and excluded. There has been a marked shift towards mixed activism for example, with men increasingly included in feminist spaces; there has also been a necessary clarification of trans inclusion in women-only feminist spaces. In contrast to the early days of the Second Wave, groups today often clarify what they mean by the term 'woman', as this is no longer seen as self-evident. Groups often state that their spaces are open to 'self-identified women', thereby including transexual- or transgender-identified women. As any feminist activist will know, these sorts of decisions are fraught with controversy and have become a common fault line in the modern WLM. This is just one reason why these debates do matter, and why it is important to engage with the challenges from queer theory, a body of work which actually has a lot more in common with feminist theory than is often acknowledged.

## *The new woman question*

The category of woman itself has come under fire from queer theory, and so also have the categories of gender and even sex. Judith Butler's important theory of gender performativity defines gender as a social construction. By gender, I mean masculinity and femininity. Butler asserts that gender is a phenomenon that is brought into existence only by the repeated, high-quality performances of the current cultural norms for masculinity and femininity. It is the quality and the repetition of these performances that ironically adds to their natural appearance, and thus to their presumed naturalness. It follows then that if we all stopped 'doing' gender, it would cease to exist. The argument is that there is no 'real' gender behind your gender presentation – there is only your presentation. From this perspective, categories such as woman and man are not clear and fixed, and they certainly cannot exist outside of the cultural norms that create, label and define them. In fact, it is these cultural norms which bring the labels into being in the first place, through the act of naming, recognition and the following presumption of continued compliance and maintenance. To simplify this theory then, gender, as in masculinity and femininity, is not natural or biological, and it does not come naturally to human beings.

In fact, most people put a great deal of work into their gender; they spend a lot of time, money and effort on appearing recognisably masculine or feminine.

It is important to note that gender is not the same as biological sex. Sex currently describes at least three recognised sexes: female, male and intersex. These labels describe biological features of the body, such as reproductive capacity, hormones, chromosomes and genitalia. Intersex refers to people born with what are sometimes rather inappropriately called ambiguous genitalia, but this simply just means that they are born with different sexed characteristics which include features labelled as male and female, not just genitals and reproductive capacity, but also hormones for example. This used to wrongly be referred to in a very medicalised or pathologising way as hermaphrodite or hermaphroditic. Thankfully, there is now a growing, global intersex rights movement, which tries to stop medical institutions from performing unnecessary surgery on babies born with these bodily characteristics. Too often the response has been a brutal one, which sought to forcibly 'normalise' these babies, determined to fit them into one sexed box or another with medical interventions that often resulted in a lifetime of ill health, scrutiny and painful surgeries on one's most intimate body parts.

Very different to biological features of the sexed body however, gender most simply describes masculinity and femininity. There are actually many more than two genders though; the term can also be used to describe any individual's expression of their own sense of gender identity. For example, we could say that androgynous, macho or camp might also be gender expressions, as might be a mixture of these, or something else entirely of someone's own creation. There are also many people, including many feminists, who do not wish to be defined by gender at all, or to define themselves as one gender or another. In fact, for many feminists, the existence of gender at all is a problem; I will go into this in more detail later. For now, to return to the most common, narrow sense of these terms, sex and gender are usually assumed to be congruent; that is, to be matching. Matching, in contemporary Western society, usually means of course that females are supposed to be feminine and males are supposed to be masculine. If we think of current stereotypes or ideal types of masculinity, we can see what men are *meant* to be, usually strong in wealth, power or physicality for example, perhaps preferably all three. Gender can therefore certainly be expressed through the body, in terms of physicality in the definition of masculinity above, but it does not depend on the body or lie dormant within it like some sort of genetic feature or inherent essence. Gender is not born. No baby is born masculine or feminine. Although we may hear such terms often, especially in policy, legal and employment documents, there is no such thing as a 'birth gender' or a 'gender acquired at birth'. Gender is a set of learnt behaviours; it is the cultural roles and expectations of behaviour, dress, work, appearance and physicality that are attached to males and females.

We can say that most female people have the biological capacity to give birth, but we cannot say, for example, that most female people biologically have long hair or sit with their legs crossed. There is no biological link between being female and having long hair, wearing make-up or wearing dresses, while there is a biological link between being female and having the capacity to give birth. Likewise, there is no biological link between being male and having short hair, or liking football or being violent. Of course, scientific studies emerge periodically, usually very well received and publicised, which seek to 'prove' such gendered couplings: that girls like pink, that boys like blue, that men are biologically incapable of ironing and so the list goes on. There is often an accompanying lack of reflexivity as to the irony in these studies, which on the one hand portray men as naturally physical, practically minded, logical providers and protectors, while simultaneously claiming they are naturally unable to cook for themselves or wash their own pants. Such pop psychology has been beautifully branded by the scientist and author Cordelia Fine as neuro-sexism; same old sexism, wrapped up in peer review.

The gender binary that so many seek to prove, maintain and justify scientifically or otherwise, is what Judith Butler calls the 'heterosexual matrix'. This matrix depends on humans being organised by sex and gender, and then living up to their sexed and gendered labels. Female babies are called girls and are supposed to grow up to be feminine; male babies are called boys and are supposed to grow up to be masculine. When a baby is born, the question usually asked first is whether the baby is a boy or a girl – this is seen as an intrinsic part of being human. As it stands, society may have a hard time adjusting to human beings who were not sexed and gendered because this is such a fundamental distinction. Butler argues then, that, in contemporary Western society at least, being sexed and gendered is compulsory, and, taking on from the work of feminist poet and writer Adrienne Rich (1980), that this system is also marked by compulsory heterosexuality. This phrase refers to societies where heterosexuality is taken as the norm and assumed to be the norm, but also, where that status quo is enforced. Heterosexuality is enforced by being aggrandised, actively promoted, rewarded and maintained above other sexual identities and expressions which are silenced, discouraged and punished.

We can see this in hate crimes against lesbian, bisexual and gay people for example, in homophobic bullying within schools and in tragic murders, such as the fatal assault against 62-year-old gay man Ian Baynham in 2009, punched and kicked to death in the middle of Trafalgar Square in central London simply for holding hands with another man. In order for heterosexuality to be promoted and maintained, individuals need to be divided up by sex and gender into polar opposites and they need to comply with those labels visibly and unmistakably if heterosexuality is to continue as an institution in its present form. It should be noted then that it follows that, like gender, heterosexuality is also a social construction; it too is neither natural nor biological.

Butler questions the relationship between feminism and the heterosexual matrix. Firstly, she argues that the category of 'woman' cannot possibly contain all the diverse human beings that may be identified as, or identify as, women. Therefore, attempting to draw borders around the identity inevitably invokes cases which will not fit, or which will refuse to fit, within those boundaries. Secondly, Butler suggests that by building a political movement and a politics around and for this category 'woman', feminism also constructs the category itself and brings it into being, while claiming simply to represent it. Thus, Butler raises the highly provocative question as to whether feminism is complicit in the very system it claims to oppose, by using predefined, narrow concepts of men and women, rather than searching for more radical alternatives or rather than rejecting the heterosexual matrix and its labels outright. The argument follows then, that every time feminism invokes the idea of woman as a category, we bring it into being, we buy into and maintain the heterosexual matrix. 'The suggestion that feminism can seek wider representation for a subject that it itself constructs has the ironic consequence that feminist goals risk failure by refusing to take account of the constitutive powers of their own representational claims' (1990:4). Or, as transexual activist and writer Kate Bornstein puts it more simply, to accept women and men as two distinct, pre-existing or a priori gendered categories, and to identify with one or the other, only serves to construct and maintain those categories. 'Once we choose one or the other, we've bought into the system that perpetuates the binary' (1995:101).

So, if we take Butler's theory then, if gender is performative and a social construct, does this mean that gender is not 'real'? Is it just an act that we can choose to take on or take off? The answer to the latter question is definitely no. Butler's theory of gender performativity is not the same thing as performance. Performance suggests voluntarism – it suggests choice, temporality, diversity and play, whereas in the heterosexual matrix, none of these is generally present. Exceptions to the rule do occur of course. I am not trying to suggest that everyone goes through life like some kind of robotic Barbie or Ken doll. However, sometimes any exceptions that do occur only further solidify the rule. To take an example, say a person assumes that a baby dressed in blue is male, or that an individual with short hair and trousers is a man, their reading, or assumption, may not always be right. The baby may be female; the individual in trousers may identify as a woman. Such an incidence will often be seen as a 'mistake'. When such a mistake or misreading occurs, people rarely use the event to reflect on the wonderful variety of human identity and expression. They simply think to themselves that they made a mistake due to the individual's sex and/or gender presentation being unclear. Of course, what they are comparing this unclear presentation to is an assumed norm, the binary, narrow, rigid gender norm of female femininity and male masculinity. Thus bodies are seen not to 'fit', or to have the 'wrong' presentation, or to be unclear or unreadable to viewers, resulting in 'mistakes' which, strangely, usually only further entrench people's belief in the naturalness of the norm. Or to put it more simply, we need to believe that one way of being and appearing is the 'right' way in order to view any other way as 'wrong'.

To return to the earlier question then, does all of this theorising mean that gender is not 'real'? I think it probably does. Gender is clearly a very social construction. This is proven in the fact that gender changes over time and space, whereas biological sex stays pretty much the same. Gender is historically, culturally and geographically specific – by which I just mean that it looks different in different countries and cultures and that it has looked different throughout history. In Britain, in the 1900s for example, pink was often considered too bold and brash a colour for girls to wear, being seen as more suitable for boys. Today however, pink is not considered a very masculine colour, and toys and clothing seem to have become more gender segregated over the years, rather than less. If gender were biological, then we would expect masculine appearance, roles and behaviours to stay the same over time and place. The fact that this is not the case should surely make us doubt the fixity of gender. None of this suggests that gender is not lived and experienced though. It does not mean that our gendered lives and experiences are not 'real'.

In her 1993 book *Bodies That Matter*, Butler attempted to address some of the misreadings and simplifications that had developed around her earlier work. She clarified that she never suggested that gendered categories did not matter, or that we can all freely play around with gender like children at some giant pick and mix sweetie stand. As Butler reiterated more recently in a 2014 interview, we must not lose track, amongst all our theorising, of the right to live out our own sex and gender identity, whatever that may be and whether we personally experience it as biological or not. Nor must we forget that doing just that, living one's preferred personal identity, can sometimes be dangerous and can actually lead to loss of life.

> No matter whether one feels one's gendered and sexed reality to be firmly fixed or less so, every person should have the right to determine the legal and linguistic terms of their embodied lives. So whether one wants to be free to live out a 'hard-wired' sense of sex or a more fluid sense of gender, is less important than the right to be free to live it out, without discrimination, harassment, injury, pathologization or criminalization – and with full institutional and community support.
>
> Butler, 2014

All of us live in real bodies, bodies that are policed and trained by the social norms which surround us. Ours are bodies that can be hurt through trying to tow the line, as well as hurt for stepping out of line. Gender may be a fiction, but it is not a joke; it can mean life and death. We live gender therefore, we live it out in our human bodies, just as it also acts upon us and shapes us accordingly, moulding us into acceptable displays of masculinity and femininity.

Significantly for my discussion about the definition of the category of 'woman', Butler also asserted that this particular identity category is necessary for feminist political reasons. Butler clarified that she never

suggested that the category of woman did not matter, or
that subjects within it did not have a bodily materiality,
albeit under/within the current binary gender system.
She does repeat however, that there are dangers associated with mobilising politically under terms constructed
by the system which that very mobilisation is against.
Therefore, she argues, for our part, feminists can open
up the category of 'woman', or at least leave it open, not
pin it down or fence it off. This does not just mean that
we leave open what it means to be a woman, it also means
we leave open what a woman even is in the first place
and how, or whether, we could define all women. Butler
sees this as an exciting emancipatory project, one that
could make feminism change and grow to become more
relevant to more people.

This deconstruction could also co-exist with a strategic use of the term 'woman' when politically necessary
though. We could do both – use the term, but still continue to recognise and challenge the limits of it. Echoing
the important scholar Spivak's (2008) useful theory of
'strategic essentialism', Butler insists that it must be possible to use the term 'woman' while still critiquing it,
because we acknowledge we are positioned and limited
by it. To summarise then, as feminists we often reject
the patriarchal definitions of what a woman should be
and is, but we still use this very term 'woman' to rise
up against that patriarchal system. Using a particular
term like this, strategically and practically, as a mobiliser
or a banner to unite under should always be done
cautiously and consciously and it should always be temporary. Spivak reminds that we should always consider
the 'dangerousness of something one cannot not use'
(2008:5).

Butler was wrong however when she stated that
'the question is not whether or not there ought to be

reference to matter, just as the question never has been whether or not there ought to be speaking about women' (1993:29). In fact, this is just what has happened, the latter has become perhaps *the* question within feminism, at least for those immersed in, researching or studying this movement. In what could be seen as a reformulation of what was called in the nineteenth century the 'woman question', the newer, new woman question is literally the question of what is a woman. Debates about the deconstruction of sex and gender have been interpreted by many feminists as an accusation that the WLM is built on sand, on a fictional category. If there is no such stable, unifying class or group category as 'woman', then how can there be such a thing as women's oppression or a women's movement to end it?

## *Reclaiming radical feminism*

How can radical feminism respond to these challenging and important debates? Firstly, it is useful to remember the key components of radical feminism. I have identified four key defining features which can distinguish it from other schools of feminism. These are the acknowledgement and analysis of patriarchy, the prioritisation of women-only political organising, a focus on male violence against women as a keystone of women's oppression and, fourthly, the extension of the analysis of male violence against women to include the industries of pornography and prostitution. It is important to understand that these are only distinguishing features; they are some aspects that arguably set apart or define radical feminism's particular foci when compared to other recognisable schools of feminism. This definition in no way precludes radical feminist analysis of, or attention to all other social justice issues. For example, the masculinisation of wealth and power, capitalism, war and militarism, racism, environmentalism, reproductive rights, class struggles, caring work, parenthood, childcare and animal rights; all of these and so many more are issues that radical feminist theory, rightly and urgently, has and does address.

The focus of this particular school of feminism certainly does not end at rape, or porn or domestic abuse, it has merely worked tirelessly to ensure that those issues are included in broader political analysis, are on the agenda, are in focus at all. In return for that effort, those of us proud to identify as radical feminists are often assumed to be blinkered to any other kind of human suffering or injustice, as if we do not care about women's poverty, as if we do not care about men exploited in sweatshops, forced into war, or raped or killed. Some people really believe that radical feminists only care about the issue of male violence against women, simply because we are the ones who have arguably done most to raise awareness of that issue. At the root of this common assumption lies the problem that all too often prioritising women is seen as excluding men. This is just another of the ongoing challenges for feminism in general of course: the difficulty of focussing on women in a phallocentric or male-focussed society. Our work can often invoke a knee-jerk discomfort which kicks against this movement for the less powerful half of humanity. Such discomfort was identified, recounted and commented on frequently by the contemporary feminists I spoke to in my research on RTN activism. It was this discomfort that sometimes appeared to lurk in the background of some resistance to women-only RTN marches for example and it also could be found behind concerns over sexism towards men. I will outline and explore these issues in more detail later in this book, but it is important to note that these very live and current issues can be related back to the fundamental practical questions of borders and definitions which are being addressed in this chapter. These seemingly theoretical debates translate into real and urgent questions such as why should feminism separate out women and men anyway? Why should feminism continue to use a binary division which we know has stereotyped men just as much as women?

From a radical feminist perspective, it is not necessary to advocate that gender is inherent and biological in order to accept that these categories were not created equal. I disagree with the former and agree with the latter. As already discussed, gender arguably has no basis in biology. Even biological sex may not be as fixed and binary as has been assumed, as in the case of infants born intersex for example. However, as mentioned earlier, this does not mean that sex and gender are not experienced as lived identities, by humans who often have little or no choice whether they adopt gendered roles or not, within a heterosexual matrix that uses sex and gender as a marker of humanity itself.

It is possible then to say that 'women' exist. They are adult human beings who have been defined within patriarchy as women and as female, usually based on a cursory exam of their genitals at birth when they were labelled female and girls. But, all these women are also all unique individuals; it would be difficult to decide on any one defining feature of women. Most often, attempts at any such definition would resort to biology and indeed women as a group do share things because of their biology, or rather, and this is important, because of how their biology is treated within patriarchy. Women as a group, not every individual woman, but women as a group, share the capacity to give birth for example. This raises the potential of unwanted pregnancies, which gives rise to concerns around access to free, safe, legal and non-stigmatised abortion. Pregnancy and child rearing can also be a common site of experience between women, both positive and negative. Women as a group, not every single individual woman, but generally, women also share menstruation for example, which is stigmatised within patriarchy. Women are also subject to misogynistic attacks on their bodily integrity, such as sexual violence or female genital mutilation. However, as has been explored already, biology is not always so simple a marker. Many women cannot give birth for example, and there are women who do not have wombs, or ovaries or breasts, not every woman chooses pregnancy or experiences pregnancy and not every woman menstruates. Women's bodies take many diverse forms and change throughout a lifetime. Perhaps the only thing that women share beyond doubt or question is the lived experience of being treated as women in a society where that means second class; and that includes how our bodies are treated. In a sense then, the only thing that unites us as women in all our diversity is our shared experiences of resisting and surviving sexism in its many and changing forms, however conscious of that process we may be. I am then asserting that women and men are two distinct groups, but that this is a political, rather than a biological divide.

There will be many women who are loathe to think of themselves as belonging to a political group or social class purely by nature of their sex; this is also anathema to many contemporary queer activists who view such a dichotomy as simplistic and deterministic. Yet, I would argue that this understanding of sex class is a prerequisite for feminist identification, for feminist action and for change. As Kate Millett has argued, 'the emergence of a

positive collective identity proceeds revolutionary awareness and marks the difference between it and pointless
uprisings which only spin back into further reaction'
([1969]1972:355). This is also a key requirement for
all identity-based social movements of course, not just
feminism, but Black civil rights movements, lesbian and
gay movements or disability rights movements for example. Social movement scholars have studied what they
call collective identity or class identity in such uprisings, a feature which obviously relies upon individuals
considering themselves part of a class or identity in the
first place.

Statistics evidence women's inferior position compared to men around the globe. This is therefore a
structural inequality which does exist and which has
not gone away. This unequal sexual status quo benefits
men, not every man as an individual, but men as a
group. The status quo does not benefit women, not every
woman as an individual, but women as a group. Wherever you look in the world, this hierarchy between men
and women is present. Amongst poor and oppressed
peoples, women in those groups will be poorer. Amongst
the uneducated and the displaced, women will be there
in higher number than men. In times of civil war or
other conflict, women will make up high numbers of
those displaced. Women are also highly represented in
casualties and fatalities of war, though they are less likely
to be fighting themselves as combatants, much less making political and economic decisions to go to war. Women
and children also face sexual violence in war, such as
the use of rape as a weapon, and they can then face
further problems such as accessing health care or safe
legal abortions. In countries and cultures where education is hard to come by, girls will often be the ones
most likely to be denied an education. Even if you look

at the higher echelons of society, if we look at the gender pay gap in banking in the UK for example, we find that privileged educated women are still being paid thousands of pounds less compared to their male colleagues. Women are not equal to men. This probably seems an uncontroversial claim, but what many rarely do is move on from that to conclude that women are unequal because of men. The workings of patriarchy, which is made up of the actions of men as a social class, oppress women as a class - that is precisely how patriarchy rules and has done so for so long.

Women are then in the peculiar position of not being a minority, yet being oppressed in a way we commonly associate with the treatment of minority groups. Oppressed may seem a strong word, many may associate this term more with political repression, for example the treatment of certain ethnic or religious groups in dictatorial or unstable regimes. When I use the term, like most feminists I refer to the common dictionary definition. Last time I checked in my Oxford English, the term 'oppression' referred to prolonged cruel or unjust treatment or exercise of authority. I believe it is not a misuse of the term then to suggest that women as a group have been subject to cruel and unjust treatment for millennia, simply for being born female, under the exercise of male authority. This oppression is not good for women; obviously, oppression is not good for anybody, it has an effect on the oppressed and that effect is not pretty. In studies of inequality, the effect of being oppressed, usually applied to minority groups, leads to something called minority group status – an inferiority complex, an internalised belief in the lies the ruling group tells you about yourself. This is basically the playing out of what the sociologist Robert Merton called a self-fulfilling prophecy. In other words, if you are given a particular label replete with certain expectations and treated accordingly, eventually you will start to act exactly as that label defines.

Millett points out that with the label of woman, the expectations and beliefs of that label are mediated to us through every area of our lives from birth.

> When in any group of persons, the ego is subjected to such invidious versions of itself through social beliefs, ideology, and tradition, the effect is bound to be pernicious. This coupled with the persistent through frequently subtle denigration women encounter daily through personal contacts, the impressions gathered from the images and media about them, and the discrimination in matters of behaviour, employment, and education which they endure, should make it no very special cause for surprise that women develop group characteristics common to those who suffer minority status and a marginal existence
>
> Millett, [1969]1972:55

The category of woman does indeed matter therefore. There is a justifiable need for a politics around this category, a politics around this mystery that is woman which philosophers struggle to define. It is striking of course that while all these academic and theoretical debates unfurl, our enemies seem to have no problem defining us. Despite our postmodern pondering, somehow women in their billions all over the world are still successfully distinguished from men and earmarked for lower pay, fewer legal rights, male ownership and a denial of bodily integrity. I suggest then that we accept that the binary gender system is a social construction, but also appreciate that it is a construction with ancient and still strong foundations. The effects of it are real. As long as it exists, there will be many individuals committed to chipping it away, to changing it and, like many feminists, to demolishing it altogether. But, to emphasise once again, our paying attention to this system, contrary to the challenges from queer theory outlined earlier, does not mean that we built it or that we seek to maintain it; quite the contrary. To blame feminists like that is just a case of shooting the messenger. As the wonderful and inspiring radical feminist writer and activist, the late Andrea Dworkin summarises so passionately,

> [t]o be a feminist means recognising that one is asso-
> ciated with all women not as an act of choice but as a
> matter of fact. The sex-class system creates the fact.
> When that system is broken, there will be no such
> fact. Feminists do not create this common condition
> by making alliances: feminists recognise this common
> condition because it exists as an intrinsic part of sex
> oppression.
>
> 1983:221

Earlier I pointed out that Butler has argued that decon-structing woman could be a positive project, but this has by no means been seen as inevitable by many feminists. Incidentally, this is not just a concern for feminism, but for all social movements which are mobilising around a particular identity. It is a concern because we are all then uprising politically around a category that also limits and oppresses us, a category we are seeking to challenge. These were the dangers pointed out in the discussion earlier by theorists such as Butler and Spivak. But some feminists have argued that while we can acknowledge the limitations of the label of woman and challenge what it represents within patriarchy, deconstructing the category woman may be far from exciting or liberatory. There is a danger looming, the danger that we could get lost in such a project, and that it will only become confusing and all consuming, without presenting any challenge at all to patriarchy. As feminist commentator Croson warns in an article on the importance of women-only organising, 'deconstructing woman is of absolutely no help in deconstructing male power' (2001:9). It is the latter which I assert is, or should be, the project of feminism – by which I mean all feminism/s. This is a project which did not create gender categories, but which arises as one response to them. It is a political response to a social structure where power and privilege is accorded to one half of humanity over another, based purely on their assigned sex and attached gender at birth.

To conclude then, mobilising around the category of woman does not mean that feminism has been blinkered to the constructed nature of this category. In fact, feminism generally, and radical feminism in particular, has been extremely progressive in its analysis of gender as a social construction. This is highlighted not least by the important radical feminist analyses of male violence as political rather than biological; it can also be seen in the understanding of patriarchy as political rather than biological. The aim to continuously interrogate and challenge social divisions and markers like sex and gender is indeed an important project; it is an important project today for queer theorists, but it has always been so for radical feminism.

## *Returning to the classics*

In the early radical feminist publication *The Dialectic of Sex* for example, written by the late Shulamith Firestone in 1970, gender, as in masculinity and femininity, is not presented as biological. Nor is patriarchy presented as biological, inherent or immutable. Firestone is most commonly known amongst feminists for having argued the case for so-called mechanical wombs, to free women from the biological burden of childbirth. Her argument is in fact far more subtle than this crude summary which abounds about her work. Her focus on reproduction was perhaps also misplaced, as childbirth does not have to lead to childrearing necessarily. Society could easily decide to organise childcare and childrearing quite differently to what we do currently. There is nothing inherent in reproductive capacity which lends itself to oppression of course. Early revolutionary and radical feminists actually emphasised this when they explained the importance of considering sex as a political class and this was fundamental to their theory. This is illustrated in this quote from papers on women and sex class, printed in the Second Wave journal *Scarlet Women* in 1977 and written by now famous names like Sheila Jeffreys and Jalna Hanmer. 'It is not our biology that oppresses us, it is the value that men place on it ... Our biology oppresses us because of the value men place on it, per se it is not oppressive' (Hanmer et al., 1977:9).

The point about patriarchy being political rather than biological is argued most persuasively in the work of pioneering radical feminist theorist Kate Millett. Millett's *Sexual Politics*, published in 1969, still stands as one of the most extensive and thorough exposés of the long history of the workings and effects of patriarchy. It was also impressively forward thinking in analysing gender as a cultural construct, and in exploring the emerging work on gender and sexed identity by well-known researchers such as Robert Stoller, and the far less renowned John Money.

Millett refers to patriarchy as a form of social government and to sex roles as a product of this 'nakedly oppressive social system' ([1969]1972:343). One of the critiques of feminism that I looked at earlier is the suggestion that it universalises patriarchy. Is this true then in Millett's classic analysis? Millett does indeed define patriarchy as universal, asserting that male supremacy is a feature of societies worldwide. 'Perhaps patriarchy's greatest psychological weapon is simply its universality and longevity... While the same might be said of class, patriarchy has a still more tenacious or powerful hold through its successful habit of passing itself off as nature' (Millett, [1969]1972:58). Here she is stressing that it is precisely because of its longevity and universality in fact, that patriarchy increasingly resists challenge by presenting itself as natural. As the famous philosopher John Stuart Mill, whom Millett refers to in her book, argued much earlier in his 1869 treatise on *The Subjection of Women*, 'The subjection of women to men being a universal custom, any departure from it quite naturally appears unnatural' (1984:270). The longer the system endures therefore, the more it will be defended on the grounds of its apparent suitability and naturalness.

As Millett points out though, assertions that things have always been this way can only ever be assertions, because studies of social organising in pre-history remain largely speculation. The historian Gerda Lerner, introduced earlier in this book, argues that male supremacy appears as a constant throughout available histories, across the globe, therefore highlighting the universality of patriarchy. To defend this position, Lerner asserts that in contrast, female supremacy has never existed anywhere.

> There is not a single society known where women-as-a-group have decision-making power over men or where they define the rules of sexual conduct

or control marriage exchanges...when that power
includes the public domain and foreign relations and
when women make essential decisions not only for
their kinfolk but for the community.

1986:30

It should be possible then, to acknowledge that
patriarchy is universal; though to do so does not,
and should not, entail homogenising the form that
patriarchy takes in different cultures and communities around the world. It seems that it is the latter,
rather than the former, that leads to critiques of feminism, particularly of its analysis of patriarchy. Of course,
patriarchy looks different in different countries and
cultures; that does not mean it does not exist. Radical feminists were far from unaware that gendered
and sexed relations and dynamics take different forms
globally and culturally – it would be patronising to
suggest they were so unaware and so unrealistic. But
the global shifting, adapting and fracturing forms of
patriarchy throughout history and space in no way pre-
clude the identification of the continuing dominance of
male supremacy and female subordination as a system of
social organisation and governance.

Millett ([1969]1972) argues that without the sex-class
system of patriarchy, sex would no longer matter as a
marker, so sex and gender roles would cease to exist
in their present state at least. Women can therefore
be seen as a product of patriarchy, not only politically,
but bodily too. With similarities to the sociologist Pierre
Bourdieu's theory of habitus (1986), Millett explains
how women's physicality is inscribed on them, a process
whereby their bodies are literally fitted into the requirements of their sex role, as patriarchy acts on and shapes
their bodies. JS Mill mentioned this too in his 1869

treatise when he spoke of women of the upper and middle classes being treated like greenhouse or hothouse plants, being confined in pots, trimmed, kept indoors, trained to grow in a certain way and kept sheltered from the weather. His point was that girls are grown to be the fairer sex and that if boys were treated in the same way, they may well be fairer, gentler and less physical and muscular. We can see habitus in the way that women take up space for example, or not, often taking up less space than men do. To give a very simple example, I often see women sitting on the bus with their legs crossed, while men take up almost a whole seat with their legs spread apart. Women sometimes walk differently to men, taking shorter strides and keeping their bodies more contained. The point here is that this is not due to biology; the bodies of women and men have just been trained in certain ways. 'The heavier musculature of the male, a secondary sexual characteristic and common among mammals, is biological in origin but is also culturally encouraged through breeding, diet and exercise' (Millett, [1969]1972:27). Thus the gender system does not just affect our minds, as I said earlier, it actually affects our physical bodies too – men as well as women. In her classic text Millett therefore troubles the presumed naturalness of gender and sex roles, highlighting that appearance, mannerisms, physique, attitudes and behaviours are in fact socially constructed and manipulated in patriarchy's image.

To summarise, the category of woman can arguably be seen from a radical feminist analysis as a political rather than biological category. 'The patriarchal mentality has concocted a whole series of rationales about women...And these traditional beliefs still invade our consciousness and affect our thinking to an extent few of us would be willing to admit' (Millett, [1969]1972:46).

Feminism generally, and radical feminism in particular, invokes this identity in the process of founding a resistance movement to the oppression attached to the category; that does not mean we are wedded to the category. It does not mean we see the category as immutable. As a movement based on identity, feminism has indeed emphasised the borders of that identity, but those borders are rarely based on biology. More often, as stated earlier in this section, they are based on shared experiences of oppression for those marked as female and as women, within male supremacy.

To conclude then, I propose that radical feminist theory is in fact fully congruent with a Butlerian understanding of gender as a social construct and is certainly far from the essentialist project it is often accused of being. How then do all these theoretical, political and academic debates play out in the actual organisation of feminist activism today and just how relevant are they? I shall now turn to look at the work of contemporary feminist activists themselves, and highlight how such debates influence and shape their motivations and practice.

# Chapter 6

# Repetitions per decade: Voices of activists past and present

In the next chapters, you will hear from some of the many activists across the UK who are giving up their time and energy to attend, organise and fundraise for RTN and many other causes for social justice. These are the women who keep the tradition of RTN alive. They have taken on the flaming torch from our sisters who went before us and with it, the responsibility to ensure this march continues onwards; for as long as it remains necessary. Throughout my research and through my own activism, I have been privileged to meet many of these committed activists. I have also been lucky enough to join and even lead many RTN marches in different towns and cities. Some of these marches followed tragic events; they were angry protests at recent rapes perpetrated by men against women in their city for example. Others were in response to all too common police 'advice' after such cases, suggesting effectively that women should not go out if they did not want to be raped. The defence of local services was another reason to march, protesting against funding or closure threats for Women's Aid refuges or Rape Crisis Centres. The marches are always a mixture of defiance, celebration and anger. They are also tinted with a sadness, the sadness that we still have to keep marching like this against rape and sexual violence.

The type of people involved in feminist activism are a diverse bunch, it takes all sorts, and the activists I met came from many different backgrounds. In the next section, I will outline some basic demographics, so you can get a picture of their ages, the length of time they have been involved in activism and their own political identifications for example. The activists are identified with pseudonyms only, and in most cases, I have not listed the town or city in which they live and work. This is to protect their anonymity, as the activists took part in my doctoral research under academic conditions and ethical frameworks which assured they would not be identified. I have therefore respected that here in this book too. The feminist scene is a small world and so I have tried to make sure that nobody is too easily identifiable by their description, while at the same time giving you, the reader, a picture of who these activists are.

I travelled all over England to meet and interview RTN activists, 25 in total, with over 100 taking part in an online survey as well. Their contributions covered all the key issues alive in feminism today, including some of the tensions. I met activists in squatted social spaces, Student Union bars, art galleries and cafes and we talked about inclusion and exclusion. We talked about the Whiteness of feminist events, the definition of 'woman', the division in the movement between those pro or anti-pornography and prostitution and we wrestled with the pros and cons of involving men in feminist activism. RTN marches are a site where many of these contemporary feminist fault lines converge, particularly for activist organisers of course. Those organisers are making decisions about whether or not to hold mixed RTN marches where men are invited, whether to have women-only space and how they will define the terms and borders of that space if they do. They are also making practical plans about whether to march past and protest against lap dancing clubs in their town for example, or whether to take a total detour around the fierce debates in feminism over the sex industry, choice and agency. Regardless of what decisions these organising groups make, each march receives criticism; sometimes it is constructive and other times less so. Committed to organising successful and inclusive events, the activists continue their work, trying to build on mistakes and successes and aspiring to that ideal in politics – pleasing most of the people, most of the time.

## *Introducing the activists*

Who then are these activists who take time away from their families, jobs and studies to organise a night-time march, often in the cold British weather, to protest against rape and all forms of male violence? The activists I met were from a wide range of backgrounds, ages and political identifications. Their ages ranged from teens to sixties and the vast majority were female, with only one man taking part in the interviews I carried out. Most activists identified their ethnicity as White, and this does raise a significant absence in this book, as well as affect the representativeness of the sample presented here. I have to acknowledge that as a White feminist, working in a sector dominated by White women, it is possible that my own profile discouraged Black women from taking part in my research. However, silences such as this in my small sample are by no means representative of the diversity of women involved in feminism today and in the past. RTN organising groups and the marches themselves have always and still do attract women of all ages, sexualities, faiths and ethnicities. It is a sad fact that male violence against women knows no borders of race, religion, class or status; it is an issue which unites all women. Many activists pointed this out, and many were also positive about inclusion on RTN and felt that over the years it had become more representative particularly in terms of ethnicity. This view was summarised by Babette for example, a young anti-capitalist and queer activist in her twenties. She praised

> the positive move towards greater inclusivity, particularly for Black women and people of colour. Feminism has historically been criticised for excluding these women, but in recent years appears to have been changing.
>
> (Babette)

It is a shame that the received wisdom about not only RTN, but the movement as a whole, is that this is a movement for White women. There is an important difference between stating that feminism is a movement for White women and pointing out that it is White dominated. It has been, and is still the latter here in the UK, but that does not mean Black women have not been active in feminist struggles for centuries or that Black feminists did not play a key role during the Second Wave here in the UK; indeed they did, as was highlighted earlier in Chapter 2.

As well as ethnic identification, I also asked activists in my research about their sexual identity. Given the important role that lesbian women have always played in the Feminist Movement, I was interested to see if this was still the case. As a lesbian myself, active in the movement and observing its changes and membership, I held a perception that lesbians were less visible today than they were in the Second Wave. I have a few ideas about why this might be the case, as did the activists I discussed the issue with. Not all of them raised it however, and overall there seemed to be a general opinion that the movement today is far more inclusive to all groups. Sexuality was not actually mentioned as an issue of inclusion or exclusion, and I was not surprised that the majority of activists identified as heterosexual, though several lesbians did also take part. A minority preferred to identify their sexuality as queer, and some identified as bisexual. When they used the identifier of 'queer', most activists meant by this that they did not want to be labelled, or that they experienced their sexuality as fluid and so could not fence themselves off in neat tick boxes as either gay, straight or bisexual.

Despite their different backgrounds and different identities, the activists had very similar motivations for marching on RTN marches. They all spoke about empowerment and solidarity. Bette, in her late twenties, said she was radical and left wing in her feminism; she said that it was the sense of togetherness with other feminists which kept her coming back to RTN and the sense of unity over a shared cause.

> The sense of solidarity and empowerment you get from marching alongside other women in public to make a stand on an issue that affects women.
>
> (Bette)

Activists also thought that RTN provides an important public relations role for feminism; showcasing to the general public that the Feminist Movement is currently alive and well, and recruiting, as Lucy, a 24-year-old feminist illustrated.

> If people are in the pub and they see a whole load of women marching, they see the Women's Liberation Movement is not over, it's not a historical thing.

So I think it's a physical manifestation of that and it raises awareness.

(Lucy)

Most obviously of course, RTN raises awareness about male violence against women, and this is its focus. But the march was seen as an opportunity to do this on the activist's own terms, on feminist's own terms. This was seen as rare, rare that is outside of the now rather mainstream but often conservative debates and policy discussions on violence against women which make it into the media and are very much framed by the agenda of the government of the day. For some activists, the march was a chance to highlight all the lives lost to male violence, and to honour and remember those women. This was the feeling of Bronwyn, a young anti-capitalist feminist in her twenties who defined politically as a radical feminist.

The march to me is like a remembrance. There are women who can't march, they have already either lost their lives or are living lost lives. I have to march every year because they can't. To me, the march is saying – we haven't forgotten you. That's a vital part of the movement. No other event has that significance for me.

(Bronwyn)

I asked all the activists about how they would identify themselves politically. As I discussed in Chapter 3, there are so many different schools and types of feminism and this used to be quite important during the Second Wave, with different theories and methods being fought out between different tendencies. I was interested to note that these herstorical divisions seemed far less important to younger activists today. Although many did have quite fixed ideas about which type of feminism suited them best, opinions often seemed broadly united on several topics, no matter which particular school of feminism was signed up to. However, it was also clear that some of the well-known theoretical divides were still playing out, and this was particularly the case between radical and socialist feminists. These also happened to be the two most popular political identifications given. When I asked activists how they would define if they had to pick a particular kind of feminism, it was those answers they gave most often: socialist feminist or radical feminist.

Although many of the activists were younger feminists, making up the new generation that so much of the popular feminist commentary focusses on, few actually identified as third wave feminists. 'Third wave' is the term so often used to describe contemporary feminist activity, although it seems that the precise number of waves rises every week, with some suggestions that we are now in a fourth wave of feminism. Despite such media hysteria, several activists were far from positive about the wave metaphor in general and decidedly negative about the third wave in particular. While this term was used as a purely chronological referent by some, for others it carried political ramifications, many of which they disagreed with, as I shall outline later.

In my sample group of activists were those who had been involved with the original RTN back in the 1970s and 1980s, and also those who had only been on contemporary marches since 2004. Activists who had been involved with the original UK RTN tended to be aged between 45 and 65, the contemporary marchers were usually younger, with most giving their ages between 25 and 30 years old. When it came to questions about tactics and methods, as well as political questions about aims and motivations, there was marked agreement between both these groups – the original and contemporary marchers. Both gave their opinions on how RTN has changed over the decades; some had obviously seen this happen themselves, while younger activists had gleaned their views from reading about past marches and from talking to older activists about Second Wave feminism. Starting with the practical questions first, I will now begin to introduce the activist voices by exploring some of the changes that have been observed in the RTN march over the years.

## Practicalities and passion: How has Reclaim the Night changed?

The level of passion amongst the marchers is the same. Ways of organising are very different now.

(Al Garthwaite)

Some of the changes in RTN are obvious and practical, namely the huge influence of the internet on organising methods, not just for feminism of course but for all social movements. Marches are now organised mainly through social media, rather than through word of mouth or newsletters. Previously, our foremothers had to slave for days over a hot printing press to get ideas and events out in leaflets and newsletters, which even then had a relatively limited circulation. Their reach also depended on some degree of insider knowledge or access to women's centres or other alternative spaces where these materials could be picked up. Other practical changes that activists noted were perceived changes in the responses of bystanders to the RTN marches. These are the members of the public whose evening is interrupted by a slow and noisy political march wending its way through their city centre. Whether shoppers, commuters or tourists, most are at least interested and many will stop and line the route of the march either just to be curious or to clap and shout encouragement. It was heartening that several of the original marchers noted that bystanders today are far more knowledgeable than in the past and far more sympathetic to the aims and sentiments of the march. Vivienne had noticed this shift on the recent marches she had been on. I chatted with Vivienne on the phone because she was a full-time carer and we never managed to find a convenient time to meet at a base in the Midlands where she was from. Vivienne was 51, she had been quite involved in feminism in the past and she identified proudly as a radical lesbian feminist.

> I don't recall ever in the past seeing such a strong positive response from women we bumped into, and there was a real strong positive reaction [on a recent march she attended]. And they seemed to know what was going on. I mean, I don't remember that in the past.
>
> (Vivienne)

However, even from my own experience on RTN I know that this is sadly not always the case, and several activists did point out that the reaction from bystanders today is by no means always positive. Unfortunately, there have even been cases of violence and harassment on RTN marches, and it is normal to hear heckling and jeers from some observers of the march, usually men. I will come back to this issue later when I explore the arguments activists made in favour of women-only marches. As well as worrying about the mood of bystanders though, some activists felt that the mood of the marchers

themselves might not always be as positive as it could be.
There was a perception that the RTN of the past was
more loud, angry, radical and challenging. This was a
perception held by activists both young and old, and
it linked to a more general refrain, common in activist
circles, that feminism as a movement is not as radical
as it was in the Second Wave. There was a sense that
this might just be a part of a much broader institutionalisation and neo-liberal professionalisation affecting all
political movements. There were views for and against
such a shift, as well as differing views on whether it has
even taken place.

The activists in my research had attended RTN
marches all over the UK and thus they brought a huge
wealth of experience, reflection and insight. Between
them, they had attended marches in over 22 different
towns and cities from Inverness to Plymouth. Many of
these locations were firsts for RTN, being places that
never held marches in the heyday of the 1970s and
1980s. In fact, contrary to all those assumptions that feminism was bigger, better and badder in the old days, the
RTN of today is in fact larger and more popular than
it ever has been in the UK. Since 2004, marches have
grown from one or two every year to 20 or more. For
some though, this growth has come at a price.

### *The dimming of the flaming torch: Reclaim the Night and institutionalisation*

Many activists expressed frustration that the contemporary Feminist Movement, including RTN, is institutionalised when compared to the movement of the Second
Wave. Iphra, who was in her sixties, had been on both
original and contemporary RTN marches; she was thus

in a good position to describe any changes over this period and she felt that most of them had been negative.

> a lot of feminism has become co-opted, as it has become institutionalised into weakening its aims of getting rid of male dominance and gender itself as a hierarchical power relationship.
>
> (Iphra)

Several different signs and symptoms of this institutionalisation were identified, and they included formal sponsorship and funding for RTN marches, as well as police involvement on the protest of course.

It is important to note that institutionalisation was not always seen negatively however. Some activists felt that while there had indeed been a process of institutionalisation in feminist activism, this could be seen as a sign of the acceptance for RTN and for the message and aims of the march.

> In a way they're a lot more institutionalised now, and I don't mean that negatively, I mean that as a compliment. Like, with the trade union support, they've moved on to something that's seen as important and something that's included now, not just as bra-burners and crazies like it was before.
>
> (Sheila)

Large organisations, such as trade union branches or local Community Safety Units placed within local authorities, do indeed often support and sponsor local RTN marches. Usually this support was welcome, and it was seen as positive that such mainstream groups now see feminist events as something they want to be associated with, as radical feminist Sheila noted. But some strings or repercussions were also identified as being attached to such support. This was compared to a perception that the RTN of the past was much more autonomous, organised by independent individuals in collectives and without formal funding. Ellie, in her early forties, was critical of the contemporary RTN for this reason:

> It's mainly organised by organisations, rather than by local women. I believe the Women's Movement is more professionalised than previous and is less effective at bringing through local women to take over and influence the work.
>
> (Ellie)

Brenda, a queer socialist feminist in her twenties made similar points, and she also felt that since the 1990s, feminism generally has been becoming much more institutionalised. She saw this as a feature of the whole of the women's sector also, including campaigns against male violence against women, but also in service provisions such as refuges.

> Violence against women organisations have become a service-providing arm of the state, rather than the autonomous, self-defining feminist welfare organisations that they were set up to be.
>
> (Brenda)

The independence of the movement of the past, as well as supposedly making it more radical, was also believed to have enabled it to involve non-violent direct action or NVDA on original RTN marches. To clarify matters, I asked the original marchers about the sort of direct action they got up to on their RTN marches. They would often pick march routes purposely to go past sex shops, shops selling pornography, and they would then sneak over as the march filed past and close the locks shut with superglue. Grace, who identified as a Black radical revolutionary feminist, recalled her experiences of spray-painting graffiti on buildings while the march went past, as well as supergluing locks. She had not seen any similar direct action on the modern RTN marches in her city though, and indeed contemporary marchers did not recount any such activity on any present-day marches.

> less direct action on the night, like spray-painting and supergluing locks of sex clubs etc.
>
> (Grace)

Al Garthwaite also remembered direct action on RTN and she was usually right at the heart of it. I interviewed Al for my research in January 2012, at her home in Leeds. Relaxing on her sofa and covered by her two cuddly cats, she told me all about one particular incident on an RTN in Leeds in 1980 where the march took a detour into an Odeon cinema. A group of activists had prepared leaflets in advance – these were outlining reasons to boycott a film being shown at the time called *Dressed to Kill* – which marchers felt glamourised male violence against women. Importantly, this was at a time of course when the city was still gripped with the then still unsuccessful search for the Yorkshire Ripper, Peter Sutcliffe, who murdered his final victim that year.

> We were on Yorkshire TV at the time, and a break-away group went into a cinema showing *Dressed to Kill* and threw leaflets, and we certainly got coverage for that.
>
> (Al Garthwaite)

Sheila also recalled more direct action in the past, not just on RTN but as a regular practice of feminist groups in general. She told me about how she and others in one feminist group in the 1970s tried new and creative ways to protest against sexual harassment for example.

> We'd all wander out behind men in the streets and pinch their bums and say: give us a smile darling.
>
> (Sheila)

Compared to this type of lively, humorous and media-grabbing direct action recounted by Grace, Al and Sheila, many activists felt that the contemporary RTN was slightly 'tame' and less radical.

> they were more adventurous and militant in the early days, now they are pretty tame.
>
> (Iphra)

Being 'tame' then involved a lack of NVDA, but, as noted, also a level of cooperation with the police that was not felt to have been the case in original RTN marches. The modern marches were seen to be generally more organised, more professional and less anarchic. For many of the activists I spoke to, nothing symbolised this declining radicalism better than the demise of the flaming torch. Time and again, younger activists in particular would hold this example up as a symbol of a more fiery past, a herstory now dampened and dimmed.

> the original one was more confrontational, and they had their flaming torches. We wouldn't get away with that now.
>
> (Sylvia)

But talking to other women, it seems there was a lot more freedom then. It was a lot more anarchic.

They had their flaming torches and they didn't stick to routes. Maybe now we are more concerned about what the state thinks of us, maybe, I don't know, maybe we have lost a more radical stance.

(Christabel)

Of course, many activists rightly pointed out that it is a fact that there are just more public order restrictions on political demonstrations today, not to mention health and safety regulations against flaming torches. I remember having to take out professional public liability insurance when organising an RTN assembly point one year in Trafalgar Square in central London. This was just in case anyone brought candles and wax happened to find its way onto the paving stones of the square. Wax is apparently very difficult to remove from heritage stone and the process would have been a costly affair for us had such a travesty occurred. Several suited Heritage Wardens patrolled our event just in case we forgot our commitment to ancient monuments. This is the sort of climate in which activists are trying to organise lively, imaginative and inspiring protests; it is no wonder that they find themselves more restricted than colleagues of the past. In this climate, there is also the fact of CCTV of course, which is everywhere in our town and city centres today, and again a new feature, one which heavily restricts actions such as spray-painting graffiti, flyposting posters or supergluing locks on offending porn shops. Radical feminist and socialist Cordelia, who was in her sixties, explained how this constant observation limits opportunities for action today.

But then we never had CCTV see, when we used to do things we were out with the wallpaper paste every weekend. Whatever you're protesting about, take the flyers slap them on the walls. Unless you

were actually seen by a real policeman, but now, you
know, you wouldn't dare do anything. You're being
photographed all the time.

(Cordelia)

As well as these practical matters though, there was also
a more abstract cause identified for declining radicalism, and this was a reduction of feminist anger. Perhaps
the two things go hand in hand of course; the increasing state crackdown of protests may, over time, reduce
the levels of direct action and any outlet for showing
anger in the first place. As I mentioned, it was usually
the younger activists in particular who were more likely
to say that they felt that the RTN of the past was more
'angry', more radical, and that they felt that this anger
had been lost. Anger was an emotion that many wanted
to maintain though, and they saw it as their job to try
and rekindle it, waking this mysterious righteous anger
from the embers of the flaming torches that our sisters
have handed to us down the generations.

I hope that when we march on RTN today we're keeping the spirit of these aims alive, and keeping the
anger against these things alive.

(Kira)

Whether the marches were more angry in the past
or not, it is true that the RTN marches of today do
indeed involve less or no NVDA, they do receive formal
sponsorship from large organisations, including local
authorities and they do have police involvement. On
marches today, roads are often closed by local police,
and RTN collectives provide stewards to work alongside the police in ensuring marcher safety and directing
traffic. While everyone appreciated being able to take

back their streets in this way, through the roads being formally closed, for some activists, the involvement of the police was just another negative example of the institutionalisation of RTN.

## *Policing Reclaim the Night: A contradiction in terms?*

Contrary to marches today, the original RTN marches appear to have been organised with very little police input. In my discussions with original marchers, I always asked them whether they had gained or sought police permission for their event. Each time the responses were similarly vague. Most could not recall seeking or asking for police permission. Several stated that they most definitely would not have asked for police permission, as at that time popular opinion in the WLM was against such state involvement.

A minority of activists, of a variety of ages, were openly hostile to a police presence on RTN. They raised police presence as a critique of contemporary RTN, and even stated that the police presence ran counter to the aims of RTN and made the march redundant. Clevedon was in her early thirties and she identified as an anti-capitalist feminist; she made this criticism of RTN organising groups today:

> working with groups or organisations that actually promote violence against women, like the police, simply to increase the numbers on the march.
>
> (Clevedon)

Other activists pointed out though that even when it was sought, police permission was by no means a given anyway. Sometimes RTN marches were refused permission

to march, such as Exeter RTN in 2010 in the South
West of England. Or marches were forced to change the
date or route of their march, such as in Scotland at the
Edinburgh RTN of 2010. In Exeter, a march had to be
cancelled when the local police force withdrew their support on the grounds that officers could not be spared
from their duties for a protest they did not see as being of
national significance. In Edinburgh, local police forced
the RTN organising committee to postpone and re-route
their march to avoid potential clashes with football supporters in the Grassmarket area of the city, a central area
populated with many bars and clubs. Despite such problems though, many activist organisers still saw gaining
police permission as simply a pragmatic move, and a
necessity in order for the march to go ahead, albeit a feature that many activists were ambivalent about. Without
fail, all the activists expressed frustration with the irony
of having to ask a male-dominated institution for permission and protection while holding a march demanding
that women be safe and free from male violence in public
space.

The issue of safety is relevant here though, and
this was significant for activist organisers in particular. Despite Vivienne's positive observations and experience of friendly bystanders, as mentioned earlier, some
activists had unfortunately seen or heard of aggression
and violence on RTN marches. The safety of marchers
was thus put forward as another reason for reluctantly
seeking police involvement, as Christabel, a 37-year-old
feminist explained.

> I mean, obviously, you don't want a whole load of
> police chaperoning women around, but then, we do
> get a lot of hassle, and we get stuff thrown at us. And
> I thought, well hang on, why should we just go around

the streets and get assaulted, and the people doing it have no repercussions, 'cos they're not going to get arrested, 'cos there's no police there.

(Christabel)

Police involvement was also seen as pragmatic not just for the safety of marchers, but to ensure a large and successful march and enable as many women as possible to attend. It was recognised that some women might not be able to risk attending an illegal march for example, perhaps due to their immigration status, current occupation, previous involvement with the criminal justice system or due to their caring responsibilities. Organisers often felt then, regardless of their own personal views, that they had no choice but to acquire police permission.

If you want to do anything big these days then it seems getting permission appears the only way of it actually happening.

(Sophie)

However, the potential for disruption by police or even police harassment was also a cause for concern. Activists often pointed to cases of bad policing and police brutality at large demonstrations, such as the policing of student marches against rising tuition fees in London in November 2010.

Well, police are not always supportive of women and have been aggressive, and around protests they can cause a lot of problems, like, the G20 and the student 'riots' you know. They're not necessarily on our sides all the time.

(Shelley)

Other activists considered police facilitation a right, and saw this as part of the civic duty of local police which feminists should demand be extended to their protests and events. Mary for example, a 44-year-old radical feminist, emphasised that women have a right to organise RTN marches. I met Mary in a busy coffee shop near her office where she manages a large charity; she took time out of her hectic schedule to talk to me about the changes she had seen in RTN from when she first got involved as a student organiser in the 1980s. She was keen to emphasise that feminists have a right to public protest just like any other political group. Thus, she insisted that the police should facilitate such demonstrations to take place peacefully and safely.

> I don't really take that sort of 'them and us' view of the police. I think it's more effective to get at it from all angles, and you know, we're the majority of the population, you know. The state should work for us. I think they should be engaging with us.
>
> (Mary)

Even Mary understood police involvement as a sign of changing times in the Feminist Movement though and recognised that this would have been an anathema to organisers on the original marches. To summarise then, for many of the new generation of activist organisers, police permission was just a necessary part of successful event management. Activist organisers abided by health and safety rules, they routed their march in line with police requirements and they wrote their publicity materials in accessible, often gender-neutral terms in order to ensure funding from generic organisations such as a local councils and trade unions. This does represent a break with the past, a change of direction from the previous do-it-yourself, anarchic attitude of the Second Wave. This new, professionalised and managerialised version of feminism was seen by some as symptomatic of what they understood as the third wave phase or style of feminism.

## *Dipping into the third wave*

I asked all the activists whether they identified as or with third wave feminism, including Kira, who was a younger activist in her late twenties. Kira was also a committed RTN organiser, though she had been taking some time out to focus on other interests such as writing. She identified as a radical feminist politically, but said she was also a socialist and that was important to her. Chatting in a café one evening after work in her city in the South West of England, she explained to me that she did not identify with the third wave, she did not like the term and she did not like the whole wave metaphor either. She felt it just separated her and others of her generation from fellow older activists.

> I don't like the idea of waves, 'cos I just feel it creates a false barrier between women of the 70s and me.
>
> (Kira)

None of the activists I spoke to actually had any clear definition of third wave feminism, but nevertheless they often had their own quite fixed ideas of what it was. Many associated it with negative characteristics and this view came from feminists of all ages, including younger feminists, who are the very people most commonly associated with or assumed to be third wave feminists. Babette for example was one of the younger activists, in her twenties, she identified as queer and as an anti-capitalist feminist. For her, third wave feminism was a sort of:

> *light* feminism.

> (Babette)

This was in fact a common theme, and several activists used similar language to Babette when describing the third wave. Many agreed that third wave feminism was feminism-lite, a sort of watered down, modern but less radical version of the movement. Some went as far as to describe it as post-feminist. Post-feminism is the term used for neo-liberal anti-feminism, which is individualistic rather than collective and which relies on consumer culture for a disappointingly mainstream identity expression. It is 'feminism' for those who believe feminism is over because it is no longer needed and its aim is to make feminism history. Many of those who self-identify as third wave would dispute this link of course, and indeed there are noticeable differences between the two and a great deal of scholarship which sets out to demonstrate that (Evans, 2015; Budgeon, 2011; Dean, 2010). Nevertheless, several of the activists I met felt that there were indeed overlaps between post-feminism and the third wave, and that these two were not always so easily distinguishable. Charlotte for example, a 34-year-old radical feminist, defined third wave feminism as:

> glib, depoliticised post-feminist claptrap.

> (Charlotte)

These activists painted a picture of third wave feminism as naïve; they suggested that, in their opinion, it was a kind of feminism so keen and desperate to see women as empowered and liberated, it had forgotten to acknowledge the fact that oppression against women still exists. Another one of the younger feminist activists, Kyleen, a socialist feminist who was in her teens, had been to some events that she catagorised as third wave. She thought the events she had attended:

> have the pretence that we [women] are already liberated, and free agents.
>
> (Kyleen)

For young activists like Kyleen, there was much dismay with how feminism generally is portrayed in the media and perceived by the public. They expressed a sense that modern feminism has become depoliticised, or at least that this depoliticised version is the preferred image portrayed in the media. These portrayals in the media were also considered to focus obsessively on individual 'choice', a mantra in our current neo-liberal society of course, and to make links between feminism and choice constantly. Activists felt that feminism was often in fact simply represented as just and solely being about women's right to make choices, whatever those choices may be, and regardless of what bumpy and un-level playing field they are made on. In this way, any choice that is made by a woman can then become portrayed in the media as a feminist choice, whatever it may be, even if it is completely unrelated to feminist theory, activism or politics.

Importantly, choices made by women to comply with narrow beauty standards for example, can also be presented as feminist choices simply because a woman has made them and she has a right to make that choice, and thus matters are therefore closed off for any critique or debate. The false logic follows that it would, after all, be anti-feminist to question a woman's choice, when feminism is about choice. This is actually a twisted post-feminist version of 'feminism' for which the feminist scholar Michelle Ferguson has coined a new term: 'choice feminism' (2010). Two activists both described this phenomenon perfectly, though they did not use that exact academic term. They were generations apart, Helen in her late fifties and Boreland in her late twenties, but they both emphasised an exasperation with a crippling focus on choice at all costs, even when the chooser pays the price.

> I think there is a misunderstanding that whatever a woman 'chooses' is feminist simply by virtue of the fact a woman 'chose' it.
>
> (Helen)

> It's more about 'choice' rather than rebellion.
>
> (Boreland)

Kira also talked about this notion of choice when she too described third wave feminism as simply choice feminism.

> I think the third wave in particular are perhaps related to a liberal, libertarian idea of feminism that's very pro-porn; and about, this is my choice, you know. If a woman does it it's a feminist choice, even if it's just a choice to have a glass of white wine. So I don't identify as third wave myself.
>
> (Kira)

For some activists, it was this sort of depoliticisation and obsessive media focus on what they saw as false notions of choice and agency that partly lay behind the general hostility that they encountered towards women-only feminist space. Often, women-only events were seen as outdated, as a practice of a closed off, narrow and repressive version of feminism which was compared unfavourably to the more flexible, fluid, individual but inclusive movement of today. This leads on to one of the biggest changes observed in RTN over the years of course – the shift from women-only to mixed marches.

# Chapter 7

## From 'women' to 'mixed'

One shift in RTN which was not disputed but which was controversial was the increasing inclusion of men on contemporary marches. On the question of whether men should be involved in RTN, there was far greater support amongst all the activists for women-only or women-led RTN marches, rather than fully mixed marches involving men. A women-led march is usually where men will march at the rear, or join the march later on in the route and stay in one section. This preference oddly appears to run counter to the practical make up of many marches today of course, with most being mixed. Although the majority expressed a preference for women-only or women-led RTN though, several activists did voice objection to women-only marches or discomfort with any borders at all being set around who could attend, and these views do represent those held by large sections of the movement today. In this chapter, I shall explore the reasons behind these often strongly held views and the competing arguments for and against men's inclusion on RTN.

When defending women-only RTN, a subtle point was made about inclusion and exclusion. This argument was summarised perfectly by one activist I spoke to in the North of England. Eve, a radical feminist, worked as a university lecturer and for the previous few years had helped to organise the RTN in her city. We met in a convenient café in the city centre, which actually turned out to be on the route of the RTN march, as Eve showed me. After updating me on the success of their most recent march and the positive local response, Eve moved on to explain this point about inclusion and exclusion.

> well, if it's mixed then you're not including everyone. You're always excluding someone, and you're choosing to exclude women who are survivors and who don't want to march next to men, and you are making a decision to exclude them. So it's not like you can include everyone, you're always making a choice to exclude someone.
>
> (Eve)

Eve said that a choice therefore always has to be made, because any act of inclusion will necessarily exclude. Several RTN organisers who I interviewed felt that it was impossible to include everyone anyway and that someone would always feel excluded. They felt that given this unavoidable situation, women should always be prioritised over men. In fact, the prioritisation of women was often seen as an aim of RTN in itself. Out of the many hours of discussions I had with activists on this issue, I was able to identify three main arguments in favour of mixed marches and six key arguments against. These were the arguments that arose most often in defence or rejection of the involvement of men on RTN marches.

## Arguments for male inclusion

1. Violence against women should be of concern to men. It is a 'men's issue' so men should be welcome at RTN

to demonstrate their opposition to male violence against women and children and to show solidarity with women. Violence against women was seen as a men's issue for two reasons: firstly, because men can be affected by sexual violence and intimate partner abuse themselves, including rape. Secondly, men are also affected by male violence against women through their loved ones becoming victimised or through the fear of this happening.

2. Violence against women and children will never end unless men are actively encouraged to be part of ending it, through attending events such as RTN.

3. In order to build the broadest possible support for RTN, men should not be excluded, but can be included in a minimal way, for example by being at the rear of a women-led march, which was seen as a tactical compromise.

## *Arguments against male inclusion*

1. RTN is about male violence against women. This type of violence does not affect men as victims directly, so the march should be women-only to keep this emphasis and specificity clear.

2. Women marchers gain more sense of empowerment, release of anger, jubilation and solidarity in a women-only march and this should be one aim of RTN.

3. RTN is a feminist march and feminist events should always be organised, led, attended and directed by women.

4. One objective of RTN is highlighting women's fears or anxieties regards their safety when alone in public space at night. Having men on the march provides male security, 'chaperones', 'escorts' or 'protection' and therefore defeats the object of the march.

5. If men are included, there is the potential that perpetrators of violence against women, including sexual violence, may attend. This would potentially threaten the safety of marchers and breach the spirit of the event.

6. Men's support for RTN should be welcomed, but men should express their support by being 'back office staff', helping at a crèche/rally/parallel vigil or in other behind the scenes roles. This was seen as preferable to men taking visible leadership roles, being 'glory stewards' or 'peacocks'.

In the next section, I will explore these arguments in more depth, considering the merits of each and discovering just why activists on both sides are so passionate about this issue.

### *Why should men be included on Reclaim the Night marches?*

The first of the most common arguments raised in favour of male inclusion maintained that male violence against women is a men's issue too and that RTN needs all the allies it can get. In addition, many activists rightly drew attention to the sad fact that men are more affected by street violence for example, and are actually more at risk than women are when out in their town and city centres at night. Men are also not immune to rape and sexual assault, with figures from the 2010 Stern Review in the UK for example finding that around 8 per cent of reported rapes concern a male victim.

As well as being the potential victims of rape and sexual violence, activists in favour of male inclusion also pointed out that men can be affected by male violence against women by proxy. This can happen through their loved ones being affected; men too feel the pain and loss of male violence, they also are alert to the threat of this violence through the fear that their female loved ones may be victimised. This point was actually raised by the only male activist I spoke to in my research. I had not met John before and he had at that point only attended one RTN march in his home city in the South West of England. He had volunteered to take part in my research because he identified as a feminist and was committed to RTN for many reasons, including the future of his two young daughters, one of whom he had taken along on the march with him.

> it doesn't just affect women does it, you know. I have to worry about my wife going out, you know, in the same way; so of course it affects me. So I would sort of, I feel strongly I should be able to march on that subject. It would seem, if not, then that would be sexist.
>
> (John)

Several other activists made the same point on behalf of men, suggesting that excluding men would be sexist and therefore anti-feminist.

Like John, many women felt strongly that most men are just as passionately opposed to male violence against women and children as women are. One activist called Bonnie, who was in her late thirties, defended this view. Bonnie argued for male inclusion, but, like many others, only within a women-led march. This was a fairly common stance and it appeared as some sort of acceptable middle ground to many activists who clearly felt uncomfortable excluding anyone from RTN, but who also felt on some level that the march should be an opportunity for, or statement about women's leadership.

Men have mothers, sisters, daughters and grand-
daughters and they shouldn't be stopped from par-
ticipating. I do believe that the marches should be
women-led through.

(Bonnie)

Illustrating some of the differences between schools
of feminism, explored in Chapter 3, Dolores, a 63-
year-old socialist feminist, had no problem reconciling
men's involvement with women's leadership and did not
see this as any sort of compromise or middle ground.
Dolores had been involved in feminism for decades and
shared many great stories with me about the National
Women's Liberation Conferences she had attended and
various demonstrations she had been on. She was actually living in Oxford at the time of the famous Ruskin
Conference, the influential and pivotal conference I
mentioned earlier in Chapter 2, but she had not
attended due to having two very young children. She
made up for it later by taking her children along with
her to political conferences when they were a bit older.

Dolores was still involved in equalities work in the
public sector and is one of the many truly principled
people who can be found in feminism; she is still living her politics and she benefitted from being active at
a time when that congruence mattered. I met Dolores
at her home to interview her, and we left her husband
working quietly while we sat in the sun on her balcony
amongst the plants. Dolores argued that male involvement was actually crucial to her socialist feminist politics,
but that this would 'obviously' have to go alongside
female leadership.

as a socialist feminist I think it's really important to
work with male allies, we've always worked with male

allies. I mean, I don't have a problem if some women want to have a women-only thing, but I personally, I prefer mixed, but women-led. You know, women at the front obviously, I think that's only right.

(Dolores)

It was therefore seen as counterproductive to exclude male allies for this cause and also to miss out on a great boost or even doubling of the numbers on RTN marches.

Activists also argued that men who are opposed to male violence against women could usefully challenge public assumptions that this is only a women's issue. They could also potentially be positive role models for men and boys.

Good to get men and boys involved, as many are opposed to violence against women and can influence other men's behaviour and attitudes.

(Fiona)

Fiona was in her late forties and she emphasised that she was not aligned with any one school or type of feminism. Another activist, who also identified as just a feminist, Lucy, also supported male involvement, and was also positive about the example this could set for other men, through bystanders watching the RTN march or perhaps through seeing the event covered in the media. Twenty-four-year-old Lucy also felt that men being involved could change the perception of feminism more broadly, giving a positive impression of this political stance.

I think I do quite like it when men are there as well, 'cos in a way that challenges people's perceptions too about what feminism is and who feminists are. But I think probably having it part and part is the best compromise.

(Lucy)

Here again the caveat of female leadership is emphasised. Lucy even uses the word 'compromise', suggesting that she feels some sympathy with male inclusion but also with the idea of women's visible leadership and is trying to reconcile these two preferences.

What was not commonly voiced, and this was surprising, was the argument that men are victims of violence too and therefore this should be a justification for them attending RTN. Many of the activists I spoke to, both those in favour of male inclusion and those against, described frequently being accused of not being aware of, or not caring about, violence against men. Regularly, activists would say that whenever they tried to raise awareness about RTN, recruit marchers or promote the march to their peers, colleagues and friends, they would inevitably be asked why they were focussing on violence against women, when men are affected by violence too. This is an example of a zero-sum approach, a naïve and simplistic assumption that one cannot be for one cause alongside another or many, or that rights for one group must come at the expense of another. Shelley was an RTN organiser from the South West of England and was frustrated with these assumptions. Shelley was 30 years old and identified her ethnicity as Dual Heritage. She helped to organise a mixed, women-led RTN in her city.

> straight away people are like, well men get beaten up too you know and we're like, yeah, we know that and we're not denying that and go and organise something

about it if you want, but today we're talking about women. But people just don't want to talk about that you know. And even collecting money for stopping violence against women, people will say they don't donate 'cos what about the men. But if you were collecting for polar bears, people wouldn't go, well, what about grizzly bears!

(Shelley)

Yet only three activists explicitly used this argument themselves in favour of male inclusion; that is, the argument that violence can affect anybody regardless of sex or gender identity. For example, Brooke and Carrie both made this point; they were in their late twenties and early thirties. Brooke identified as a Marxist and a feminist, and Carrie as a leftie.

I think a modern attitude towards gender nowadays means that we shouldn't stress too much about the gender identity of those who identify as feminists, but should allow anyone who can follow the requirements of a female-led environment and remain sensitive to privilege, should be allowed to come. In London sexual violence and street violence is by no means limited to biological or self-identifying women, and so a march against it needs to be flexible about everyone who may want to come. However, in general, feminism needs to be women-led to achieve its political aims.

(Brooke)

Where I come from 1 in 8 victims of rape are male. I feel unable to commit myself to a campaign which excludes that group.

(Carrie)

As I mentioned earlier, the arguments that men should be included often rested on a strong belief that feminism should not exclude anyone and that to do so would be counter-feminist and even patriarchal. This was argued by Amelia, who felt that the sex segregation on the RTN in her city was just divisive. She was in her early twenties and she identified as a feminist and also as a leftie.

> I don't like that the main march is women-only. I believe men can (and should be) feminists too and that dividing by gender is part of the problem of patriarchy. That said, I do understand that some women may feel more comfortable at women-only events. It's a tricky one!
>
> (Amelia)

Although Amelia was uncomfortable with excluding men, like so many other activists I spoke to she also expressed a slight anxiety or unease about women not being able to attend a women-only space. Often when activists mentioned these 'some women' who may be uncomfortable, they meant survivors of male violence or separatist feminists who consciously sought out women-only space. There was usually less sympathy for the latter though, and sometimes it almost felt that the former was a form of pathologisation; hinting that the only valid reason a woman could have for opposing male involvement was if she personally was a survivor of male violence and felt 'uncomfortable' around men. The problem with this view, often unquestioned, is that it delegitimises or hides political discomfort or opposition. Many women, including, but not only survivors, have political reasons for preferring and promoting women-only space and this does not by default mean that they have past experiences of abuse or that they have some sort of personal problem or fear of being around men. It was clear though, that for many activists, especially RTN organisers, they felt pushed to come up with a defence of women-led or women-only protests and found that citing the presence of survivors was a way to avoid the most harsh critiques and opposition.

As Amelia said, all RTN organisers found issues of exclusion and inclusion tricky. For many, it was seen as tactical to include men because this would create a broader and stronger movement. This stance formed the basis of the second key argument used to promote mixed RTN marches. This was the argument that it is logical that a movement against violence against women should include the group overrepresented as perpetrators – men – because this is the group that needs to change. Benjamina for example, a feminist in her late twenties, explained this stance.

I feel that the movement against violence against women also needs men to agree not to commit the violence, and to support our cause. We need to show people that this movement is for everyone. Unless everyone supports it, it won't work.

(Benjamina)

Caz, a leftie in her early thirties, also took this position. She argued that it was simply strategic to include men and she also pointed out the educational purpose as others did, suggesting that men could educate other men and help society to evolve away from sexist assumptions which attach masculinity to violence.

I understand and appreciate why the marches are sometimes women-only. I however feel that this means that men feel unable to support a march and that it reinforces the view that 'all men are violent'. Personally, I feel that we need to involve everyone if society is to change. I also feel that this march needs to be women-led; I am very firm on this.

(Caz)

As can be seen in the selection of quotes above, even these activists who provided spirited and passionate arguments for men's involvement in RTN still felt that the protest should be women-led. The conceivable or imaginable forms of male involvement were therefore limited, and conditional upon the men present respecting women's leadership and direction. In fact, this collaboration between women and men was also seen as another opportunity for education and a chance to present a positive example of gender relations publically.

The third and final argument made in favour of male inclusion was mainly a tactical one. Not tactical in the way outlined above, through being an opportunity to educate the public or play a public relations role for feminism for example, but tactical in that it is simply a way to keep everyone happy. As with so many things however, this is of course impossible. Just like Eve said in earlier quotations, some group is always going to feel excluded or unrepresented, and whatever decision is made about the form of the march, there will always be critique. In efforts to minimise this though and to involve as many potential allies as possible, several activist organisers saw men's involvement as a pragmatic compromise between a women-only RTN or a completely mixed RTN.

One RTN activist in the North of England, Christabel, made this point. She was 37 and identified politically as a radical feminist. She was part of an organising collective in her city. Their march was split into two halves, with men joining at a later point on the route and staying at the rear.

> I think probably we have a compromise, you know, a balance. We have men join us towards the end of the march; this was the compromise we came up with.
>
> (Christabel)

Compromise did not always work though, as Charlotte pointed out. Charlotte was also an RTN organiser in the same city, 34 and also a radical feminist.

> we've tried this compromise and we've upset everyone. We've upset the men who feel like a token and women who feel it should be women-only, and so, well, the group we don't want to upset is women, you know.
>
> (Charlotte)

However, even those activists who saw male involvement as a tactical move, or a compromise necessary in a climate of hostility to women-only events, still hoped that as a side effect, men's involvement could aid the building of a broad-based, large and successful protest with higher numbers than women-only marches may attract or enable. For those opposed to men's involvement though, the pursuit of such a broad base and higher numbers was at the expense of the very principles and aims of RTN, and was seen as entirely counterproductive. The numbers on the march were considered far less important than protecting the principle of women-only space. I shall now turn then to look at the six key arguments raised against male inclusion and in favour of women-only RTN.

## *Why should Reclaim the Night be women-only?*

One common argument made in favour of women-only marches, and perhaps the most obvious one, is that the march is about violence against women and, as men are not women and so not victim to violence against women, they should not attend. Charlie, in her early thirties, made this point, also highlighting that as men are not affected, they also do not carry with them the fears and anxieties that women do about using public space at night for example.

> men have not, and don't, experience the unspoken sanctions that women do.
>
> (Charlie)

This stance relied on activists identifying one aim of RTN being awareness raising about male violence against women specifically, and it not being about public safety in general. For those who saw this awareness raising and focus on women as victims as key, it was precisely the women-only element which was tactical. They argued that the women-only element of RTN is its unique selling point, it is what makes this march stand out from other political protests and therefore it would be impractical to miss out on this interesting feature. As Sheila said of mixed marches:

> and it just makes it look like an ordinary march, like all the others.
>
> (Sheila)

Sheila was 65 and identified as a radical lesbian feminist and a socialist. Sheila had been involved in feminism for decades and was still active in feminism as well as in socialist groups against government cutbacks and anti-war organisations. She was retired and therefore had the freedom to spend her time tackling the capitalist patriarchal status quo and enriched the groups she was in with her feminist theory and activist experience.

Several activists felt that by keeping RTN women-only, a clear focus is maintained on male violence against women and thus the message to bystanders is clear and unmistakable. Eight activists actually used the word 'diluted' when they critiqued mixed marches. Debbie for example, an anarcho-feminist in her late thirties, argued that:

> I feel that 'open-gender' or mixed marches dilute the message and un-gender the very gendered phenomenon of sexual violence against women.
>
> (Debbie)

For those in favour of a women-only RTN, the aim of the march was to highlight women's demand to live free from the threat and reality of male violence. To have men on the march detracted from this, and sent 'mixed messages' to the bystanders watching or those hearing about a local march through the media. Rosa also emphasised this, another anarcho-feminist from the North of England; she had experiences of both mixed and women-only RTN. I met Rosa in a veggie café near to where I was staying with a friend in the city. After arriving late due to getting the wrong bus, we were able to chat about Rosa's experiences of different RTN marches and the different approaches that had been taken in her city. Rosa worked as a therapist in a women's centre, and was very committed to women's empowerment through actively doing politics and because of this, she preferred to be involved in do-it-yourself or DIY activism, where, like during the

Second Wave, people very much do it for themselves, and organise their own events independently from the state and from mainstream organisations and funding.

> I've been on both women and mixed. I've noticed differences. Like I said, I think that on mixed marches there's mixed messages, the messages are diluted. Reclaim the night, well, who's reclaiming the night from who? I guess when you're raising awareness of violence against women by men, which is the majority of sexual violence and domestic abuse anyway, for men to join it, I think it confuses the issue to the public.
>
> (Rosa)

Al Garthwaite had similar views. While she understood that men are also affected by violence, she felt that when men are physically assaulted or mugged for example, they do not face the same victim-blaming culture that women do when they are sexually harassed, assaulted or even raped and that this is an important distinction between women and men's experiences.

> Men are also subject to violence, but are not blamed or disbelieved if they get attacked.
>
> (Al Garthwaite)

John recounted that he personally had been in such positions where he feared physical violence from other men when out in public space, but added that generally he did not carry fears about being raped or sexually assaulted.

> I read things talking about that [sexual violence by men against men], but I don't think I have any perception of it really. Nobody talks about that

particularly. No, I've never felt at risk of sexual violence, no. But yeah, physical violence, from other men, yeah, sure.

(John)

John mentions in this extract above that he has no perception of sexual violence against men being a real threat to him, that he does not think about it or talk about it and that he does not feel at risk of it. This of course means that he will understand his personal safety in a different way to how women understand their own personal safety. Like Charlie, Al and John, Rosa felt that men use public space, especially at night, without the same fears and anxieties about sexual violence. She felt that men actually tended to dominate public spaces at night and therefore already 'owned' the night, so had no need to reclaim it from anyone.

what I thought was really nice about the London march, when there was some men along the route with banners saying that they supported it. And to me, that is males supporting RTN marches. They don't have to take it over, they're standing there for all to see and they agree with us as well, but they're not pretending to reclaim the night; 'cos, like, who are they reclaiming it from? Themselves, you know.

(Rosa)

As well as the argument that male violence against women does not affect men directly or cause them to curb their liberty in the use of public space, the second common defence of women-only RTN was that the march should be a site of, and opportunity for women's empowerment. Empowerment was not just an intended outcome for the women on each RTN, but also for women bystanders to the marches. Christabel questioned whether this empowerment could even occur at all within a mixed march.

> It is empowering with women, and, would that empowerment be there otherwise?
>
> (Christabel)

Supporters of women-only RTN believed strongly that RTN is a place for women to release their righteous anger, frustration and passion in a safe environment, alongside other like-minded women. This links back to the points raised earlier about the supposed decline of anger on the RTN marches, and the belief of younger activists that this radicalism needs a protected space in which to be maintained and fanned. Many felt that such an environment was rare. Buffy, a feminist in her late twenties, stated that:

> It is extremely empowering to be in a large crowd of women and also highly unusual. It is more relaxed.
>
> (Buffy)

It was also suggested that many women often feel unable, as individuals on their own, to publically express their anger and resentment towards sexual harassment, everyday sexism or threats and acts of violence. This is because they fear reprisals if they challenge those men who perpetrate these acts against them, as Vivienne recounted.

> When I was younger, like most other women I received a lot of sexual harassment in the streets. So going on the march, there was meaning for me being there. You know, often you can't respond

angrily or in any way in case, 'cos of what men might do. So, like other women, it was about putting all those experiences in and getting all the anger out about them safely, that had happened all over the year.

(Vivienne)

As well as being a safe space to release anger like this, a women-only RTN was also seen as a space for solidarity to be built between women. The march was seen as a rare chance to experience this group solidarity, as Epstein, a radical feminist and separatist in her early forties, maintained.

Women are uniquely oppressed as women. It's important that we develop solidarity amongst ourselves to stand up to oppression. It's not possible to do that with men on the marches.

(Epstein)

Like Epstein, Vivienne also felt that solidarity was built particularly in women-only spaces and she suggested that women would not be able to be, as she put it, radical, if men were around. She thought that women would temper themselves or reign in their anger if male allies were marching alongside them.

Women can't be as radical when men are around. I went with a heterosexual friend of mine and she was with me on men not being there. And she was saying, you know, you can't help it. The dynamics if you have men there are going to change, and make women less radical.

(Vivienne)

As well as releasing anger, creating solidarity and allowing women to be radical, several activists made a complex point about identity and protest. Mary for example highlighted that most protest marches are about an issue that is, in some ways, outside one's own direct personal experience or identity. A march for animal rights is about a cause, a march about global warming is a cause, but the people marching are not animals affected by vivisection. They may also be lucky enough not to feel particularly affected by global warming personally, depending on their location of course and their resources. RTN on the other hand is also a protest march for a cause, but the cause is women, and the marchers are women, who are the victims and targets of male violence against women. RTN is therefore a protest march that is intrinsically linked to the marcher's own identity, in a very direct way. Mary saw this conjoining triad of protestor, identity and cause resulting in empowerment. She also believed that it sent a vital and powerful image of women's solidarity to bystanders and the public.

> I just kind of think that there's a place for men, but not on my RTN march thank you very much. You've kind of missed the point haven't you? I mean, I think there's a difference between it being an empowering and liberating activity with a personal meaning for the women on the march to be in that space, which is powerful. And then, the: I want to support your cause thing. Which is the traditional understanding of a demo.
>
> (Mary)

The third point made in defence of women-only RTN applied to all feminist events in general. This was the assertion that feminist events should always be led by women because feminism is a movement for the liberation of women. The activists who held this view advocated that political self-organisation should

be a right for all oppressed groups, including women.
Chantelle, a radical feminist in her early thirties,
explained:

> A movement needs to be led by the oppressed
> group. [male] Supporters need to recognise this, and
> if they feel strongly about fighting violence against
> women they could find out if there is any support they
> can offer, rather than demand a place on the march.
>
> (Chantelle)

Removing the element of women's leadership was therefore seen to depoliticise RTN and also turn it away from
being an explicitly feminist event. This was not just seen
as damaging for RTN potentially, but for feminism as a
whole. Eve insisted that RTN should maintain a commitment to women's leadership and women's space. Eve
was an organiser in her city. She recounted many long
discussions in her organising committee about whether
and how men should be involved on RTN. She was frustrated with the shift towards mixed feminist events that
she saw happening across the board in feminism, not
just in RTN. She thought this shift had put pressure on
RTN marches to follow suit and made them vulnerable
to hostility if they did not.

> RTN becomes about a night out, and it's for everyone,
> but I think if we did make it for women-only, I think
> that would change it. It would mean more, or become
> more serious again. I think we're in an age now when
> that depoliticisation is part of the wider movement,
> and it's been used to nullify feminism.
>
> (Eve)

Cher made a similar point. She was in her early thirties
and also a radical feminist. Cher asserted that women's

leadership and space is a key component of feminism, because it stands as a visible exception to what she felt is a very male-dominated culture. In this way, feminist events being led by women for women are a rare example of what women can do and what they can achieve together.

> I would prefer women-only. This is mainly on political principle. Our entire culture has so strong a habit of valuing messages more when they come from men, and of attributing the capacity for political thought, will and action mainly to men, that I honestly think that the best thing supportive men can do in this case is to enable the women in their lives to attend RTN without those men being there.
>
> (Cher)

Another reason why activists felt men should stay at home rather than attend RTN formed the fourth key argument in favour of women-only marches. This argument was to do with perceptions of women's safety and women's restricted use of public space, particularly at night. It moves on from the issues raised by marchers such as John about how men's sense of personal safety is generally different to that of women's. Activists felt that if men were present on an RTN they could be seen as chaperones or protectors for women marchers and thus undermine the point that the march is about women on their own reclaiming the night to feel safe in spaces they usually do not. If the point of the march is to raise awareness that often women do not feel safe on their own, without a man to accompany them, then logically it was seen as counterproductive to include men. It will be recalled of course that RTN first started amidst a man-hunt for the Yorkshire Ripper, partly because of anger against sexist police advice that women should not go

out at night or that they should have a man to accompany them if they did. Activists stated that it 'defeated
the purpose' to include men on the march. This argument was made by Sheila, and also by Bryony, a younger
radical feminist in her late twenties.

> It would be absurd to reclaim the night with male
> chaperones.
>
> (Bryony)

> The whole point of the marches is women taking back
> their space, and demonstrating that they have a right
> to walk around un-accosted by men, so they lose their
> purpose if men are involved. Men marching sort of
> reinforces that women need men to walk with them
> on the streets to keep them safe.
>
> (Sheila)

The founder of the original RTN London, Sandra
McNeill, agreed. She also worried that if men marched
on RTN, then they may be perceived by bystanders
as being there to protect the women, or accompany
the women, even if marchers certainly did not feel
this themselves. Sandra argued that many women often
just do feel safer out at night if they are with a
man they know, and if that is the case, then surely
RTN should be a chance to protest that very point by
going out alone for once, without a chaperone, without
protection.

> It's nonsense to have men on them, when you have
> men on International Women's Day marches and
> every other place; but not on RTN. Reclaim the right
> to walk along with my boyfriend, so what?
>
> (Sandra McNeill)

Fallon was a 32-year-old RTN organiser from the South of England and was one of the few activists who I already knew before I interviewed her for my research. She and I have been on many protests together since she first attended a feminist meeting I organised. We became friends and allies when at only her second meeting she offered to arrange a fundraiser for the group with another friend who also came along. Many people begin with such ideas when they first get involved in activism but often do not have time to follow through on all of them, and so initially, I did not actually expect the promised fundraiser to materialise. I was reprimanded for my cynicism when the event was a huge success and that was just the beginning of Fallon's commitment to feminism. While other members came and went, Fallon became a key organiser of RTN in her city. Her words echo and emphasise Sandra's points by confirming that she does indeed feel safer when out in her city at night if she is with her boyfriend or her brother. But for Fallon, RTN was therefore a chance to do things differently, to be out at night just with other women and feel safe.

> I don't feel I can go home late and not feel threatened, and not worry about it. And I think that is the time [on RTN] when you're out and it's dark and it's rainy, but you feel a hundred per cent safe. I do feel safer walking down the street with my brother or my boyfriend. I feel safer with men, and that annoys me. And I think that night is one night you don't have to have that, you know, you've closed the streets and you're all women.
>
> (Fallon)

The effect of women's fears of crime on their use of public space has actually been long and well studied in the areas of geography, criminology and urban studies for example. There is much professional research looking at women's tactics for avoiding and managing the fear and risk of male violence, such as sexual harassment or assault in public. This literature suggests that women are affected by what is called 'spatial segregation'. This is just a fancy academic term to refer to an observable tendency for women to limit, segregate or manage their participation in public space based on a fear of crime, in particular male violence. A tendency I am sure we can all recognise, and likely may have experienced and felt ourselves. Scholars studying this have pointed out that in many cases, women interviewed in research about such avoidance practices may not even be aware of them, as they have just incorporated certain strategies into their lives from an early age and they have become normal. 'While relatively few women spontaneously say they are afraid to go out alone, study of their actual practices and the content of their discourse enables us to qualify this assessment' (Condon et al., 2007:110).

RTN organiser Shelley, who was 30 years old and who lived in the South West, spoke about just this kind of avoidance practice and spatial segregation, though she did not use this precise academic term. Like many of the other younger women, she noted that she took care over identifying her routes around her city at night. She picked better lit ways home, she avoided bridges and underpasses, she would not walk over parks, she texted friends her estimated time of arrival, she would not walk on the pavement where it is often in shadow and hidden by parked cars but would walk down the middle of the road under the street lights, she walked with her keys in her hand or would pretend to be on the phone. Some women said they carried rape alarms or pepper spray, and yet these are young women who have benefitted from changes in the urban landscape, who have grown up amongst a lively night-time economy and leisure industry which is essentially open to all and which women are certainly more present and visible in than they perhaps ever were.

> My boyfriend doesn't really get it. We were walking home once and there was this group of lads and he said: would you be scared now walking here if I wasn't with you? And I said: I wouldn't be walking here if you weren't with me. Because, like, it's a quiet road, I'd be on the main road, walking down the middle of the road.
>
> (Shelley)

Analysis of the media coverage of male violence against women brings up another spatial link, the idea that women are affected by what is called in the textbooks and policy documents 'spatial provocation' (Walby et al., 1983:89). This phrase refers to the tendency for the media to over report male violence against women when it occurs in public space, often focussing on the location, time of day or more often night and the clothing of the alleged victim, as well as alcohol consumption for example. The point here is that the location and details of the space itself become the focus of the reporting, rather than the male perpetrator. This promotes a sense that women themselves provoke crimes against them by being in those spaces at certain times, particularly after dark. As Joanna Bourke highlights in her extensive history of rape, this focus misses the point that the space itself is not the cause of the violence. 'It is also to encourage the illusion that sexual danger loiters in social spaces, like some agentless germ that a woman can "catch". The rapist is not a "social virus". He is human' (2007:6). As I said, issues of spatial provocation and segregation did indeed emerge in my research with young contemporary activists like Fallon and Shelley, with many recounting their own fears when out in the streets on their own, particularly at night, and their strategies for managing the risk they perceived. In all cases, the activists felt that they were made to carry the burden of this risk management, and that if something did happen to them, they would be the ones to be blamed for being in the 'wrong' space at the 'wrong' time. This was the culture of victim-blaming which the activists raised and named throughout my research. Catherine for example, another younger feminist in her early thirties, explained that like Fallon, she too felt at risk when going out at night, and she felt that the social messages she received told her it was dangerous for her to do so and that she should limit her activities. Like her sisters before her in Leeds in the 1970s, she said she still felt under a sexed curfew in the modern city.

> I feel very much under a siege, a curfew, when I am told I must not go out alone or in the dark. It's like everything is my fault because I'm alive.
>
> (Catherine)

In fact, these fears were often cited as motivators for attending RTN marches, which many saw as a 'trespass' into male space. Public space was often felt by default to be sexed; it was seen as male. Dolores made this point when she emphasised her motivations for marching on RTN.

> The point of it is, that we live in a society where it's not possible for women to use the streets with as much freedom as men. Men behave as if the streets are their terrain. And I just like the title, you know, reclaim,

reclaim. Let us women take back the streets, it's not their bloody streets to do what they feel like.

(Dolores)

Even the most hardened of activists, like Dolores, pretty much left this spatial assumption unquestioned, they spoke of the urban night-time landscape as male and as in need of 'takeback' or 'incursion', 'storming' or 'reclaiming'; interestingly using quite territorial and militaristic terms.

The fifth argument made for women-only RTN was the concern that perpetrators of male violence may attend if the marches were mixed. This could threaten marchers in terms of their safety and anonymity. For example, the leaflet for the Dorchester RTN in 2011 stated:

Due to the nature of this event it is women-only – no disrespect to men, but we do have people attending who are fleeing domestic violence and who wish to remain anonymous.

(Dorchester RTN)

Epstein also highlighted this risk

allowing men in means that statistically there is a possibility that some of those men will have committed sexual offences against women.

(Epstein)

Relating back to the point I noted earlier about worries over inclusion and exclusion, many activists were aware that including men on RTN would exclude some women and potentially make some women marchers feel unsafe, particularly women who may have experienced sexual violence or intimate partner abuse. It was felt that RTN should be a place for those women.

> women attending RTN may well have been sexually, physically, emotionally attacked by men. Marching on RTN is exposing enough, without having to deal with extra interactions from men at the same time. RTN should be a protected space for women, I really think that the pro-feminist man's best symbolic action at an RTN march is to get off the streets!
>
> (Cher)

Two survivors of male violence, Bethan and Buffy, who were both in their twenties, did state that they would prefer RTN to be women-only. This was partly because they thought they could feel more comfortable and safe, but also more empowered when marching in solidarity with other women and this was a motivation that many activists gave for attending RTN.

> Marches are busy and people bump up against each other. I was abducted from a busy shopping centre when I was gang raped – people jostling me can be triggering if I'm aware that men are around, whereas it isn't the same in a women-only march.
>
> (Bethan)

> A women-only space preserves the message of Reclaim the Night, that women are reclaiming the right to walk safely at night. It also provides a safe space for survivors, such as myself, who do not feel comfortable with large groups of men.
>
> (Buffy)

It was not only survivors of male violence who stated that they would feel safer on a women-only RTN though.

Billie was in her late twenties and identified politically as a radical feminist.

> I do not like marches that have men attending. It makes me feel unsafe and seems to defeat the object of *women* and *girls* Reclaiming the Night!
>
> (Billie)

Meanwhile, Faith recounted not just a sense of threat, but a case of actual violence on a mixed RTN by men watching the march or targeting it. Unfortunately, this does happen occasionally as I mentioned earlier in this book, and it has affected a few marches. Faith was in her late forties, she described herself politically as a feministic dyke, though she did not elaborate further on exactly what she meant by that political label; it was just one of the several creative political titles that activists used to describe themselves. Incidences of violence and aggression, although rare, when they occur, often only further instil the view that RTN should be women-only, that men are a potential risk and that the march should be a protected and safe space for women.

> I don't like the stupid bastard blokes that run into us marchers and grab at women. Police are never to be seen at those points. Happened every time I've marched.
>
> (Faith)

Another marcher, Lucy, spoke of how male bystanders, even if they were not physically violent, often treated the march precisely as if it was some sort of incursion into their male territory; adding weight to the activist's own perceptions of RTN as a takeover of male space. Lucy recounted a group of young men reacting angrily to seeing the march go by. I have also witnessed this myself, I have actually heard men shouting at women marchers 'these are our streets' and 'get off our streets'. Perhaps the activists were right then to use such militaristic and territorial terms to explain the purpose of RTN.

> Another year we had a group of lads on a night out, purposely walking through us on the march, like it was – no, we're men, we can reclaim this space, we can go wherever we want to and walk through the middle of your march. And, like, this one man asked my friend where the nearest brothel was.
>
> (Lucy)

Marchers were not just passive however; several had humorous accounts of dealing with aggressive male bystanders.

> And there was one bit, we were going past this pub, and these blokes came out and started shouting various shite, and one of the marchers sort of whopped him over the head with a placard. And then one of the policewomen arrested him for threatening behaviour, to great cheers from the crowd.
>
> (Mary)

In a possible suggestion that the urban landscape is not always on the side of men, sometimes marchers did not need to intervene themselves, and street furniture interrupted aggressive heckling and threats from male bystanders.

> Some guy started heckling the drummers at the front of the march, and then he walked into a lamppost.
>
> (Kira)

Returning to a more serious note, as well as a real and justified concern for the safety of women marchers, including survivors, there was also a suggestion from some activists that men should not be allowed on RTN because men may be more likely than women are to be aggressive, either with bystanders or with the police. This was seen to be another potential risk, making the march unsafe for women as well as other men. When activists voiced this concern, they often used arguments similar to eco-feminist theories and to scholarship on the Women's Peace Movement for example. These arguments rested on a contention that women have been socialised to be homemakers, carers and society builders, and that through that socialisation, they are more likely to be pacifist than men are, as men have generally not been socialised in the same way. Cait, who described herself as a fun feminist, was in her late thirties, and she touched on this issue. But she added that because of such socialisation, men may actually be more at risk than women, ergo it would not be a good idea for them to be on an RTN march. She particularly thought that men might be targeted by aggressive bystanders for example.

> It's about making women safe. Men on the march may be more aggressive and start fights with people who disagree on the street, or be more likely to be punched by those people.
>
> (Cait)

The final argument made in favour of women-only RTN highlighted that male support was always welcome, just in ways other than actually being on the march itself. All the activists unanimously welcomed male support in what they called back office roles, or supportive behind the scenes tasks.

There are lots of things men can do to oppose violence against women and children and joining an
RTN march doesn't have to be one of them. They
can serve the refreshments at the rally, I'm not against
that.

(Al Garthwaite)

Fallon had recruited her brother to help with the
women-only RTN march in her city in the South of
England. He helped at the after-march rally, setting up
stalls, collecting placards and arranging the stage and
sound system for speakers at the mixed rally which was
open to all. In many cities and towns, small groups of
male volunteers often take on such tasks. Fallon emphasised that her brother enjoyed his support role, and
indeed found it empowering. He enjoyed his part in
making the march happen.

men can come to the rally and they can do their
own bit, I like that. I remember my brother saying
it's amazing hearing the noise of you lot all coming
down the street and it's like, there was something
scary for him about this group of men waiting for
this onslaught of noisy women! But he always says
it's an amazing sound to hear all these women. You
know, and I think it's important men experience that.
It makes it feel like it's possible you know, that women
can go out and we can be threatening, and we can be
in control.

(Fallon)

Here Fallon highlights the benefits to men of supporting a women-only event, but also the benefits for women
of being on such an event on their own, as women.
For her, to be in such large numbers of women on
a successful political demonstration, with men waiting

for them in a purely supportive role, made her believe
that change could be possible. It gave her hope that
it could be possible for women to take political leadership and be powerful and in control alongside men as
equals.

As mentioned at the start of this section, it was suggested by some activists that those men who do seek out
leadership roles in RTN may not be doing so for the
best or most honourable reasons, whether intentionally
or not. Some activists felt those men may be volunteering
just to boost their own ego, or to be seen by others to be
right-on and doing the right thing. This was what Sheila
called 'peacock' behaviour, showing off to aggrandise
themselves in the eyes of others.

> I get really irritated with men supporting women, 'cos
> I think they'd support women by not being there.
> I think they're there to be peacocks really, to say: look
> at me supporting women.
>
> (Sheila)

One RTN organiser, Eve, recounted actually having her
leadership challenged by a male volunteer stewarding
an RTN, what she referred to as the phenomenon of the
'glory steward'.

> I was talking to one male steward and asking him to
> move down a road, 'cos I was in charge, and I'd done
> it before and I was a chief steward. And I asked him
> to move and he was just looking at me and saying,
> erm, no, what, why? And I just thought, 'cos I'm a
> chief steward and I'm telling you to, that's why. But
> I just thought, well, why are they here? They're here
> just sort of showing how great they are, they're here
> as glory stewards.
>
> (Eve)

Just as there were lots of competing and often con-
flicted and overlapping views about the pros and cons
of involving men on RTN, there were also many different explanations put forward to explain the general shift
towards mixed events within feminism. For some it was
seen as an overdue and progressive move, a sign that
feminism had moved on from a past seen as backward
and retrograde. For others it was a symptom of declining
radicalism in the movement and increasing institutionalisation affecting all social movements. The growth of
what is called queer theory and queer activism from the
1990s in particular was also partly seen to have influenced this shift, as was the popularity of certain versions
of self-defined third wave feminism.

*What about teh menz? Contextualising the decline of women-
only marches*

Given the high occurrence of mixed RTN marches, for
the sorts of reasons the activists outlined in the previous
section, it was interesting that the majority of activists
I spoke to were in favour of women-only marches or at
least women-led marches. Many of the activists I interviewed were also organisers of marches; they thus had
some control over the demographic of RTN. Yet even
those organisers who expressed a personal preference
for women-only space often organised a mixed RTN;
why was this? Their argument for doing so mainly
appeared to be pragmatic, reflecting a concern to attract
the broadest numbers possible. High attendance was of
course seen as a sign of a successful march, but there
was also a concern to avoid exclusion of any group at
all. There was a general distaste for excluding men. For
some the exclusion of men was just a form of sexism, as
bad as sexism against women, for others it was exclusion

generally, of any group, that was the problem and both were seen as antithetical to feminism.

It should be noted that although my focus here in this book is on RTN, this shift towards male involvement in RTN is not unique. It has happened across the whole Feminist Movement in the UK and several of the largest feminist activist organisations are mixed. For example, Object, who secured changes in the licensing of lap-dancing clubs and also reforms in the law on prostitution, are a mixed organisation. The dynamic campaign group No More Page 3, lobbying for the voluntary removal of glamour model photographs of topless women in the popular daily British newspaper *The Sun*, are also a mixed organisation. The umbrella group UK Feminista is also mixed and is directed by a mixed management board of women and men, as well as having employed male staff.

Whether feminist groups are mixed or women-only is influenced by individual beliefs about the aims of feminism and the appropriate means to achieve them. Activists both for and against male inclusion both justified their stance by referencing what they saw as the correct aims and methods of feminism. For those who believed that one aim of feminism was to empower and politicise women, women-only space was seen as a tactical way to achieve that. Meanwhile, those influenced by post-structuralism and queer theory often saw women-only space as divisive, and this was usually because they found the category of 'woman' problematic generally, due to the theoretical debates I discussed earlier in Chapter 5. Therefore, those activists did not want to separate out allies for equality on what they saw as essentialist biological grounds, unfairly splitting people up into 'women' and 'men' and saying one type of person can join a march, but another type of person cannot.

Many of the activists more favourable to women-only space made a link between a move towards third wave feminism as they saw it and a shift towards mixed RTN marches open to all. In line with many of the definitions in literature on the subject, several activists emphasised that third wave feminism is more inclusive and more aware of intersectionality, with the result that self-defined third wave feminist events will be mixed and open to all. As mentioned when I introduced the activists earlier though, many of the activists I spoke to did not identify with the term at all, yet third wave is a term frequently attached to the feminism of younger women. This association with younger women has only added to well-worn generational explanations for divides within feminism. But, as many of the activists I talked with made clear, the differences within contemporary feminism are political and not generational. In relation to third wave, these political differences are usually around pornography and prostitution, but also men's involvement in feminism, with third wave feminism being seen as favourable to both.

Perhaps partly because of the popularity of this sort of standpoint, many activists recounted experiencing hostility from their peers when they tried to organise women-only events. This hostility often had the result of further discouraging them from organising women-only events and thus they saw this as a sort of vicious circle. As already outlined in the earlier sections, this hostility took the form of accusing activists of not caring about men, or being sexist against men. Activists found that there was little understanding amongst their peers of any need to prioritise women at all. To do so was viewed negatively as patronising to women, as reducing women's 'choices', 'agency' and turning them into 'victims'. Instead, a gender-blind inclusion was aggrandised above all else and seen as the most progressive stance, as Charlotte explained.

> I say I go to my feminist book group, and it's a women-only book group, and friends will say: 'oh I thought it was a feminist book group'. And I'll say: 'well yes it is, and this one's women-only and if you want to organise a mixed one then why don't you go and do it. I just started this one up on my own'. Well, my friend used to work on an anti-vivisection stall and she said nobody ever came up to her and said: 'what about the dolphins'.
>
> (Charlotte)

For many of the activists I met, these arguments and accusations were all-consuming. As a result, some found it easier to just deflect this flack and avoid it happening in the first place by including men on limited terms, such as at the rear of a march.

Activists also told me that, perhaps ironically given the modern neo-liberal focus on choice, that they felt they really had no choice about the demographic of RTN. They felt that feminism as a social movement was in a weakened state, weathered by the elements of third wave or post-feminism which they identified. Of course, the backlash against feminism was also mentioned here, a kickback from the patriarchal status quo against any claim to equality which appears to hold a potential to succeed. Susan Faludi has written about this in her 1992 book, *Backlash*, which uses examples from America and the UK. This backlash has been seen whenever feminism goes through a resurgence; it is in the premature claims that feminism is dead for example, and it is in the media focus on limited examples of feminism and feminists – usually educated, White and heterosexual young women for example. The backlash is also clear in the fierce sexual objectification of women which often follows feminist wins or high points. For example, today it is the rise and rise of the pornography and prostitution industries that we have witnessed growing since the 1990s in particular; it is also the narrow and degrading images of women which we see in advertising and culture. Other elements of the backlash include the perpetual mockery of feminism alongside wilful misrepresentation, especially this focus on individualism and 'choice'. This is an attempt to reduce the potency of feminism not by ignoring it, but by acknowledging it and dismissing it at the same time as no longer needed in our supposed liberated times. The feminist scholar Angela McRobbie has written about this process of disavowal in her excellent book *The Aftermath of Feminism* (2009).

In this hostile environment then, many activists told me that while they personally may have all kinds of views about the importance of women-only space, they felt that they just could not afford to put people off feminism any more than they already were put off. Unfortunately, they regularly found that women-only events were one of the things that put people off feminism, albeit for problematic misogynistic, homophobic and unfounded reasons, which the activists of course acknowledged. Linked to this, while the great majority of activists supported the idea of intersectionality, an approach focussed on inclusion, they also thought that this had sometimes been mistakenly taken to mean that women could not self-organise and that to do so was sexist against men or anti-intersectional.

## One for all, and all for women-only

As a radical feminist committed to the promotion and maintenance of women-only space, I obviously find the arguments outlined against male inclusion to be more convincing. I agree that the best way men can support RTN is to get off the streets and allow women to take up space for themselves. Men do indeed experience street violence and harassment, in fact, they are more vulnerable to it; but RTN is not about random street violence and harassment or men's macho or drunken aggression towards other men. RTN is about male violence against women, and men are not affected directly by that. Men also do not experience blame and stigma in the same way when they are assaulted or attacked, as Al Garthwaite pointed out. Nobody would ask a young man how tight his jeans were when he was mugged or if he had been drinking when another man bottled him in the face. As the activists highlighted themselves, if the message of RTN is to be kept clear, then this cannot be done more powerfully than through the feature of it being women-only. How many political demonstrations do you see going through your town or city centre that are made up just of women? Not many, I expect. This is what makes RTN stand out. It showcases the whole point of the march and, if nothing else, it grabs attention and that is so important for a protest aimed at awareness raising.

I know some women who say that they personally do not like women-only space because they feel that women-only space is not safe. Many find it intimidating and alienating. This is perhaps because it is so unusual and unfamiliar and so many lies are spread about it. But our job as feminists is surely not to pander to myths about women-only space, but actively to challenge them by proving them wrong. So many women have been taught that all women are 'bitches', that women are the worst bosses, that women compete with other women, are 'their own worst enemies' and are the harshest judges of each other. It is no wonder that so many women are reticent about women-only space. But we need to remember that these messages are meant to represent all women. This is what patriarchy says all women are, because in labelling women as this way or that way in propaganda and gossip, all women are labelled, including you.

For anyone who believes that these messages are lies when applied to themselves, the task is to extend that same degree of doubt and scepticism to your perceptions of fellow women and have some feminist faith. If some women reading this do not feel that they are 'bitchy', competitive, manipulative or critically judgemental about other women, then perhaps other women are not either. I am not saying that working politically in women-only space is easy. Women are not saints or angels and they bring their own baggage to the committee table. Many women in feminism have been harmed by the very wrongs that we are struggling against, those brave resisters who have survived appalling violence often at the hands of those men who should have loved and protected them the most. In a way, all women are survivors of course, for all of us know what it is to grow up in a patriarchal world where being a woman equals second class. Women are taught by our culture to hate their bodies, told they are too fat, too thin, too hairy and otherwise not good enough for the male gaze. Yet women are also damned even when they do what they are told, when they do dress and act the way they are supposed to and follow the dictates of fashion, celebrity and the plethora of women's so-called lifestyle magazines. Women are blamed for playing the game, even though they never wrote the rules; they are seen as too sexy, too much and made to carry men's shame for turning them into sex objects in the first place. This takes its toll.

I have of course known women who have struggled in women-only spaces, this does happen. I know women who have found some other feminists hostile and judgemental. I am sure we have all experienced that; I know I have. But I have also known mixed feminist spaces where men have shared details of their porn addiction or recounted how they bravely managed to get over a phobia of female sexual partners with unshaved genitals. That is not safe; it does not make for a safe space. Women should not have to hear that. We do not need to know how men get over their fear, fascination and disgust of the female body. The important thing for us is that they get over it and traumatise as few women as possible in the process. Creating women-only space is often difficult, but nobody said saving the world was going to be easy. The efforts put into stopping women sharing political, cultural and domestic space together as women should alert us to the inherent potential power in that organising method. I believe that in a patriarchal society, the most dangerous and revolutionary thing women can do is remove, however temporarily, some of their energies from men, be that politically, culturally, socially, domestically or sexually. This will never be seen by the patriarchal status quo as anything other than a threat, because such a society depends on the support of women to prop it up. This perception of threat is therefore well founded.

While I promote and encourage women-only space, I am not saying that men should not support RTN or feminism generally. I know plenty of women who would like to bring their male partners, friends or family and march alongside them in solidarity on RTN for example.

I understand that admirable aspiration. But RTN is not about excluding men; it is about including women. One point of the march, as argued throughout this chapter, is that it takes place specifically to protest the sad fact that so many women do not feel safe when out at night on their own or with female friends. They feel vulnerable to sexual harassment, assault or worse just because they are too often seen as fair game by men if they are not being chaperoned by another man, or if they have breached the spatial segregation that they are supposed to adhere to. This treatment harks back to ancient patriarchal stereotypes about women as men's property and it is high time we broke those stereotypes down.

Due to these very stereotypes, women often do feel safer and less vulnerable to sexual harassment when they are with another man; so what is the political point of having men on RTN marches? The protest is meant to be an opportunity for women to experience the very opposite of that chaperoned fragile half-freedom. It is a chance to enjoy their town or city without a male protector, to get a sense of what it is like to feel powerful and to dominate space as a woman and with other women. After all, men reclaim the streets all the time, they dominate public spaces outside pubs and clubs, they swarm the streets following football matches for example and other sporting events. They enjoy public space together in groups of other men and they fill up those spaces with noise and bodily presence. RTN is a chance for women to do that, not in worship of a few men scoring goals in a field, but in pursuit of grander political goals in the whole of society.

While I do not want men on my RTN march, as I said, I do think men have a place in feminism, and I welcome support from pro-feminists. Male volunteers have always helped at the London RTN rally for example.

On that night, women march through the centre of the city to the rally location at which they are greeted by men who gather up their placards and stack them safely for storage until next year. The men collect the high-visibility tabards worn by the stewards and fold and bag them so they can be reused on other protests, they distribute rubbish bags and dispose of any glass bottles before marchers enter the venue. I think there is something powerful and empowering in this process and in what it represents and symbolises. It is a rare occasion when women have been in the lead politically, women have organised, stewarded and led their own successful national political demonstration and men have aided them in supportive and behind the scenes roles. Men have taken a back seat, while women have led. How rarely this happens in political spaces, and yet how urgent it is if we are to truly work towards liberating ourselves and the rest of the world from our history of chains.

Men have a role in the WLM, but the clue is in the name. This is the WLM, and it should be led and directed by women and it should always prioritise women. There is plenty men can do to support women's activism, without taking it over. If they want to walk their political talk then they can take the opportunity to prioritise women by allowing women to lead and direct their own movement. As for the argument that men can change other men's behaviour, I agree; I wait patiently for the day when men picket lap-dancing clubs and brothels and stop other men from buying and exploiting women. There is much men can do in the struggle for women's rights if they choose to do so; some of these are quite dramatic. Men can stop rape for example, by not raping women. They can bring the sex industry to its knees by removing their patriarchal pound from this brutal institution founded on the inequalities of sex, race and class.

But we women have not got time to persuade men to do this or to teach them about feminism in some time-consuming maternal way. Nor should women have to thank men when they do behave like decent human beings. Most men do not rape women or children, or abuse their partners or use women in prostitution. They do not deserve a medal for that. We do not need to waste our time thanking men, praising them or worrying about making our politics amenable to them. We have a hard enough job on our hands engaging women in feminism, in a context of backlash where women risk ridicule, exclusion and worse for identifying with a politics of their own. That is the engagement that should be the focus of feminism – the rest will follow.

Of course, in my discussions with RTN activists, men were not the only group over which there were concerns about inclusion or exclusion. Reflecting one of the big fault lines in feminism, several activists were concerned at the exclusion of transgender/transexual-identified people on RTN marches. Others felt that people involved in prostitution or those with a history in the 'sex industry' were also not actively welcomed on marches. These topics often took up just as much of my time with activists as did the conversation about whether or not men should be allowed. They continue to be debated online and offline and they incur into the work of activists organising RTN marches. These issues split RTN organising groups and individual activists. They cause dissenting groups to organise differing marches in the same year or in concurrent years. They cause some RTN marches to lose their funding, while others receive more support. They result in some RTN marches being boycotted, picketed and loudly protested.

Given the importance of these feminist fault lines, I shall now move to focus firstly on the feminist differences around the issue of the 'sex industry' and secondly, to the inclusion of trans people, meaning transgender or transexual-identified individuals, on RTN marches and in the wider Feminist Movement.

# Chapter 8

# Inclusion and exclusion on Reclaim the Night

In this chapter, I will consider the inclusion or exclusion of groups other than men on RTN; namely, trans people and also people involved in or supportive of the industry of prostitution. These two issues rest on the more theoretical debates I explored earlier in Chapter 5. They are an example of how seemingly very abstract and academic conflicts can have real ramifications in practical activism. In this chapter, I will try to outline, for those not immersed in the feminist scene, just what these conflicts are all about. For those activist organisers reading this book, I will try to provide some possible arguments that could be useful when defending RTN marching, specifically women-only RTN marching. I will also provide some feminist arguments against the industry of prostitution, though these will not please those queer or third wave activists who see that industry as a potentially positive site of women's empowerment, economic and otherwise. In fact, it may be the case that my views on this industry will only fulfil stereotypes about radical feminists, because indeed I do consider the so-called sex industry to be a form of male violence against women and a symptom of patriarchy. That does not mean I am anti-sex or anti-women's agency, as I shall attempt to explain. Hopefully, this analysis will help others reading this who also share those views, who are also forced to justify them on a regular basis and who are sick of being called prudes or otherwise as a result. In this chapter, I will also state my own stance on the very controversial issue of trans inclusion in feminism and provide my own take on the supposed, and surprisingly well publicised, current rift or dispute between some trans activists and some feminist activists.

The perceived exclusion from RTN of trans people, that is, people who identify as transexual or transgender, and of people involved in the sex industry, form two of the current feminist fault lines I have observed in the contemporary Feminist Movement. It was often the case that those activists who were concerned about trans exclusion were also concerned at the potential exclusion of people involved in prostitution or the sex industry. Often they linked these two issues, usually because they felt that feminism, or at least some types of feminism, were jointly hostile to these groups of people. Those aligned to queer politics often held this view, such as these quotes from activists Corrie and Brooke illustrate.

... trans women and sex workers have been excluded in the past and there has not been enough conversation and working together to ensure that *all* those who experience discrimination and violence are included.

(Corrie)

Sometimes people on the march are not very tolerant, particularly when it comes to showing open support of women who identify with sex workers. I have been shoved, sworn at and threatened with the police because I walk with the sex-worker contingent.

(Brooke)

Some RTN marches in a variety of cities do purposely choose routes past lap-dancing clubs, for example the London RTN, which for several years marched past the Spearmint Rhino lap-dancing and pole-dancing club. This club is situated on Tottenham Court Road in central London and was planning an expansion into other UK cities. For some activists, marching past these sorts of venues is difficult though, and they were opposed to marchers shouting slogans or chants against the sex industry. This was partly because they felt such shouting could be seen to be blaming or shaming the women working in such premises, something nobody would want to do. It was also partly because they felt such opposition was misguided and lacking in critiques of the role of capitalism in creating the sex industry.

> I also *hate* the shouting at the lap-dancing clubs that happens in my city. They do this yet completely ignore the bars paying below a living wage, meaning that often for some women it makes more economic sense to become a sex worker. There is such a powerful anti sex-work lobby, which is fine, but no acknowledgement of the economic reasons behind this.
>
> (Babin)

For several activists though, it was the divisions between feminists of different standpoints on this issue which caused them most discomfort, rather than the complex arguments for and against the industry of prostitution. Some activists also described anger or disappointment when groups in support of the 'sex industry' attended RTN. For example, groups such as the International Union of Sex Workers or IUSW, whose campaigning tool is to protest while carrying red umbrellas and forming a bloc on marches and events. Also, the English

Collective of Prostitutes, who are a sub-group of W4H, a long-standing organisation described earlier in the chapter on the history of the UK Second Wave. W4H frequently distribute their flyers at feminist events, including at RTN, and particularly in London where they are based. Danielle for example had attended several RTN marches and did not like to see such groups on the marches at all because of her political stance on the global 'sex industry'.

> ... there is nothing right about it, and prostitution in my opinion cannot be defended as a job. It is a form of exploitation, slavery; and a very specific one. I don't like the red umbrellas one bit.
>
> (Danielle)

It is hard to explain to those not involved in activism just what a fierce divide this is in the Feminist Movement. It is not a new one. It goes back to the 1980s and 1990s and what were misleadingly called the 'sex wars', where feminists were divided on issues of prostitution, pornography and sexual practices such as sado-masochism (Long, 2012). During that time, it became common to refer to feminists who were positive about prostitution and pornography as 'sex positive'. Therefore, feminists who problematised these industries were often rewarded for their troubles by being called 'anti-sex'. This is a misleading and mistaken label of course, as feminists who take this standpoint do not generally see the industry of prostitution as being much about sex, but instead about power and exploitation. It is worth going over this simplistic pro- and anti-sex binary, because, like most things, it is not that simple.

As you will remember from the Seven Demands, since 1974, the UK WLM has been profoundly positive about sexual liberation; it was never and is not in any way anti-sex. In 1974, at one of their national conferences, that year held in Scotland, the Sixth Demand was agreed – this called for the right of all women to define their own sexuality and for an end to discrimination against lesbians. Our movement has never been against sex, it has been for women's rights to explore, enjoy, express and identify their own sexuality free from the patriarchal double standards that try to police their behaviour. This double standard aggrandises men for engaging in sexual behaviour, while shaming women for doing the same. It is the patriarchal standard that requires women to walk a tightrope between slut and prude, judging them at every turn. Throughout the ages of patriarchy, all across the world in fact, it is clear that men as a class hold a fear and fascination of the female body and female sexuality. This fascination and fear has led to men trying to control women's bodies and their sexuality in varying degrees from blunt to subtle. Feminism has always struggled against this and continues to do so. This is why so many feminists oppose the multibillion-dollar global 'sex industry', not because they are against sex, but because they are against the presumption of a male right to sexual access to women's bodies.

This is not an agreed standpoint however, far from it. Not all feminists take that view on the so-called oldest profession (which incidentally is not the oldest occupation, as that honour goes to agriculture). Regardless of its age, the length of time an oppression has been in existence is not grounds for its continuation, it is surely more reason to overcome it. The problem is that feminists are not even agreed whether it is an oppression in the first place, and so prostitution has long been a contentious issue in the WLM, splitting feminist individuals and groups. This division can be summarised briefly as being between those who have the aim of abolishing prostitution versus those who promote prostitution as work like any other. This division is often known as an abolitionist versus legalisation dichotomy. This is a reductionist and misleading split however, because prostitution is not technically illegal in the UK anyway, although most activities associated with it are, and also because many feminists cannot fit easily into one side or the other. To provide some background to this feminist fault line, put into context for those not familiar with the activist scene and also for those activists who would just like to know more about the arguments on either side, I shall now explore this dichotomy in more depth. This should also hopefully provide some useful arguments for those activists who are facing conflicts in their RTN organising or other activist groups and hopefully set the record straight on some of the lies and myths which surround this division in the movement.

## *Beyond the binary: How to argue against prostitution and for women in prostitution*

Abolitionists are those who believe in the criminalisation of demand for prostitution, with a view to reducing prostitution, or perhaps ending it in the future. This is not just a feminist argument; many socialists and anti-capitalists also subscribe to this view and look towards a future without the prostitution industry. Abolitionists usually view prostitution as a cause and consequence of inequality, including gender inequality; they do not view it as work like any other. This is a political stance – it is not a religious, moralistic or conservative stance.

Many feminists, including abolitionists like myself, advocate what is called the Nordic approach, calling for the complete decriminalisation of all those exploited in prostitution and instead for the criminalisation of demand. In 1999, Sweden outlawed the purchase of sexual acts in prostitution, effectively criminalising punters, while decriminalising all those selling 'sexual services'. Other countries, such as Norway and Iceland, followed suit in later years and more are considering adopting such a law. What does this law mean then, in practice? To put it plainly, because statistically speaking this is a profoundly gendered industry, the law means that women are not criminalised, but the men are. This move was in line with Sweden's understanding of prostitution as a form of violence against women and a symptom of inequality, as well as being part of their commitment towards tackling global sex trafficking. Any such legal move must of course go alongside a large and dedicated financial investment in both harm-minimisation and exit services, and this is no less than what those people exploited and harmed in prostitution deserve, many of whom have been let down consistently by the very state services that should have protected them. I will cover what harm-minimisation and exit services are later in this section.

On the other side of the debate is the so-called legalisation argument. This is the argument for prostitution to be viewed as a legitimate business and for the whole of the 'sex industry' to be able to operate legally, for example in legal brothels. It is an argument usually made by groups referred to as sex-worker lobby groups, sex-worker rights groups or self-titled 'sex-positive' groups. These groups usually view prostitution as work like any other. These groups are usually opposed to abolitionist groups. They often argue that only the full legalisation of the whole of the 'sex industry' can make women – and men and young people, and trans or queer people and indeed all those people involved – in prostitution safer.

However, given the current legal situation, where in the UK prostitution is not illegal anyway, this 'legalisation' approach is perhaps better and more accurately referred to as an argument for brothelisation – for the establishment of legal brothels operating as businesses. The argument that prostitution is work like any other is usually followed by the assertion that the decision to enter this industry is a matter of individual choice with which the state or anyone else should not interfere, but should only facilitate that choice to be enacted as safely as possible. Such a stance harks back of course to the earlier discussions in this book about the importance and reification of 'choice' in some third wave and post-feminist approaches. Groups like the English Collective of Prostitutes (ECP) or W4H describe prostitution as 'consenting sex', which 'should not be the business of the criminal law' (ECP, 2014). Groups like the IUSW also view prostitution as a worker's rights issue and promote prostitution as a legitimate business. Both groups commend the approach taken in New Zealand, where brothels of varying sizes from small owner-operated ventures to larger chains are allowed to operate legally, though the ECP favour small owner-operated ventures over larger big business brothel chains. The latter are thriving however under this regime. Recent news coverage in local papers in Auckland, New Zealand details planning applications for a 15-storey brothel to be developed in the city's main business district for example; a brainchild of two entrepreneurial brothers in the brothel industry, a plan they have currently put on hold (Dougan & Fletcher, 2014; Gibson, 2012).

It can be enlightening in fact to study the local newspapers of towns and cities in all countries where brothels have been legalised to see what is happening on the ground. In Queensland, Australia for example, local papers recently reported on complaints from legal brothels regarding being undercut by the illegal sector, resulting in the closure of three legal brothels (Solomons, 2011). The legal sector is not a panacea however, it does not guarantee women's safety; for example, a woman is reportedly suing a legal brothel in Melbourne, Australia after being threatened with a gun for refusing to have unprotected sex (Medew, 2011). A survey in Australia found physical safety still the highest concern for women in legal brothels (Norma, 2011). Women are still raped, assaulted and attacked in legal brothels and tolerance zones. And, in countries which have legalised, this happens behind the closed doors of legal profit-making brothels paying a licence fee to the state; therefore making the state a pimp.

If the UK were to follow the example of legalised brothels, such as in New Zealand, Amsterdam and Australia, what do we expect would happen to this so-called industry? Is it not common business sense to assume that when an industry is legalised and promoted, when it can freely advertise and set up anywhere in our towns and cities, that it will therefore grow, that it will expand? And, if the industry grows, who will fill the new 'vacancies' that will be created? More women, children and men in prostitution; we have to ask ourselves if that is the sort of outcome we want. There is also the argument that wherever there is a legal sector there will always be an illegal or so-called underground sector. There will always be those that do not wish to register as sex workers, those that do not want to or cannot afford to pay taxes, those that are working illegally without papers, those who are immigrants or trafficked, pimped or under age.

Legalising prostitution turns it into a business, turns it into a career option and turns pimps and traffickers into legitimate businessmen overnight. Legalising prostitution removes any obligations to provide exit services from what becomes a profession like any other. It can give a green light to organised crime and it formally defines women as commodities, as objects of exchange for men's presumed natural needs. Yet many sex-industry lobby groups and individuals see no need to reduce or end prostitution, and believe it should be a legitimate business – just made safer than it currently is. This is where what is called harm minimisation comes in. This term refers to practical interventions, such as CCTV and other security measures, better police responses to crimes against those in prostitution, free contraception, specialist sexual health care etc.

There is probably agreement, regardless of political stance, that those in prostitution have a right to this kind of protection and support. People in the UK for example are entitled to their rights as citizens generally, and to their human rights whatever their immigration status, regardless of how they make an income. This is where what is called harm minimisation can play a role. No feminist that I know would argue against harm minimisation. Nor are feminists arguing against a better police response when prostituted women report crimes, including rape. All women deserve a better police response when reporting rape. Everybody has the right to support after rape, including support to prosecute if they so choose. Feminists are certainly not arguing against services such as free contraception, drug and alcohol counselling, access to safe legal abortion, benefits advice, housing, laundries, refuges, needle exchanges etc.

All these examples of harm-minimisation services are sadly vital as long as prostitution continues to exist – whether legal or illegal. But importantly, the feminist argument highlights that we must always and also look towards harm ending, alongside harm minimisation. Society cannot, and should not, be satisfied for ever more with merely piecemeal and temporary fixes to the scars that prostitution leaves on our society and on the bodies of those chewed up within it: the women murdered, missing, raped, battered and those who find tragically that the only way to exit this industry is to take their own lives. To continue with only harm-minimisation approaches is to merely maintain a whole class of people in sexual service to the other half of the population and thus sustain this fundamental injustice; an injustice which makes a mockery of claims to equality. And while these debates go on, back and forth and fiercely contested in Student Union debates and as the topics of women's groups and CR groups, the situation continues. Tonight on our streets, up to 5000 young people will be exploited in prostitution (HO, 2010) to fulfil a demand we are told to accept as inevitable. Children continue to be groomed and pimped, with the average age of entry into prostitution worldwide estimated at around only 14 years old (Silbert & Pines, 1982). Women, children and men in this industry continue to be disproportionately affected by violence, including sexual violence, with Canadian studies suggesting that women in prostitution face a homicide risk 40 times higher than the national average (SPC, 1985).

Abolitionist feminists view the industry of prostitution as a cause and consequence of inequality, not as work like any other. There is of course, the familiar anti-capitalist argument that all of us are coerced to work, regardless of what job we are in. This argument asks what choice or consent any of us can really have or give in a world blighted by inequality, by sexism, racism and homophobia. Ours is a world scarred by the masculinisation of wealth and power, where all too often women and children pay the highest price. In such a world there is certainly a question over the extent of our agency, when the vast majority of us have to work for a living at best and survival at worst, whether we like it or not.

Some sex-industry lobby groups that subscribe to this valid anti-capitalist stance then use this argument to classify prostitution therefore as work like any other. They argue that all workers sell their labour, whether they are journalists, waiters, academics or prostitutes. To argue in this way removes any gendered analysis from debate about prostitution, which is wrong, because prostitution is markedly gendered. The vast majority of those in prostitution are women and the vast majority of punters are men. This, and other signs of the symptoms of structural inequalities, cannot be overlooked. It is also offensive to people earning money through prostitution whose 'job' is very different to the more privileged life of a journalist or academic.

We should save powerful words and terms to describe what they are meant to describe lest we dilute or demean the meaning, but unfortunately, this is often not common practice. To take just a few examples, currently so many things are referred to as 'rape' which are not rape, such as 'Facebook rape' when someone hijacks a logged-in Facebook page and posts inappropriate material or jokes, or environmental destruction referred to as 'the rape of the earth' or even, football matches, such as the German defeat of Brazil at the 2014 World Cup, referred to as 'the rape of Brazil'. The same is true of the word 'pimp', which has tragically come to refer to the practice of making something better or improving something, such as 'pimp my ride', meaning souping up or customising a car, or trainers that are 'pimped'; there was even a soft drink for a while called 'Pimp Juice' sponsored by a US rapper called Nelly. The term 'pimp' actually describes someone who makes money out of the prostitution of others; it can describe a controlling or violent person who actively prostitutes others. The fact that this term has become so glamorised is telling and should highlight the importance of language. Let us call prostitution prostitution and nothing else; let us call rape rape, and nothing else.

Unfortunately, activists reported time and again that terms such as prostitution were generalised and minimised; that debates around the violence of prostitution were reduced to issues of worker's rights alone. To return to the common refrain that prostitution is work like any other then, this was actually one of the most frequent arguments that activist organisers in local RTN groups told me they faced and they were often unsure how to respond to this challenge. Feminist arguments against the industry of prostitution hold that there is a difference between selling one's labour and selling access to one's body. Survivors of prostitution often say the same. A builder or plumber labours with his or her body, she sells her labour which is a product of her physicality, including her mind. A journalist or academic labours with their body too, thinking, writing, delivering lectures, travelling to conferences etc. But this is not the same as selling access to one's body. Goods are produced by labourers through the labouring of their body – their body is not the good itself. Some would then point to dancers, or artists who use their own bodies in their art. But the same argument can apply, as dancers produce dance, and artists produce art with their bodies – their body is not the good in and of itself.

The boundaries of the body are enshrined in law, our bodily integrity is universally understood; everywhere but in debates about prostitution it seems. Most of us would understand that there is a difference between being punched in the face and being raped. Our law treats these two violent assaults differently, because the latter is understood to have breached bodily integrity – it is a violation of bodily boundaries. We understand the body as a possession in some ways, but we do not understand it as a possession in the same way as a car, or a mobile phone or a house. If your house is burgled, this is a violation on your property and is treated seriously in law, but it is not treated the same in law as a violation on your body, as common assault, as rape or sexual assault. Most of us would be very upset and angry if our computer or car was stolen for example, but we would understand that this is a very different crime to a crime on our body, and the two would be treated differently under the law. Therefore, it should become clear that the body is not commonly understood as just a tool, or possession or product. This is partly why labouring with one's body and making one's body into a good itself are two very different things. To put it bluntly, being a builder does not involve making one's body sexually available to one's employers; the same is true of journalists, academics, waiters etc.

Feminists who take the abolitionist stance, which includes many radical feminists, are not saying that earning a living through prostitution does not involve labour of the body and mind, it certainly does. It is probably one of the most difficult ways to earn a living and many people struggle to even earn a living in this 'industry'; many experience it as merely survival, and all too many do not survive it. But debate around prostitution cannot and should not be shut down by turning to the refrain that all work is like prostitution – because it patently is not; and the great majority of people understand this. I remember one survivor who is now a writer and campaigner summarising this argument well when she was asked if prostitution was not just a job like any other that nobody particularly likes but does for the money, as with cleaning. She replied that perhaps prostitution was a little like cleaning – if all cleaners were forced to do their cleaning work with only their tongues (Mott, 2009). Therefore, I disagree with the supposedly socialist sentiment expressed by some that all work is prostitution, because it is not. Prostitution is prostitution, and it is demeaning to those involved in it to argue any otherwise and to do so only minimises the struggles those people face.

Those of us who take the abolitionist stance are also often accused of removing agency from women, of making women into victims and stigmatising people who earn money through prostitution. It is argued that any legal controls of prostitution just further stigmatise the people in it, making their lives harder and more marginalised and this sentiment is used against feminists expressing uncertainty or doubt about the continuation of the prostitution industry. It is important to understand that it is not feminists though, but patriarchal society, obsessed as it is with a fear of and fascination with women's sexuality, which attaches a stigma to those in prostitution. It is a form of what the late feminist academic Mary Daly would call a 'patriarchal reversal' that this stigma is not also attached to those who buy sexual services in prostitution – punters, who are overwhelmingly men. Within patriarchy, men's sexuality is not degraded by buying sexual access to others, whereas women in prostitution are degraded. This patriarchal reversal is visible in other areas too of course, though it often goes uncommented, proof itself of its grip on culture. Take for example so-called celebrity sex-tape scandals involving singers such as Tulisa Contostavlos in 2012, or reality TV star Lauren Goodger in 2014. It is the case that, although usually ex-boyfriends publicise such footage without the knowledge and permission of the woman involved, the woman is the one expected to be somehow shamed, embarrassed, 'caught out' or 'exposed' by such material; and indeed often is. Questions are asked in the media about whether such tapes will hurt, launch or hinder careers or how women may 'recover', 'come back from' or 'take control' of the fall-out from this exposure. Yet nobody stops to wonder why we do not have the same expectations and assumptions about the man appearing in the film, and his various body parts and sexual acts which are suddenly publicised to the world for all to see.

Patriarchy has constructed women generally as object to men's subjectivity, and associated women with nature, with the body and with sex. Women in prostitution are forced to bear the brunt of this dualism. This is not a construct of feminists. Feminists oppose such patriarchal constructs. Feminists do not support campaigns that stigmatise or attempt to shame women in prostitution. Feminists do not think that being in prostitution or having once been in prostitution is anything to be ashamed of. It is the men who choose to buy access to women in prostitution who are stigmatising people in prostitution by commodifying another human being. In fact, in a hopeful display of some kind of conscious or unconscious realisation of this inequality, punters themselves often report feeling ashamed of buying sexual services in prostitution (Bindel, 2010b).

As well as supposedly stigmatising people in prostitution, radical feminists with an abolitionist stance are also accused of supporting the criminalisation of women, through police controls. In fact, the history of RTN even plays out in these charges, with some groups using RTN as an example of radical feminist demands for increased policing. I have already dealt with these charges however, in Chapter 4, and shown how this was never a demand of the early RTN marches or the broader Feminist Movement during the Second Wave. No feminist I know is arguing for those in prostitution to be criminalised. This is just one matter on which I am sure there is agreement, regardless of political stance. I am sure that whatever approach one takes, even if one is firmly on one or the other side of this divide, we can all agree that those involved/exploited/working in this industry should not be criminalised. Feminist groups are in fact calling for decriminalisation of those in prostitution. We would like to see crimes such as soliciting to be removed from the statute and for any records for these offences to be wiped, as having such a record only further inhibits women from entry into the formal labour market, training or education and unfairly brands them a criminal. Feminist groups are not calling for women in prostitution to be criminalised, and feminist groups do not support the fining or imprisoning of women or the serving of anti-social behaviour orders on women in prostitution.

Radical feminists are also accused of suggesting that everyone in the sex industry is a powerless and passive victim devoid of any choice or agency. No feminist I know is arguing this. It would be nonsensical to suggest that *all* those people – women, young people, men – earning an income through prostitution are forced or coerced in the bluntest sense. However, the fact that there are probably some people successfully navigating the 'sex industry' without any negative experiences, for both the love and the money of it, should not negate the fact that research suggests this is far from the experience of the majority.

It is possible to be against sweatshop labour for example, but still acknowledge that countless families depend on an income from it; ditto with child labour. It is possible to be against the global illegal trade in body organs, but acknowledge that for too many people, this illegal industry sometimes becomes a choice in an environment of very limited options. Presumably, nobody would seriously argue that an illegal trade in body organs is fine, as long as people are operated on with sterile instruments. The fact that people find ways to make money when they need it in our imperfect world does not render those ways unquestionable – the exchange of money does not make everything ok.

While prostitution seems to have become some sort of liberal ideal, often heralded as a haven of choice and empowerment for women, trafficking for the purposes of prostitution is generally seen as undesirable. It is usually acceptable to say that one is against trafficking, although some sex-industry lobby groups do try to suggest that this is extremely rare and they prefer to talk about 'migration for sex work'. Indeed, reliable statistics are hard to find when dealing with an illegal trade where people are hidden or hiding and I do not deny that some government attempts at statistics can never be anything else than guesses. Difficulties in measurement do not mean it does not happen though, and sometimes the efforts of sex-industry lobby groups to dismiss research and policy on trafficking read like denials. Whatever stance one takes however, it is fact that both prostitution and trafficking have one key thing in common, and that is demand. If men in Britain did not wish to buy sexual access to women, children and young men, then nobody would be trafficked into or within the 'sex industry' in this country; in fact, prostitution as an institution would cease to exist.

Abolitionist feminists are also accused of not caring about the safety of women in prostitution. We are told that only full legalisation can protect people in this industry. Yet there are other ways to protect people in the industry as long as it exists. For example, it is possible to implement both harm-minimisation *and* exit services. This is not an either/or argument, though it is often reduced to such by proponents of the sex industry. It is not necessary to legalise and normalise the whole of the sex industry in order to provide exit and harm-minimisation services, and we should be wary of those groups who frame the debate in this way and threaten such an ultimatum. Exit services are interventions aimed at supporting those who want to get out of the 'sex industry' to get out. Interventions can provide support with housing, education, training, benefits, counselling, family mediation, police support to prosecute abusers be they pimps or punters etc.

Exit services are important and necessary because the so-called sex industry is an industry built on the inequality of women, it is built on the deep fissures of inequality that in fact characterise society at every level, inequalities of class, race and wealth. It cannot be coincidence that evidence suggests that the majority of those in prostitution around the globe are women, are poor women, are Women of Colour, are migrant women, are young women, are mothers, are homeless women, are First Nation women, are women without papers. The 'sex industry' is an industry that harms those in it, which damages those in it and it is not surprising then that global research finds that around 90 per cent of those in it would leave if they had the economic freedom to do so (Farley et al., 2003). A 2007 study in Germany also found that most of those surveyed in the prostitution industry said it was only a temporary solution to a difficult financial situation and they wanted to get out as soon as they possibly could. Securing this economic freedom must then be one element of all feminist campaigns against the industry of prostitution.

The answer to poverty and marginalisation is not to negate our social responsibilities and hand over this authority to the multibillion-dollar 'sex industry'. Brothels and strip clubs in our communities are not providers of drug rehabilitation, of rape trauma counselling, of housing. Lap-dancing clubs in our communities are not providers of higher education and they are not providing a public service by recruiting young student women struggling to pay the high fees and expenses now associated with completing a university education. The answer to the latter situation for example, is to unite together and fight for the return of the student grant and for free education for all – not to turn to the often criminal 'sex industry' as if it is some sort of safety net for women, when it is usually the very opposite.

It is time to envision a society, and a world, without prostitution. This may sound idealistic, but the theory matters, the direction of travel matters, the aspiration matters, because if we can't envision such a society, then we cannot even begin to build it. Those of us who accept that prostitution is not a positive feature of society, and those that agree that it is not a positive career option for women, children or young men, must then tackle and reverse the social and economic conditions that enable prostitution to thrive. Our society has failed people who need refuge, who need safe housing, who need food, who need health services, who need money to survive, who need childcare, who need justice to be served on rapists and abusers. We have raised girls who think their worth is based on their attractiveness to the opposite sex, we have reduced women to nothing more than sex objects; we have brought up boys to believe that women are second class. Thus, we have created a conducive environment for prostitution. This is not natural, it is not inevitable and it can be reduced, maybe ended; at the very least it can be challenged, rather than glamourised, normalised and condoned.

The real question about prostitution is the question of men's rights and, whether we as a society believe that men have a right to buy and sell women's bodies or whether they do not. We know that people will do what they have to do to survive and to make money, this is not rocket science, it is not a feature of people's sexuality or sexual identity. People make desperate choices to provide for their children, to keep a roof over their heads, to feed their families or just to make an income – and they should not be criminalised for doing so when their situation and/or vulnerability is exploited within prostitution. But why do men choose to buy women's bodies, men who are often in full-time employment, in relationships and in a position of relative privilege? And why do we as a nation protect and condone that choice as if it cannot be helped, as if it is a feature of our human biology that some of us are born with a price on our head and others with a birth right to buy us?

Imagine if every country stood up and said that this is not acceptable, as Sweden has done, stood up and said that every woman is worth more than what some man will pay for her and that we will criminalise rather than condone men who assume a right to buy the body of another human being. If our laws are lines in the sand, if they define collective aspirations, then ours are clearly lacking on this issue. This is despite the changes in the Policing and Crime Act 2009 under the last Labour government, which were indeed a step forward, for the first time directing the eyes of the law onto those who fuel prostitution – punters. This victory was a result of tireless campaigning by women's groups, led by the feminist, abolitionist 'Demand Change' campaign. Nevertheless, these changes did not go far enough and those exploited in the 'sex industry' are still being branded as, and treated as, criminals, with all the increased vulnerability that engenders.

Rather than simply throw our hands in the air and legalise the whole of the 'sex industry', some genuine vision and ambition is needed here. It is time to choose which side we are on, because the multibillion-dollar 'sex industry' is doing fine and well; it does not need our support, it certainly does not need our protection. But around the world, exploited in prostitution, there are women, children and men who do, many of whom can see no end to their situation, so we must. We must make it happen; we must end one of the oldest human rights violations our world has known and relegate this blot on our humanity to history.

I do not expect everyone to agree, and even in the small sample of activists I met, the views differed greatly as their own voices show. On both sides, it seemed there was shared frustration with the way the debates are held, with some activists saying they just tried to avoid the issue because they could not handle aggressive critiques from either stance. I do think there are meeting places between the different sides though, particularly over demands to stop criminalising those in prostitution and for better safety and exit services. I hope this brief discussion of some of the arguments aids in the pursuit of that goal, and also reassures all those feminist activists out there who feel uncomfortable about the so-called sex-positive approach to prostitution, and all those readers who on a common sense and gut level know that prostitution is not something they would wish on anyone and is not an 'industry' they would like to see normalised or expanded. However, it is indeed difficult to build shared platforms across this feminist fault line when the destination is not agreed upon. As long as groups continue to promote the idea that a world with prostitution is preferable to one without it, it will be difficult for many feminists to get on board, especially radical feminists.

Another area of disagreement between activists and within the feminist scene generally is on trans inclusion. There was a perception, voiced by a minority of the activists, that as well as being unwelcoming to those in prostitution, RTN marches and feminist spaces more broadly are implicitly or explicitly closed to trans-identified people – by which they sometimes meant trans women, and other times meant transgender or non-gender normative identified people more broadly. This was another area, like that discussed above, where often there were shared views and common ground, but where many sidestepped the issue altogether whenever they could because the debates on this topic have become so fierce, especially online. Again, it is difficult to explain to readers not immersed in feminist activism just how controversial this topic has become. Feminist conferences are being picketed and boycotted when they are not open to trans women – meaning transexual women, and others are being attacked for perceived exclusion or lack of welcome. Some feminists refuse to include trans women in women-only space and some trans people disagree with women-only space at all. RTN marches are being counter-protested, with alternative marches following formally organised ones and regular calls for boycotts of certain RTN marches appear across feminist blogs, publications and commentary in mainstream media. There are insults and harsh words on both sides, with some activist organisers and feminist commentators receiving death threats and rape threats from queer and trans rights groups and individuals on the grounds of transphobia. It is hard to uncover what exactly lies behind such animosity, but it has become simplified as a battle between trans activists and radical feminists. This is yet another misleading reduction of the actual and more complex debates and disagreements which are unfolding. It also unfortunately serves to cordon off a surprising amount of shared ground as well as divert attention from shared enemies.

### *Boundary changes: The inclusion of trans women on Reclaim the Night*

Many RTN marches today are explicitly advertised as trans inclusive or as open gender. This means that it is made clear in the publicity and advertising materials that those who identify as trans men or trans women, as transexual or transgender, or those who reject any sex or gender label, are welcome on RTN, and in women-only spaces, all 'self-defined women' are usually invited. As I stated in Chapter 5, there is a difference between the terms 'transexual' and 'transgender'. In this book, I use the term 'transgender' to refer to those people who identify as non-binary and who cross the lines of socially constructed gender. I use the term 'transexual' to refer to those people who are legally and socially recognised as the opposite sex to that which they were labelled at birth. The term 'trans' has however become a shorthand to refer to both transgender and transexual people, and indeed anyone who considers their presentation and identity to be non-gender normative. In my mapping of RTN marches over the years from 2004 to 2012, I recorded that 20 marches made explicit statements about trans inclusion generally. The shift towards the breaking down of borders around the category of 'woman' and the expanding of boundaries around RTN was a shift that was seen as both positive and negative by the activists I met. Often, those who argued in favour of the inclusion of men on RTN were also the most passionate advocates for trans inclusion. In fact, the two issues were often conflated because those in favour of male involvement were usually against excluding any allies for RTN, regardless of their sex or gender identity. In all the discussions I had, I identified three key arguments which were raised in favour of explicit trans inclusion on RTN – usually referring to transexual women, but sometimes referring to any transgender or non-binary identified people, including people identifying as men, male or as trans men.

1. Trans women are disproportionately affected by violence and harassment, at least as much, if not more so, than women who were assigned female at birth. Given their experiences of street harassment and violence, the RTN march is highly relevant to trans women.
2. Trans women identify as women and have likely experienced discrimination on the grounds of their identity as women. As such, they should be welcome on RTN to protest against sexist discrimination and harassment.
3. Trans women are women; RTN should be inclusive to all women. To exclude this particular group of women would be bigoted and prejudiced.

None of the activists I spoke to stated explicitly that women who identify as trans women should be barred from RTN. However, there were a small minority of activists who raised concerns about trans inclusion. It was common for there to be tensions around this issue generally though, regardless of personal view or stance; and these tensions were most often raised by organisers who struggled to build a mass march and appeal to an audience of many different political standpoints.

Activists themselves sometimes used terms such as gender queer or non-binary to refer to their own sex or gender identities. Some also used such terms to refer to their politics. When discussing trans inclusion, some activists used the term 'cis' to describe their identity too. They used this term to refer to women assigned female at birth who still currently identify as women and as female. The term 'cis' was used to differentiate between trans women and non-trans women, by which I mean transexual women and women who are not transexual. The use of this clarifying precursor subjects the category of 'woman' to the same treatment as that of 'trans woman', requiring a defining term before any reference to the category of 'woman' at all. The use of the term 'cis' is also intended to highlight the supposed privilege of women who have been recognised as female since birth. Such women are not seen as generally having their sex or gender questioned in daily life or in official contexts. This is in stark contrast to trans women, who may experience such questioning regularly. For many queer-identified activists, the terms 'cis' and 'trans' carry the same meaning of hierarchy as the terms 'gay' and 'straight'. That is to say that cis is to trans as straight is to gay.

For some activists, the shift towards greater inclusion on RTN and in feminism generally was positive and overdue. Twenty-year-old Heidi, who identified as a queer feminist, was in a relationship with a trans woman when I met her and particularly welcomed changes in feminist spaces and organisations that made trans women feel welcome. She argued that this was not always the case, historically or currently.

> ... the thing I don't like about the Feminist Movement is that loads of them are horribly transphobic.
>
> (Heidi)

I met Heidi in a Student Union café as she was currently studying for an undergraduate degree. She was relatively new to feminism, describing herself as being involved for around two years. She was highly critical of London RTN and of many elements of radical feminism, as she perceived them. Similarly, another young activist, Babin, also described a despondency with what she saw as a hostility to trans women, through acts of omission, which meant that trans women were not explicitly welcomed on London RTN.

> I boycotted the London RTN in 2010 after it refused to put the words 'self-identifying women' on any flyers or promotional materials. I don't go where my friends feel unsafe, and my friends because of this action felt unsafe.
>
> (Babin)

Several other activists actually singled out the London RTN in particular when discussing the issue of trans inclusion. Although the organising committee of London RTN always answered individual or press enquiries on the subject confirming that all women were welcome, including trans women, this stance was not advertised on the London RTN flyers or website. In 2011, the London RTN organising committee decided to clarify the stance by adding an inclusivity statement on the website for RTN. This statement invites all women to join RTN, and lists different types of women, such as older women, girls, religious women and trans women.

Prior to the publicising of this statement in 2011, there had been regular calls for boycotts of London RTN, counter-protests and anarchist 'black blocs' against the march for example. There were also many articles and comments on the online UK feminist magazine *The F Word*, berating London RTN as transphobic. Perhaps due to this coverage, some activists I spoke to had actively chosen to become involved in explicitly queer, or queer feminist organisations, perceiving these to be more inclusive.

There's definitely like, a different character to the feminist group I'm involved in, which is quite queer and quite focussed around including trans people and stuff you know, who are more affected by stuff to do with getting attacked at night than cis women are. So I think it's really important to include them. And I think trans men should come as well, and people of non-standard gender presentation should be able to come as well.

(Heidi)

Clevedon agreed that trans women are disproportionately affected by violence. An anti-capitalist feminist in her early thirties, she argued that:

...transwomen are disproportionately impacted by violence against women, and transphobia should not be tolerated in the Feminist Movement.

(Clevedon)

Representing quite a common view, a young activist called Abigail was not sure whether trans people were necessarily more affected by street violence, but she felt that they were at least as affected by it as non-trans women generally. Therefore, she argued for trans inclusion, including trans men.

Violence against trans people, trans women especially, but also trans men and non-binary gendered trans/genderqueer people, is at least comparable to violence against cis women. To have a march that explicitly or implicitly excludes these people, or doesn't actively include them, is something I find troubling, especially as the structures in place which allow violence against cis women are often the same which allow violence against trans people.

(Abigail)

As already mentioned, no activist explicitly stated that trans women should be barred from RTN. On the question of mixed versus women-only RTN, many activists were more concerned that RTN marches remain women-only at all. When they addressed the issue of trans inclusion, they were in favour of publicly stating that women-only included trans women. Some organisers of RTN expressed sadness and frustration with debates over inclusion, not due to the issue itself, but due to the problems that conflicts over this issue caused for busy volunteer organisers. Catherine recounted her experiences of organising RTN in her city in the North of England.

I hate being called transphobic. I have no idea where this idea comes from and I don't care. I just want the derailment of this movement to end. RTN in my city is fully inclusive to trans women as women. Cis and trans men can fully engage in the support rally. Yet I get abuse from various groups saying that we are not this at all [meaning trans inclusive], go figure. It just feels like any derailment will do, facts regardless.

(Catherine)

Charlotte also felt that the issue of trans inclusion often ended up overshadowing RTN marches and threatened the existence of any march at all due to the hostility encountered by activist organisers who were usually already overstretched.

And all we get is shit, and every time we send out a press release to *The F Word*, we just get two lines back saying 'is it open to trans women'. You know, nothing saying: hello, well done, great to see you are organising this again. No, nothing like that, just this one-liner. I just don't understand it. It just angers me; it's always that I just think, what is you have against feminism?

(Charlotte)

Only four activists raised reservations about trans inclusion in women-only RTN: Sheila, Epstein, Shulamith and Cordelia. I met Shulamith in Bristol while she was visiting family there, on a trip from her home in Yorkshire in the North of England. Aged 47, she worked in the voluntary women's sector and had been involved in feminism for over 20 years. She was concerned that the issue of trans inclusion had impacted negatively on the possibility of women-only space at all. She was exasperated with political theories and standpoints that she felt viewed sex and gender as fluid and a matter for self-definition alone. She felt that such theories, and she named queer theory in particular, had impacted negatively on her politics and her campaigning, but she did not know how to tackle such arguments.

Similarly to Shulamith, Epstein also felt that theories and politics on transgender inclusion had impacted negatively on women-only space and on the visibility of women as a political group or class.

It's been co-opted by pro sex industry, trans and postmodernist views. Women have been taken out of the picture.

(Epstein)

Sixty-five-year-old radical feminist Sheila was the activist who brought in most political theory to her standpoint on trans inclusion. Sheila was against trans inclusion, but this came from a place of wishing to protect women-only feminist space for women assigned female at birth. She was very committed to women's empowerment and advancement, and she spent most of her time working in progressive socialist organisations, and was particularly active in older people's forums and in campaigns against cuts to benefits and rights for disabled people. Many people will feel that Sheila's stance against trans inclusion in women-only feminist space is transphobic, meaning a fear or hatred of trans people. I do not believe that Sheila, or many feminists who also take her stance, are motivated by a fear or hatred of trans people.

These four activists who had reservations or mixed views about trans inclusion all expressed a great deal of compassion for people who feel bodily distress and who cannot live comfortably in their skin. They extended that compassion to everyone affected and limited by the binary gender system though, not just trans people. This is partly why much radical feminist theory is against the system of gender at all and would ideally see it demolished. In defending women-only spaces for women assigned female at birth, Sheila referred to feminist political theory on separatism, from writers such as Marilyn Frye (1983). She worried that some trans women might be motivated to join women-only spaces because of what she saw as a legacy of male privilege and she worried about what effect that lived experience of male privilege, however temporary and however varied or marked by experiences of prejudice, might have on how trans women related to other women or used women-only space. Thinking back to our earlier explorations of the term 'essentialism', and of some of the critiques of feminism, it is necessary to clarify that the phrase 'male privilege' refers not to some aspect of biology, but to all the social, cultural, institutional and legal benefits that come from being labelled male in a sexist, patriarchal culture where men as a group dominate. These sorts of difficult discussions are important, because acknowledging our backgrounds, lived experience and varying levels of privilege can help us to find common ground and enrich our own perspective. This surely is the whole point of having an intersectional approach.

These four activists were the only participants who explicitly raised reservations over trans inclusion in women-only space and Cordelia expressed that she was actually unsure of her views either for or against such inclusion. It should be noted that several of these participants had taken part in RTN marches which were either mixed or women-led mixed marches and were in fact marches explicitly open to trans women. By far the most common view among the activists I spoke to was a pragmatic concern with protecting and maintaining some women-only presence at all on RTN marches, be that through a women-only lead or a women-only section. Within that women-only space, the majority of activists were clear that trans women were and should be welcome and included.

However, RTN is a very particular event. It is a public event; a one-off march that takes place in the streets of towns and cities. I cannot speculate whether activists would have felt differently about the inclusion of trans women in other women-only spaces or settings. Certainly, this issue continues to be a contentious one in feminism, with views hotly debated for and against. Recently, these arguments were aired publicly in disputes over two events, which usefully highlight the main causes of conflict and the differing views on different sides of this fault line within feminism. The first event was a women-only radical feminist conference in London in July 2012 and held again in 2013, which were both not open to trans women. Transexual women were explicitly not eligible to attend and the conference was advertised as only being open to women who were assigned female at birth. The second such event was a women-only workshop on girlhood sexual abuse, also not open to trans women, which was within a wider mixed conference that was open to all, held in Manchester in June 2012.

The issue of trans inclusion was also in the mainstream press and the blogosphere in January 2013, due to a perceived transphobic comment made by journalist Suzanne Moore (2013a). In an article critiquing capitalism, neo-liberalism and the current coalition government in Westminster made up of the Conservative and Liberal Democrat parties since the 2010 general election, Moore urged women to unite in solidarity against austerity. She linked this to struggles against sexism and critiqued sexual objectification of women in the media, culture and advertising. Asserting that women feel pressured to fulfil an unattainable standard of beauty, she casually remarked that this standard bears a similarity to the body of a 'Brazilian transexual'. In a swift and angry response, many readers alerted Moore to the high levels of transphobic murders in Brazil, suggesting that such a serious issue should not be used humorously and casually to make a broader point about body image. Moore emphasised that she had never intended to belittle the serious issue of transphobia or transphobic murders (2013b). Unfortunately, journalist Julie Burchill then wrote an article for *The Observer* newspaper, in defence of Moore, which used offensive and transphobic terms for trans women and only succeeded in enflaming the issue.

Coverage like this moved the debate temporarily out of the activist niches in feminism, out of the corners of the World Wide Web and into the mainstream gaze. Many of the activists I spoke to considered the issue of trans inclusion a new issue and an additional fault line that activists of the resurgent generation were having to wrestle with. This is not strictly the case though, as the issue of trans inclusion can be seen to have arisen in local women's groups and collectives from the 1970s onwards. So, despite the perceptions of younger activists, this is an ongoing issue and conflict, one that continues to unfold today; indeed, perhaps the division today is worse than it ever was. Readers who are not involved in feminist activism may know nothing about this conflict and indeed may wonder what all the fuss is about. Those readers who are involved in feminism and in activist organising such as RTN may also be wondering just where this cavernous fault line began to fracture and what lies behind it. So just where did this animosity between trans activists and radical feminists begin and what is at the root of the still often hostile relationship between some trans/queer groups and some feminist groups?

## *Bridges over turf: Charting divisions between feminist and trans politics*

It is only relatively recently that feminist theory in general has started to address the inclusion of trans people in the movement. As I have stated earlier, when I use the term 'trans' in this discussion, I mean self-identified transexual people. I use this term to refer to individuals who have sought out legal and medical recognition for the sex which they identify, where that is different to the sex they were legally assigned at birth. Transexual people gain legal recognition for their identity and can alter their birth certificates to reflect the sex they identify as. These rights were won relatively recently in the UK under the Gender Recognition Act in 2004 and the rights of trans people are protected in the single, combined Equality Act of 2010. From an academic perspective, but also from a feminist perspective, the former is a clumsily worded act, because of course it is actually referring to biological sex characteristics, rather than socially constructed gender. Unfortunately, this conflation of the terms 'sex' and 'gender' is all too common, as I have already discussed in Chapter 5. This conflation has led to the term 'transgender' being widely used as an umbrella category for transexual people, but also for all those people who identify as non-gender normative. This means anyone who considers their gender as different to what society would see as the norm for their sex, so it includes queer or non-gendered identities and those people who consider themselves cross-dressers or transvestites for example. This umbrella term therefore includes an awful lot of people. However, there is in fact an important difference between the terms 'transexual' and 'transgender', and this is why I argue that the two terms be treated as distinct and are not conflated under one umbrella.

I can see why it is easier to have one overarching term that includes any individual who views their identity as non-gender normative, but my concern is that the conflation of these terms conflates biological sex and gender and therefore naturalises and essentialises gender. The word 'trans' just means to cross, as in transnational or transport. So transexual means to cross the currently recognised lines of sex and transgender means to cross the socially constructed lines of gender. It is possible to cross the lines of gender without identifying as another sex to the one assigned at birth however. Any female person who is not appropriately feminine by all the current narrow definitions is crossing the lines of gender for example. Likewise, any male who is not appropriately masculine by present standards is crossing the lines of gender.

As mentioned above, despite the Gender Recognition Act having the word 'gender' in the title, it really applies only to transexual people, as do the extended sex discrimination laws on sex reassignment and gender recognition. These include making it illegal to discriminate against people in the workplace on the grounds of their trans status for example. The act in the UK recognises individuals who have what is, again misleadingly, called a 'Gender Recognition Certificate', which is a legal document provided by a 'Gender Recognition Panel' that confirms the person's identity and legal status as male or female. That status is then binding and they will live the rest of their lives and conduct all interactions with state and other institutions as the sex they have been recognised as, including for example in the criminal justice system, pension, welfare benefits and marriage rights. To put it plainly then, a trans woman who was assigned male at birth will be legally recognised as female and a trans man who was assigned female at birth will be legally recognised as male. There are many stages to go through before then though, and individuals are required to demonstrate that they live as the sex they identify as for at least two years. They must also provide medical evidence of their status, for example a clinical diagnosis of what is called gender dysphoria.

It is not a requirement that the applicant has had surgery to transition though, which may surprise some readers, as there is often a perverse focus in our media and culture on what is bluntly and colloquially called 'sex-change surgery'. Unfortunately, the bodies of trans individuals, being seen as gender different and as breaching the social norms of sex and gender, are often pathologised and viewed almost as public property for the public gaze. This ugly attitude continues in the way that trans people frequently recount being asked about their body by peers in social situations; a rude intrusion that would rarely be asked of someone who did not identify as trans. In reality, trans individuals will have different relationships with the medical institution – some may choose to have little intervention, while others may seek extensive surgical treatment. What used to be called 'sex-change surgery' is now more correctly referred to as sex-reassignment surgery. This terminology takes into account that many individuals do not feel that they are 'changing' their sex in a way, because they have long identified and felt an identification with that sex. They are therefore using surgery, hormones and other interventions to make their bodies more congruent with how they see themselves and to make their bodies more liveable places.

Foundational early texts, from radical feminists such as Janice Raymond, in her infamous 1979 publication *The Transsexual Empire*, are now decidedly out of date in many respects. Law, policy, psychology and medicine have changed dramatically in this area since the 1970s. Yet it is this book that can perhaps be seen as the most public beginning of the great divide between feminist and trans movements, or at least the most famous symbol of it. It has been described as 'a radical feminist attack on trans people' (Whittle, 2000:59), and shortly after its publication, a defiant and angry reply was written by Sandy Stone, called 'The Empire Strikes Back: A Posttranssexual Manifesto'. Lawyer, scholar and trans activist Dr Stephen Whittle describes Stone's manifesto as a publication which 'takes apart the feminist attack on trans people' (2000:59). Why was the book so controversial? Reading the literature around it, there appear to be two main criticisms. Raymond is accused firstly of suggesting that transsexualism is a purely modern phenomenon and a construct of the medical profession. Secondly, she is accused of arguing that trans women are not 'real' women and that trans men are not 'real' men. She does indeed say both of these things in her book. She also refuses to respect the self-definition of trans writers and activists, referring to trans women with male pronouns and trans men with female pronouns, a petty act with which I cannot agree and which I feel has no valid political purpose. It is wrong to make trans people shoulder the burden of the problematic binary gender system and wrong to pointedly refuse to recognise their sexed and gendered identity while recognising that of others in this universally imperfect institution.

To start with her first argument, Raymond does not seem to be attempting to silence the long, rich and diverse history of gender variance around the world, but she is more interested in the history of the medical institution and its role in policing gender norms. That is in fact the main focus of her book. There have of course been and are still many cases where the Western binary gender system is simply not in operation, or where it is breached by its own members. Much has been written about individuals who lived as the opposite sex in the past and some who practiced bodily modification to gender the appearance of their bodies in line with cultural norms. In Victorian England there were women who joined the armed forces or other careers that would have been barred to them had their sex been known; there were female husbands and music hall male impersonators. There are numerous examples from around the world where gender looks very different to how it does in the West. There are the Native American Indian Berdache people for example, known as two-spirits, who were able to choose the sex role they wished to live in, regardless of biology (Roscoe, 1994). Or the Albanian sworn virgins, women who took on a male role in a highly patriarchal society, living as a man in cases when an heir is missing or where a family is left without a male head of household (Young, 2001). There are all the wealthy women and men in history whose status gave them the freedom to dress as they wished, including in clothing reserved for the opposite sex, as well as to relatively openly pursue same-sex relationships (Summerscale, 2012; Whitbread, 2010). These and so many more could be seen as examples of transgenderism, and can be found around the world (Feinberg, 1996).

In her book, Raymond argues that contrary to transgender examples however, transsexualism as it is currently understood is a relatively recent phenomenon and a construct of the medical profession. She argues that while there may have long been a history of people wanting to have a physically sexed body other than the one they were born with, or making attempts to change it, that desire usually remained unfulfilled until medical science made it a relatively safe possibility and the law made it official. Such medical interventions have been developing since at least the 1930s though and, by the 1960s, the famous gender identity specialist and physician Harry Benjamin had published his influential guidelines on treating transsexual-identified individuals (1966). A criticism of Raymond's book has been that her focus on the medical developments attempts to paint the medical industry as the creator of the trans identity and condition, and not only that, but as some sort of evil henchman of patriarchy jumping at the chance to actually physically construct stereotypically gender-conforming men and women through the Gender Identity Clinics and sex-reassignment surgery. This suggestion is considered to remove agency from all the trans-identified individuals who make choices about the medical services they can access and who also increasingly play a role in shaping them, including through those who are in the professions of medicine and psychology themselves. Thus it is pointed out that many people actively seek out and control the services they receive from the medical industry, and that they actively want those interventions, rather than it being foisted upon them as if they are some sort of doll-like victims of an evil patriarchal creator. As the scholar Judith Butler said in interview in 2014, 'surgical intervention can be precisely what a trans person needs – it is also not always what a trans person needs. Either way, one should be free to determine the course of one's gendered life'.

However, when reading Raymond's book it is important to remember that she was describing Gender Identity Clinics and treatments of the 1970s, which have been vastly changed since, mainly due to the commendable campaigning work of trans activists themselves. Those very trans activists also saw first-hand a system that, in some ways, needed changing. Several trans activists themselves have fiercely critiqued the medical responses of the past. Roz Kaveney wrote in 1999 that many older trans people will likely remember how 'well intentioned doctors used to be even tougher than they are now when it comes to deciding what is appropriate behaviour in our gender of preference and making access to surgery and other aids to transition dependent on meeting their requirements' (1999:150). Zachary Nataf raised similar critiques in 1996, 'the gender clinics reinforce conventional, conservative, stereotypical gender behaviour and notions of an unambiguous, fixed and coherent gender identity, although the experience of most transgendered people is that identity actually evolves and changes' (1996:20). Also in 1996, Carol Riddell complained about, 'all the ghastly gender-amendment training which transexuals have to suffer' (1996:179). The recent UK Trans Mental Health Study 2012 found that some respondents reported gender policing by UK Gender Identity Clinics and barriers being put in place by clinicians with stereotypical views of 'appropriate' gender presentations. More recently, in a radio interview in 2014, the scholar Zowie Davy, who studies the rights and recognition of transsexual people, noted that if some trans people do pursue stereotypically gendered roles and appearance this may be because they still feel pressured to do so as a condition of receiving the medical interventions they seek.

Raymond is certainly not the only one then to have made critiques of the gender-normative responses of the medical industry, but it is significant that she was not making them from first-hand experience, whereas trans activists were. While it was not raised in anything approaching a sympathetic or respectful manner in Raymond's book, the issue is one which must be raised. All of us, not just trans people, should be concerned with how gender is being defined in our institutions, laws and also with how and when individual gendered behaviour and choices can be pathologised and turned into a medical disorder, mental disorder or disease to be treated with often invasive surgery and procedures.

As for Raymond's second argument, the suggestion that trans people are not 'real' women or men, it is not difficult to see why trans activists as well as others found this offensive and sought to criticise her book and with it radical feminism. Of course, reading Raymond now, from a post-Butler and queer perspective, we can also see theoretical problems with her argument. As I explained previously in Chapter 5, if we understand that all individuals are trying hard to be the gender they have been assigned, then there is really no such thing as 'real' women or 'real' men. Sometimes the sexed and gendered identity that feels right for us matches the one we were given at birth, and then we will experience different pressures and policing to those individuals for whom that is not the case. But within a rigid sex and gender binary, almost everyone will be subject to some sort of pressure and policing to live up to and in line with gender and sex stereotypes of what 'real' women and men look like. While females who identify as women and as feminine, and males who identify as men and as masculine may experience less gender policing because they are conforming to the required congruence of sex and gender within the current status quo, their gender displays are still a result of cultural training and they still have to work at being 'real'. So how does Raymond define real women and real men?

Despite many of the criticisms that have been made of her work, she does not actually make this definition on purely biological grounds. By that, I mean she does not simply say that real women are those people born female and that real men are those people born male. Perhaps not anticipating the decades-long storm that would surround her book, she provides a rather vague definition of who real women are, simply saying that we know when we are one. 'It is important for us to realise that these [questions over the definition of woman] may well be non-questions and that the only answer we can give to them is that we know who we are' (1980:114). But we can do better than this, reading further into her work, it is clear in fact that she defines women and men mainly on the grounds of lived experience. She says that what defines a woman is the life-long experience, from birth, of being categorised as female and treated as a woman by a patriarchal society. This definition is what enables Raymond to argue that trans women are not women in the same sense as non-trans women, because they will not have had this lived experience since birth, even though some trans people do gain recognition for their identity at quite young ages. Raymond argues that what makes a woman is the 'total history of what it means to be a woman or a man, in a society that treats women and men differently on the basis of biological sex' (1980:18).

So that is just a tiny and much-simplified snippet of the tortured history. More thorough discussions can be found in some of the texts from transexual and transgender activists and scholars themselves, such as Leslie Feinberg's *Transgender Warriors* (1997) or Susan Stryker's *Transgender History* (2008). But what of these debates now and why have these tensions lasted as long as they have? Today, most of the feminist debates about the definition of woman and the inclusion of trans women take place online, like much feminist theorising and arguing. There are still feminists today who take Raymond's line, often radical feminists, such as the feminist academic Sheila Jeffreys who recently published the first comprehensive feminist text on this area since Raymond's 1979 publication with her 2014 book *Gender Hurts*. Some feminists do argue that trans women are not 'real' women, and there are feminists who therefore claim that trans women 'invade' women-only feminist space due to a sense of entitlement, based on years of socialised male privilege afforded to them while they were identified as male.

While I do not use or condone such language and while I believe it is simplistic and essentialist to claim that trans people are not 'real' men or women, life histories and trajectories do matter, including one's sexed and gendered history and trajectory. To varying degrees and extents, trans women will have spent some of their early life inhabiting the male sex class. It is this fact that some radical feminists focus on and emphasise. It is important to understand the complexity of this though, and the individual life experiences behind those words – 'to varying degrees'. Many trans women recall a youth marked by experiences of homophobia and vicious gender policing for example. If they were brave enough to express their gender and/or sex identity early, that self-expression was often read by others as inadequacy or as sheer refusal to do gender correctly in line with current norms. Many trans people therefore do not consider or experience their life as one marked by privilege and power in any way. In fact, we should expect exactly the opposite to be the case given the severity of gender policing and the impossible ideals promoted in our culture for all sexed and gendered bodies. This does not mean that trans women have not experienced some degree and extent of male privilege, however tenuous that may be, and it should not mean that these differing life experiences of power be shut off for debate, reflection or analysis in feminist space.

Another reason that some feminists argue against trans inclusion in feminist space is on the grounds that women assigned female at birth may feel unsafe with trans women. This is not because they would perceive them as a threat necessarily and not because trans women would ever necessarily be a threat, but because the fact of their history as male-bodied may be traumatising or problematic for women who have been harmed by men with male bodies. I can understand that position and it is a logical concern in a world so scarred by male violence, a backdrop that we surely cannot ignore. I can also understand why for many trans women the very idea that they would be a threat to other women is hurtful and upsetting; but there is a context which goes beyond individuals and that context should be considered in these debates. That context is the fact of sex inequality and the epidemic levels of male violence against women. I myself have worked alongside trans women as feminist sisters and comrades, women who I have never felt threatened by, women of integrity who I have found supportive and understanding. Many of the activists I spoke to recounted similar experiences. Pointing out the context of male supremacy which gives women good reason to fear or mistrust people who have previously inhabited the male sex class, however temporarily, is not the same thing as pointing the finger at individual trans women within feminism and branding them personally as a problem or a threat of any kind. It is the fact of sex class in the first place that is the problem; it is the fact of male supremacy in the first place that is the problem.

A further argument raised by feminists who promote the right to spaces for women assigned female at birth is that increasingly fluid understandings of sex and gender mean that transgender-identified people may have little or no medical intervention and thus their bodies may retain the sexed characteristics they were born with, which others may read as one sex or another. This can create problems in women-only spaces, for example at women-only festivals or in women-only accommodation. Women may justifiably not expect to see bodies they read as male in such spaces, even if the individual in question self-defines as female. The difficulty is then how to respect people's self-identification as one sex or another or neither, while also respecting the right of women assigned female at birth to self-organise in their own spaces.

I am well aware that this concern may seem slightly contradictory to a broader and more idealistic desire for an end to gender policing altogether, and for the right of all individuals to define however they wish without that definition being linked to or dictated by their physical bodily characteristics such as their genitals. However, this worthy aspiration, an aspiration I obviously adhere to, is troubled by the context of male supremacy in which we live. It is not troubled by feminists or radical feminists. This aspiration and idealistic future vision is held back by the history and present of unequal relationships between men and women, not by feminists or radical feminists. We therefore have to navigate a path between that aspiration and the current status quo. Self-identification matters, but bodies matter too. They matter because sex equals rank, because bodies have become a battleground, and because women are so often denied any integrity over theirs, in sexuality, labour and reproduction for example. Where rape is a weapon of oppression and where sexual violence is a tool of control, the male body can never be neutral. This is partly why it is necessary, right and important that space for women assigned female at birth be protected and maintained. Ultimately, the right to self-organisation must be paramount. Just as trans women should have the right to organise politically together, so should women assigned female at birth. Both are members of oppressed groups under patriarchy and taking space separately is as important as working together to defeat that shared enemy. It should be noted also that these two styles of organisation are not mutually exclusive.

Outside of the blogosphere, it is relatively rare that debates on the divisions between trans and feminist movements get an airing at all. Feminists such as journalist Julie Bindel and academic Sheila Jeffreys are two of the few feminist voices to address the issue publically. They experience much hostility for doing so. As Jeffreys wrote in a recent newspaper article: 'Whatever the topic of my presentation, and whether in Australia, the UK or the US, transgender activists bombard the organising group and the venue with emails accusing me of transhate, transphobia, hate speech and seek to have me banned' (2012). They are criticised partly because both have questioned the pathologisation of children and young people in the diagnosis of gender dysphoria, they have critiqued the early prescription of hormones and also publicised cases of trans people who felt they had been misdiagnosed. Meanwhile, for those individuals who see a diagnosis of gender dysphoria and hormone treatment for themselves or their child as vital to enable them to even continue living, it is unsurprising why critiques of this medicalised response are sometimes difficult to hear.

Complex and subtle feminist theory about the social construction of gender, the policing of gender norms and the punishment of individuals who do not conform will be cold comfort to those seeking help here and now with physical and emotional distress. Studies such as the recent Trans Mental Health Study 2012 testify to the high levels of harassment, discrimination and abuse that trans-identified people face as well as to higher than average levels of suicide. The majority of those who took part in the study, 84 per cent, reported considering ending their lives and a shocking 48 per cent reported that they had attempted suicide at some point in their lifetime. Brutal statistics such as these only confirm the urgency of feminist attention to the institution of gender, rather than providing reason to shut down that attention. It is vital that feminists, trans-identified or otherwise, consider and critique the medicalisation of gender in the case of trans-identified individuals, and scrutinise the role of the state and the medical industry in gender policing. Incidentally, we should be able to do that without setting up a picket outside Gender Identity Clinics and blockading people from accessing support and treatment – which no feminists are doing as far as I know. We must also be able to critique the social construction of gender, and the naturalising of gender, without that debate being shut down in case it offends those individuals who experience their gender as biological, or as natural and as the way they were born. We must be able to critique the essentialising of sex and gender; we must be able to disagree with the notion of hard-wired femininity in newborn babies or womanliness in the brain for example, or neurological preferences for pink dresses. While I respect that some individuals do experience their gender as biological and do feel that their brains were hard-wired from birth to be female and feminine, or male and masculine, it is certainly not everyone's experience, whether they are trans or not. In addition, many trans people do not explain their gender identity as biological; many trans people actively subvert sex and gender norms and are far removed from some stereotype of gender-essentialist dupes.

As a radical feminist, I firmly believe that the binary gender system makes life hard for everyone, not just trans-identified people. Everyone arguably has gender dysphoria to some degree because nobody finds their gender easy and nobody does it perfectly because perfection is an ideal and, by definition, unattainable. I remain positive about radical feminism, despite all the criticisms and hostility against it, because I think that radical feminist theory has answers about how we can move beyond that gender binary. I would hope that beyond the binary, should we ever see such a world, all people would feel free to identify however they wished, and would not have to conform to rigid rules or alter their healthy bodies in invasive and sometimes dangerous medical procedures. In a world beyond the gender binary, it would also be inconceivable to cross the lines of gender because there would be no gender battle lines or territories to cross in the first place. A more tolerant world might allow people to be whatever gender they wish, including none, and be a place where gender presentation is not seen as necessarily having anything to do with the biological, sexed features of bodies, much less be dependent on them. Further into the future still, stretching our imagination and vision even further, we may try to consider a world without gender at all; a world without a system of sex rank. I would hope that such a future world would mean less distress and less body hatred for all of us, including trans-identified individuals. However, we are clearly not living in that kind of fluid world right now. Under the present status quo, it is not surprising that individuals are affected by gender dysphoria. It is only right then that all individuals can use and access what institutional remedies are in place currently to navigate such an experience. Rather than focussing on the individuals who seek such remedies, it is the gender system itself that should be our focus of action; it is that which should be problematised, questioned, critiqued and challenged.

This shared enemy is an example of commonality between some radical feminist theory and some trans theory and activism. Where this commonality ends, and

where the real root of the conflict lies, is in the reclamation of gender and the positive promotion of gender.
For many feminists, any attachment to gender only weds
us further to a system which violently oppresses women
and leads to the heartbreaking statistics on male violence
that we are aware of. Yet much in queer theory attempts
to reclaim gender positively. Judith Butler for example
recently argued in an interview that gender can be a site
of rebellion, self-determination, creativity or enjoyment.
'If gender is eradicated, so too is an important domain of
pleasure for many people' (Butler, 2014). She went on to
trouble any demand for a world beyond gender, which
is a common radical feminist demand. 'I think we have
to accept a wide variety of positions on gender. Some
want to be gender-free, but others want to be free really
to be a gender that is crucial to who they are' (ibid.).
I have a problem with gender being seen as a domain
of pleasure, when for half the population it signifies
dominion under patriarchy, where masculinity inscribes
superiority and femininity inscribes inferiority. Gender
is what turns individual human beings into subjects or
objects, into oppressor and oppressed; it is unlikely it
can be reclaimed. Therefore, I support the radical feminist argument that it is gender itself that is the problem
and assert that we must aim to move beyond gender in
the future.

Meanwhile though, out there, in the real world, none
of us live in a vacuum and most of us experience our
gender identity and our sexed identity as an intrinsic
part of who we are as an individual. Judgements about
our sexed identity are made by others about us based
on a very quick reading of our gender presentation.
These judgements are often made in a nanosecond, and
they involve a brief scan for visible, recognisable gender
stereotypes. Tick tock goes the brain of the viewer and

beep beep go the ticks against various gendered features as others read our gender. Short or long hair, trousers or skirt, make-up or not, these are the sort of signs people scan for in order to make a snap assessment about our sex and gender identity. These are often harsh judgements, and they are not always right. Sometimes we do not get correctly read by others as the sex or gender we identify. This can happen to anyone of course, but it is generally seen to affect trans people in particular. This is why the term 'cis' has come to have such resonance, because it is seen as a privilege to be able to go through life and not have one's sex and gender identity questioned or misread on a regular basis, be that in daily interactions such as shopping or when engaging with institutions such as banks, local authorities, health services or schools. However, the usage of this term, 'cis', has become another site of conflict between some trans activists and some feminist activists. There are many feminists, including many radical feminists, who simply refuse to use this term, and I am one of them.

It is quite normal at feminist conferences or meetings though to hear someone stand up and describe themselves as White, straight and cis, for example, meaning that they identify as White, as heterosexual and do not identify as transexual. The term is also in common usage on feminist blogs and online magazines. It has almost become taboo not to use it, with those of us who refuse the term often labelled as transphobic and urged to 'check our privilege'. As I mentioned earlier, when the term 'cis' is taken to have the same hierarchical relationship as the latter in the straight/gay dualism, refusing to use the term is likened to a White person refusing to accept their complicity and benefits in a White supremacist society, or a heterosexual person refusing to accept their privilege when compared to a gay or lesbian person in a heterosexist culture. I do not believe such analogies hold and so, despite such assertions, I personally still choose not to use this term for two main reasons. Firstly, the usage of the term unfairly and incorrectly implies that all non-trans identified individuals are some sort of Stepford Wives – gender-normative conformers who have no trouble with the current binary status quo. In actuality, as I have already discussed, most people struggle to fit into the narrow requirements of gender and this can cause great distress for many people, women and increasingly now, men too. As a result, women diet, self-harm, spend hard-earned money on plastic surgery and vast arrays of cosmetics. Men also diet, abuse steroids and develop injuries or disorders through overtraining, struggling to look like the models on the cover of men's health magazines.

Secondly, given that women face a gender pay gap, underrepresentation, epidemic levels of sexual violence and regular harassment alongside objectification in the media, being assigned female cannot be seen as some sort of privilege for non-trans women. While not being challenged about one's sex and gender identity in inter-actions is a privilege of sorts, compared to those who do face this, it is not a privilege by default enjoyed by all non-trans individuals. Because my gender presentation is more masculine than most women for example, I am often read as male. Added to this, I look a lot younger than I actually am, and as a result of my appearance, am often read as a young man or teenage boy. In most of my daily interactions, I am not read as a woman. I regu-larly get questioned in women's toilets, I have also been questioned in doctors surgeries and hospitals and run into problems when navigating such health institutions. I have been stopped at passport control because staff did not believe I was using the correct passport, I have problems using identification and bankcards with gender pronouns and I have experienced harassment and violent assault, both verbal and physical, because of my non-normative presentation.

These arguments are rarely considered by those queer and trans activists who casually label, reject and dismiss feminists who protest this widespread and often enforced adoption of the term 'cis'. To reject this term is a political standpoint; it is not transphobic. However, around the UK, activists are experiencing abuse and harassment, and are having their activist work discredited simply because they have political problems with using the term 'cis'. It is a difficult position to take for feminists around the country, including those who are organising RTN marches which they wish to make as inclusive as possible. This is yet another example of where theory moves beyond abstract debate and actually impacts on activism and activist organising. Although these topics may often seem removed, and may seem more suited to a gender studies syllabus, they are actually at play currently in activist's daily lives and indeed have impacted on my own activism. I have been involved in organising inclusive mixed events for example, where it was clearly stated that all self-defining women were welcome and all people of any sex or gender identity were welcome, including men. I have also organised women-only events, advertised as being open to all self-defining women. Yet after the mixed events, I have been questioned about why trans men were not made to feel more welcome for example, or why the space was so unrepresentative of people with no sex or gender identity. Just like too many of the RTN activists I interviewed, I also have felt a sense of frustration, a sense that nothing will do; a sense that any women-only space at all is by default seen as reactionary in some way, as out of date and out of time.

I refuse to call time on women-only space. I applaud the efforts of those volunteer activist organisers who pri-oritise the creation and maintenance of rare women-only spaces and events, often at great personal cost to them-selves and under great suspicion and hostility. While in general I support the opening up of women-only fem-inist space to all women, including trans women, I also believe in the political right of self-organisation for all oppressed groups. In summary, I believe that women assigned female at birth have a right to organise in pro-gressive political spaces should they see a need to do so and I would not dictate to activist groups who they should and should not invite to their own events. Like-wise, trans women have a right to self-organisation in their own groups and spaces. I consider women assigned female at birth to be a group, just as I consider trans women to be a group, and as both groups are oppressed, both should have the political right to self-organisation. The fact of differences between women does not invali-date the unity of the WLM. We are used to sharing our experiences and working with other women based on some shared elements of our identity. Lesbian women work together in the broader movement, Women of Colour work together in the broader movement, older women work together in the broader movement and younger women also work together.

We know that having diverse perspectives on all the different positions of women under and within the sys-tem of patriarchy can only enrich our understanding of how to take that system apart. Having different angles on patriarchy, including different positions of personal privilege, is what will help us find cracks in the sys-tem, those places where it needs to be fixed first, as well as where it might be vulnerable. Such perspectives will help us to identify urgent targets of action and effective appropriate methods of activism. Therefore, I do question the politics of those that seek to attack and dismantle vital, powerful and useful women-only feminist spaces like RTN marches, including when they use trans inclusion as a vehicle to do this. Hostility and prejudice can go both ways of course; harsh words are exchanged by people on both sides of this so-called division or dispute. I have witnessed hostility and stereotyping by feminists towards trans individuals, as well as outright prejudice and bigotry against trans people. I have also witnessed anti-feminism from trans and queer-identified individuals and groups, including rape and death threats and misogynistic insults. None of this aggression is acceptable, from either 'side'. It also seems a desperate shame and a distraction when queer theory and trans activism has borrowed so heavily from early feminist theory, a debt rarely acknowledged, and when feminism too shares a deadly enemy in the binary Western gender system. In the next chapter, I shall move on to look at some of the ways that together, we may all begin to change that system. I shall explore and explain some of the reasons why, despite all the conflicts, feminists continue to organise against male violence against women and continue to build spaces, like RTN marches, where feminist CR and movement building can occur.

# Chapter 9

# Motivations and destinations: What do feminists want?

Focussing on the controversies within feminism, like those outlined in the previous chapter, could suggest that such conflict is the main feature of this movement; but that is far from the case. In fact, even with such lively disputes going on, activists actually noted that RTN was a fairly easy banner to unite under, and that one of the good things about this protest was that it could bring together the Feminist Movement and feminist individuals. This in turn added to the feelings of solidarity which activists valued and which inspired them not only to attend the marches, but to stay involved in feminist activism all year round. In this chapter, I shall look at what motivated activists to attend and organise RTN marches and what they felt they got from such events.

Firstly, the activists noted that even with all the lively debates going on under the broad label of feminism, the RTN march could actually serve as an important shared space or common ground on which feminists of differing stances could work together as well as walk together.

> RTN is a pretty easy banner to unite under, everyone feels comfortable opposing rape. When an RTN is organised in your city, it acts as a platform for

collaborating, networking, awareness raising, relationship building.

(Carrie)

As well as serving as a common cause, Carrie points out that an RTN march is a good route into feminism itself. Some activists actually found volunteering and job opportunities through their local RTN marches for example, and through meeting organisations and individuals who were speaking or running stalls at the rally. Christabel for example volunteered to help set up a Rape Crisis service in her city through meeting other activists at monthly RTN planning meetings, and a year later was on the board of a new successful service which is still running today.

I reckon that I wouldn't be the person I am if it wasn't for RTN, and I wouldn't be doing the things I am. Because you get the solidarity, but you get aware of all the organisations as well, like Rape Crisis, and it's great, motivating and inspiring.

(Christabel)

Through these sorts of introductions, RTN operates as a sort of easy access point or recruitment site for feminism generally and for other feminist campaigns and groups. Activists pointed out that after all, it does not require much commitment or feminist knowledge to go along on a local march. An interested person could go on their own and would not need to worry if they did not know about the issues in great detail, as a march is very different from a meeting or group where they may be asked questions or expected to contribute. Here all they have to do is take part and march along. Bridie, an activist in her twenties who identified her feminism as Christian feminism, said that for her, this was one of the really nice things about RTN and a feature which made it accessible, welcoming and important in terms of bringing new people into the movement.

> It's a place for women to gather and meet that doesn't demand such a large commitment as joining a group. It's a good way to introduce women to the movement.
>
> (Bridie)

RTN then serves several purposes. It can recruit new women and men into feminism, it can act as a morale boost for those already involved and encourages their sustained involvement, it fosters a sense of solidarity within the movement and it acts as a living, walking, marching example of the continued existence of a large, eclectic and powerful Feminist Movement. The march then speaks to those both within and without the movement, bringing benefits for those on the march as well as those watching it go by. Indeed some of those watching may next year be on their own local march or even organising one.

> It can often be the first entry point into activism for young women coming to feminism for the first time.
>
> (Bette)

Clearly then, there is much common ground on the routes of RTN and activists with sometimes differing or conflicting views end up marching together under one banner. Indeed, in many cases, feminism has more in common than in conflict, and this emerged when I asked activists about what kind of feminist future they envisioned and where they saw the movement going. Many similar motivations for marching were put forward, as well as many similar feminist destinations identified; this was regardless of any or which particular school of feminism someone was signed up to. In addition, similar milestones or short-term goals were often identified and these served as possible indicators of success on the way to ultimate feminist revolution.

## *Where are we marching to?*

For many activists, the ultimate aim of RTN is of course to end all forms of male violence against women, and while none of the activists I spoke to expressed a concrete belief that this would happen any time soon, they felt that the march could contribute to this ideal in the future. In a way, the means of this protest are as important as the ends themselves, especially when the end, being the aim or goal, is correctly identified as being a long way off. The positive features or effects that activists noted about RTN are benefits that can empower individual women and empower the Feminist Movement as a whole through maintaining and building the collective feminist identity that is necessary if the movement is to continue. RTN walks the walk as well as talks the talk, it provides an opportunity for women's leadership, for women's skill sharing and education, it practically engages women in politics and political activism. While these outcomes in themselves do not end male violence against women, they are necessary ingredients if we are ever to do so. This is what I mean when I argue that the means are as important as the ends, as the anarchist theorist Bookchin has pointed out, 'there can be no separation of the revolutionary process from the revolutionary goal' (1974:45).

Maintaining RTN, keeping the march marching and being part of organising this event in your own town or city is therefore an important and significant contribution to feminism as a whole. There are also plenty of other campaigns to keep busy with during the rest of the year. All of the activists I spoke to were engaged with other feminist groups and events, including other protest marches such as Million Women Rise and also other movements for social justice. In an effort to come up with some sort of current snapshot of feminist concerns as well as practical pointers for feminist action, I asked all the activists what their priorities were and what they thought were the most important areas feminists should focus on now. Importantly, I was interested in their practical ideas for feminist revolution. Our sisters of the past formulated their own Seven Demands and this gave them some sort of road map; I wanted to know what our direction of travel is today and whether we too can come up with some sort of wo-manifesto of our own.

The grand aim of feminism, identified by all the activists I spoke to, no matter their political tendencies, was to demolish the current system of social governance, which they identified as patriarchal and capitalist. Ultimately, they wanted to replace this exploitative system with a more sustainable and egalitarian model which would create a fairer and more peaceful future not just for women but for our planet and all life. Fortunately, they were also realistic about interim or temporary goals which might actually be achievable in their lifetime and which could build a legacy for future feminists. It is important that we in the movement discuss and identify such goals. We need to come up with our own political theory and strategies so we know where we are headed. Too often feminist events or feminist publications of the current resurgence just outline and highlight how awful everything is, provide statistics on unequal pay, on the numbers lost to male violence, on the rollback of equal rights for example; but they do not then say what on earth we can do about it all. I asked RTN activists what they would do about it.

Their signs of progress or feminist success were all remarkably similar. They included for example the demise of the beauty industry; a decline of pornography and the sex industry; the achievement of equal pay; cheaper childcare; quicker and easier access to abortion for all; longer, equal and paid maternity and paternity or parental leave; equal representation of women in politics, business and culture; a drastic reduction in male violence against women; and a sea change in how these crimes are treated by the criminal justice system and reported on in the media. Perhaps unsurprisingly, these aspirations bear striking resemblance to the Seven Demands of the Second Wave.

How would we know then when we were nearer to finally winning these demands? Twenty-four-year-old feminist Lucy said that for her, it would be when the beauty industry was no longer so severe and when young women in particular did not feel so pressured to live up to very narrow standards.

> The cosmetic and beauty industry, I just really hate it. When you go on a night out now you can tell that women have spent hours getting ready. My friend said her little sister is only 16, and she spends two hours getting ready for school every morning. I just think it's so horrible that the value of women's worth is so tied up with how they look. I think when we no longer have that, then we'll know we've had a big breakthrough.
>
> (Lucy)

When I met Lucy in the North of England in the University where she worked and studied, she was not exactly
wearing dungarees (not that there is anything wrong
with dungarees and they are very practical attire we may
all want to consider as revolutionary dress), nor did she
seem to eschew cosmetics or jewellery for example. She
was not suggesting that people should no longer enjoy
fashion or have fun expressing themselves through their
clothing and appearance. I do not think that feminism
is fighting for that, for a world where we all wear the
same things and all look the same. The irony is of course
that this particular myth is one of the many that still surrounds feminism, yet meanwhile today we have a society
where young women do indeed already all look the same
and do already all wear the same things. In contrast
to this reality, feminism is actually striving for a world
where we are no longer prisoners of advertising, fast
fashion and the big global brands. We have to imagine
what increased options for expression we may have if we
were not held to ransom like we are, and what creativity and individuality that might make space for. At the
moment, it is very difficult for people to be different
in any way. Take as one example the fundraising phenomenon of the 'no make-up selfie' which took the social
media site Twitter by storm in early 2014 and raised
tens of thousands of pounds for a cancer research charity. While I support creative awareness raising and of
course applaud the generosity of those who donated to
this cause, if we look a little further into this craze, it perhaps has some less than pretty things to say about our
culture. Why is it that one of the bravest things a woman
can do in our society is to be seen without make-up? Why
are women's faces not seen as acceptable to the outside
world without make-up, while men's faces are seen as
generally fine just as they are? Why is that women feel

exposed, or worse, at risk of ridicule or attack if they express themselves through their body unadulterated and natural?

These are not trivial questions; they are of great importance. They are questions that every feminist should ask of themselves and each other, not to judge, but to explore the chains that bind us at every level including in our personal lives. Feminism has to be more than a meeting we attend on a Wednesday night; it has to be more than a single-issue campaign we supported once at school or college. We can take a lesson from the Second Wave in the mantra that the personal is political, or rather, should be. Too often today, it seems the reverse, people's politics are seen as private but also as completely removed from their personal lives, with both being seen as realms of 'choice' and 'agency' therefore out of bounds for question or critique. Politics are not for life it seems, and they are not about lifestyles any more. Rarely do politics actually seem to influence our lives in the way that used to be the case during the Second Wave – for better or worse. Few feminist activists now live in shared housing or communes with other feminists or other progressive political people for example. Few feminists would take seriously the idea from the Leeds Revolutionary Feminists that they should analyse their own heterosexuality and seriously consider removing their focus from men in order to commit fully to the feminist cause. Few feminists analyse their own lifestyles by talking with one another in CR groups for example. Few feminists see a link between feminism and environmentalism, feminism and anti-capitalism or feminism and animal rights. Few feminists make decisions to be vegan or vegetarian following ecofeminist analysis of 'othering' and the masculinist logic which places only monetary value on all life. Few feminists today would

consider getting arrested in NVDA or living full-time
at an anti-war or environmentalist protest. These points
were not agreed in the 1970s either, but importantly,
they were at least on the agenda and feminists were
aware of these questions. Of course, I am sure I am guilty
of romanticising that period, like many other younger
feminists. I am also sure that not everything about that
period was quite as it seems from my trips through the
archives and from the trips down memory lane which
Second Wave activists recounted to me. However, it does
appear that the feminists of that time seemed to believe,
even if it did not always work out in practice, that feminism was and should be about their whole life, how they
lived it, and how they lived up to it.

We do need to question our choices and actions today
too, especially when those choices all look remarkably
similar and especially when they have the effect of prop-
ping up current machinations of patriarchy. This was
articulated by Mary, a charity director working in the
South of England and an activist of many years.

> Far be it for me to talk about such old-fashioned ideas
> as false consciousness, but if you find that your voices
> are what the patriarchy would like you to say and do
> anyway, then surely that is up for debate. I'm not say-
> ing you shouldn't do it, I'm just saying, surely, it's up
> for challenge.
>
> (Mary)

Mary was careful to explain that she was not suggesting
that women who follow mainstream heterosexualised
hyper-feminised fashions for example are suffering from
false consciousness. Gone are the days like those in
1969 when feminists suggested such women were 'sheep'
in their famous demonstration outside the Miss World

Pageant in America. Today you will see feminists of all kinds on RTN marches and at conferences and other events. There are feminists who march in high heels, just as there are those who march in steel toe-capped boots. Politics of all kinds, not just feminism, is about looking into what 'choices' are available to us and just how much of a choice they really are. We also need to look at who or what benefits from those choices. That is not the same as saying that women cannot be feminists if they dress a certain way or do not dress a certain way. There is no feminist uniform; any woman can be a feminist.

How could we begin to interrogate these kinds of choices though, or begin to try something different? Rather than no make-up selfies, how about no make-up weeks, how about no make-up months? Think of the time and money that women could save. How about women supporting one another to try out not shaving their body hair for a while? After all, men's legs and armpits are considered normal when covered in hair, likewise their genitalia. Body hair is of course a sign of an adult human body, which has passed puberty; considering the statistics on child sexual abuse, it surely is a little bit creepy that hairless bodies are so sexualised, for women in particular, but increasingly for men too. Rejecting, reducing or temporarily giving up these types of individual actions would also have a wider effect as they would make the world easier for people who reject such beauty practices and often receive unwanted attention due to the rarity of that choice. Such personal political actions would also help to make the world a less judgemental and dangerous place for people with physical disabilities, people with scars or disfigurement or just all those of us, the majority of people, who do not look like a model in a magazine, whether male or female. Because being different is so hard in our culture, many people will not want to or will feel they cannot take part in such lifestyle changes to their appearance, but they can still be aware of what forces lie behind their choices to conform. Like Mary said in the quote above, such everyday personal choices and actions should still be up for debate because that is part of raising our consciousness about all the myriad of ways that women are treated differently to men and the ways that the hierarchy between women and men is imposed.

Linked to this, many of the activists I met, though not all, felt that the decline of mainstream pornography would be a sign of feminist success and a step on the way to a more feminist future. Even when activists agreed with this stance though, only a few said that they would welcome an actual ban on mainstream pornography. The difficulty of controls and bans in the world of the internet was well understood by all the activists who raised this issue. However, the idea that porn is so widespread that it will never go away was a passive approach not supported by those I spoke to. It was felt that as feminist awareness raised and as more women became engaged in feminist activism and theory, the numbers of young men regularly accessing or using porn may decrease naturally.

> I think it's always interesting when you talk to people about pornography and they say, well you can't get rid of it. But I think if we lived in a post-patriarchy I don't think we'd have porn, because there'd be no desire to treat women as lesser, or as objects, and there'd be no presumed male right to do that.
>
> (Kira)

It is important, with this issue and many others, that we remember not to give up on tackling things that seem so widespread and irreversible. Pornography depends on consumers desiring to see certain images of women and of sexuality and sexual acts. In turn, it influences what viewers or users think is sexy, sexual or desirable in the first place. The circularity of this relationship is debatable, by which I mean that it is unclear how much influence consumers actually have in this relationship; perhaps more power is invested in the multibillion-dollar porn industry than in consumer demand, and if that is the case, then that industry shapes consumers more than the reverse. Much mainstream porn is purely and simply about the sexual objectification of women. It is often about men subjecting women to violent or degrading sexual acts; it is about eroticising men's power and women's submission. Such representations are meant to boost men's sense of power and entitlement and extend that sense of power and entitlement over women's bodies and women's sexuality. Much of mainstream pornography is misogynistic, much of it contains narratives which bear similarity to rape; and there is of course a vast and undeniable market in so-called extreme or violent pornography, in so-called revenge-pornography and in the growing amateur market.

Of course, people will point out that such a summary does not represent all pornography, and of course, there are women and men who are trying to make pornography outside of the mainstream that I speak of. There is so-called queer, alternative, amateur or feminist porn for example. However, sometimes such apples seem not to fall so far away from the mainstream tree, and copying tired old stereotypes or misogynistic violent fantasies with the only differences being all-women actors or actors with a few more tattoos and piercings than usual does not a revolution make in my opinion. To those people genuinely trying to explore and express sexual pleasure in pornography which is non-sexist, non-racist and non-exploitative, I say good luck. This is no easy task in a culture so influenced by plastic fantastic mainstream images, imagery which is often about the gendered sexualisation of violence, dominance and aggression and too often simply about men bringing women down a peg or two and putting them in their place – that place being a malleable and responsive sex object. Even McDonalds can make a salad so to speak, but that does not redeem the fast food industry as a whole. Ultimately, I believe we should indeed be part of a feminist struggle against the mainstream pornography industry and we should try to take that industry apart however we can. We cannot sit back and accept that this industry is freedom of speech, or irony or liberating, cool or modern, when it is of course one of the oldest, most predictable oppressions of women, and one of the most base. The porn industry is a gendered industry; as a rule, men are not portrayed in pornography in the way that women are, and the great majority of porn is aimed at male consumers – we cannot overlook that fact. It is not sexy, modern, fun or cool to reduce women to sexual objects and sexualise dominance, aggression and harm to women's bodies, not least in a world where male violence is far from fantasy, but a brutal reality for far too many.

In pursuit of this grand, and admittedly idealistic aim, we could start small, we could start with the so-called soft porn that surrounds us, the everyday sexist images of women as sex objects, of women as prey to men's male gaze. We can complain about sexist advertising for example, whether on billboards, bus stops or in the media. There are ombudsmen or governing bodies which regulate advertising. In the UK, it is the Advertising Standards Agency. Individual television or radio channels also usually have options for feedback and complaints. Complaining to the company itself is important, especially as women represent such a large group of consumers. Telling companies you will not shop with them unless they raise their game can be very successful and consumer power has already made changes to clothing ranges and to children's toys for example. Students are already uniting in the fantastic No More Page 3 campaign to ban the British newspaper *The Sun* from campus shops for example. Businesses could do the same, as could charities, schools, colleges, local councils. Such institutions could make all their workplaces and public buildings places that are free of sexist imagery, free of the tired old sexism in newspapers like *The Sun* and in magazines like so-called lads' mags. Parents could pressure their local schools to take such a stand. Nurses and doctors could ask that their hospital adopt such rules. This action could also be taken against other everyday sexist imagery, such as sexist slogans on clothing. Schools for example should not be a place where female pupils are allowed to wear tops with statements such as 'future footballer's wife' or 'affordable'. Likewise, boys should not be allowed to wear tops with prints of naked women or supposedly funny lines like 'future porn star'. It may seem like a drop in the ocean to prohibit such styles in the classroom, but many drops eventually fill an ocean. Even if children and young people receive messages about equality and anti-sexism nowhere else, they should certainly receive them in school. We all talk about changing the world, but that has to begin with changing minds and that takes education. For too long our children have been un-educated the other way, they have been indoctrinated with gender stereotypes and clichéd sexism presented as humour or irony. It is time we started turning that tide and made schools the safe and equal places they are supposed to be, but usually are not.

Likewise, that means that sex and relationships education should be on the curriculum in our schools. Here in the UK, the coalition government rejected an opportunity to make this compulsory. They must be made to change their minds on that and this is an important feminist campaign. There already exist copious amounts of excellent resources for schools to teach pupils about resisting sexism and gender stereotyping. Long-standing feminist organisations such as Rape Crisis, White Ribbon Campaign and Women's Aid provide lesson plans, pupil resources and whole curriculums for children and young people of all ages. Parents, teachers and school governors could bring these resources into their schools, even while we wait for leadership at government level in the Department of Education. At the end of this book, you will find a useful list of websites, including for the organisations above, and you can download examples of lesson plans. You could even use these yourself if you are part of a youth group or if you volunteer at a local youth club for example.

For young people gaining qualifications and leaving school, the workplace remains another site of unequal opportunities. Equal pay is yet another demand from the 1970s that is still yet to be won, as is the equal representation of women in mainstream positions of power and influence.

I think in terms of indicators, you know, can we try equal pay for a start; can we try equal numbers of women in power for a start. Maybe sometimes even more than 50 per cent, that would be normal.

(Shulamith)

For a law to exist on statute for over 40 years and still not be enforced is of course quite disheartening. It is testimony to the tight hold of patriarchy, to the grip that this system has on men and also on women themselves. Regularly we are fed stories in the media about how women do not put themselves forward, do not 'lean in', do not ask for pay rises or promotions as if this is a biological fact of female nature. It is sexism which stops women from believing in themselves, because eventually, we begin to believe in the hype about us instead of believing in ourselves. We begin to believe that we really cannot do maths, that we are not as good at science, that we do not have spatial awareness, that we are not as physical as men, that we lack leadership, that we are not as good as men, that we do not deserve to be paid the same as men, that our work is not of value.

Women should not have to present a special case to get paid what men get paid for doing the same or similar jobs, nor should they have to be twice as good as the next man or work extra hard to get noticed. If average men can get on in their careers, gain promotions and pay rises, then average women should be able to get on too. I refuse to believe that all the men in powerful or senior jobs really are super humans; I suspect a fair amount of 'affirmative action', 'positive discrimination', sexism and sex discrimination got them where they are. Let me be clear, I am saying that the men who rule the world are not necessarily the most skilled, experienced or suited to those jobs. I am suggesting that they got their jobs in part because they are men, because they benefited from male privilege and male nepotism which looks after its own. For every one of those men, I am arguing that there is a woman who could do the job just as well, so long as structural and institutional sexist barriers were removed from her career path. This is all women are asking for after all, not an easy route, not unfair advantage, not patronising help, just the same opportunities that men enjoy.

If the balance was redressed then capable women could move on and up, a skills addition which would have revolutionary benefits. The time has come to actually make this happen rather than just talk about it though, and governments should immediately enforce all women quotas, positive discrimination in favour of women and transparent pay reviews in workplaces so everybody knows who is being paid what and for what responsibilities. We can all take action on these steps, for example by joining our trade unions and getting active, by pressuring our elected parliamentary representatives, by joining political parties and keeping this issue on the agenda. There are also many feminist campaigns on equal pay, such as that from the long-standing organisation Fawcett, in the UK. There are campaigns for equal political representation too, like the 50:50 Parliament group founded by Frances Scott and working for equal representation in Westminster. Sometimes people misunderstand campaigns or demands such as those in favour of positive action or affirmative action, women-only shortlists or women-only quotas, and too often people wrongly assume that this means just promoting any woman to a job whether she is suitably qualified or not. That is a ridiculous assumption and is not what any feminist campaign or demand is suggesting. If two people apply for a job and they are both equally qualified and the employer feels both would fit in well to the organisation, but one is a woman and the organisation is underrepresented in terms of women, then of course the employer should consider the merits to the organisation of recruiting the female candidate. That, in fact, is what fairness would look like; though it is often seen and denounced as precisely the opposite. To many people, such a situation is read as unfair to the male candidate, but what is forgotten is the centuries of sexism that have gone the other way. Notice that nobody complains so much about, or even notices positive action when it operates in favour of men. If people do not like the idea of positive action , then they should stop doing it and supporting it to privilege and advance men, then there would be no need to redress the balance for women in the first place.

Equal representation is not just an issue for big business, positions of power and politics either, though we certainly should have representative governments which look like the people they dare to govern. The activists I spoke to also wanted to see a change in cultural representation. Cordelia, a 63-year-old activist with over 30 years of experience in the WLM was tired of seeing a White, male monologue on the television.

> It will be a sign of feminist success when I turn on the telly and I don't see identical middle-aged White men in suits in every organisation that is portrayed; whether it's journalists or politicians, or academics or University Challenge.

> (Cordelia)

At the moment, perhaps the best way to change this situation is to try and get into the mainstream, including into mainstream positions of power. Join political parties, stand for election, and not just in the main parties, but the smaller ones that are trying to do things differently, and in the parliaments of the Celtic nations that are also trying to do things differently. They too need feminist input, vision and direction. Wherever your heart leans, let your voice follow; the important thing after all, is to be heard. Apply to become local councillors, put yourself forward to speak in the media, write to local papers, call in to local and national radio talk shows, become school governors, magistrates or sit on local health or education boards. This will not be easy. It is never easy to get on inside institutions that were built to keep women outside. The old institutions of power were established in times when women were never allowed or expected to be part of them, only subject to them. In her classic feminist text *Against Our Will* (1975), Susan Brownmiller takes her last chapter to give some advice on how we can further the feminist revolution. Her advice is well worth revisiting and reiterating. Just like the modern activists I spoke to, one of the key goals Brownmiller emphasises is equal representation in power. She states that the goal of 50 per cent representation is of utmost importance for women's rights. It is worth noting that she does not see any divide here between so-called insider or outsider feminism, nor does she demean insider state feminism, as some people call it. She does not set up a hierarchy between these standpoints nor afford the moral high ground to those on the 'outside' of the system, to those who refuse to work within the state and within mainstream positions of power, because we need both insider and outsider activists. All forms of resistance are good after all, and we need all the resistance we can get, from all sides. We need to be in the town halls writing policy, and outside them with placards too when refuges are threatened or children's centres closed down. We need to be in the Courts of Appeal, in dusty wigs and gowns if necessary, being legal representatives for women who have killed violent partners in self-defence, just as we need to be outside the courts too, waving banners emblazoned with those women's names and calling for justice for women.

While many of us would hope one day not to have armies, nor police, nor prisons or any of these trappings of the imperialist state, that is what we have now. We have to ask ourselves who we want to 'man' these institutions, these sites of power, until the revolution commeth. Do we want rows of faceless bureaucrats and yes-men? Or, as long as these systems exist, should we not be in them? Should political, feminist, socialist and justice minded people not be in these very institutions working with people in our society who have usually been failed all their lives by those very institutions, which they then ironically have to depend upon? Of course, these are imperfect systems, because we live in an imperfect world. But while those systems are there, we need to be in them: lawyers, police, judges, academics, social workers, journalists, politicians, policy makers, teachers, business leaders, prison governors. We need to be in those institutions. So do not lean in – get in; get in, play patriarchy at its own game, and win for women.

Another step on the way to feminist success is of course the number of women involved in feminist campaigns and also involved in politics generally. All the activists I spoke to emphasised the importance of growing feminist activism, and of increasing spaces where women can get politicised at all, and this was seen as an aim of feminism generally. To this end, raising the participation of women in other social justice movements was also seen as key. Too often of course, women are actually already in other social justice movements, though not so often in positions of leadership within them, for the same sexist reasons activists identified at the start of the Second Wave in the 1960s. Women have long made up the backbone of organisations working for peace, for animals, for the environment, against racism, against poverty; the movement they are not so often in is their own – the

WLM. Nevertheless, it is true that our movement will only march forward on the bridges we build between complimentary social justice movements and there is no competition there because being together makes us all stronger. Feminist activists gain useful skills in the Anti-War Movement or the Anti-Racist Movement for example, which they can then also use in any feminist campaigns they are involved in. Likewise, women who have felt supported and empowered to become leaders, organisers or media spokeswomen in feminist spaces, and especially in women-only spaces, can take that political experience into other campaigns they are part of and enrich all social justice movements.

The number of women proud to call themselves feminist also stands as a barometer of feminist success. Many of the activists I met were actually positive about progress towards this particular goal, and they felt that there was more feminist awareness generally than they had seen previously. Kristen, a 63-year-old retired nurse has been involved in feminism in the North of England for over 30 years. She described her feminism as radical and also as socialist. She was active politically in her city, against austerity cuts and threats to the National Health Service, which she was part of for many years. She saw many young, political, powerful women in the campaign groups she worked for and was pleased to find out that they usually did not shy away from feminism nor the label of feminist.

> A sign of success will be when women regularly show that feminism is an important thing to them; and I think that is the most hopeful sign really nowadays.
>
> (Kristen)

Despite our resurgence and growth however, our movement is still a niche movement. We have to accept that, even though it will not seem it to those activists for whom it is their life, for those Amazon activists who are immersed in the feminist scene. That is why it remains so important that we are vocal, visible and 'out' about our feminism and that we use the label proudly. This is a key awareness-raising tool and helps to build up and recruit to our movement. Feminism always was a niche movement after all, even during the Second Wave, which so many young women look back on now as if it was some sort of golden time. In reality, activists should take heart at the statistics I have presented here in this book, such as the fact that there are more RTN marches today than ever before and more people on them than ever before. Feminist commentary is in the media today in a way it never was just a few years ago; our movement has influenced not only laws and policies but the very language we use to discuss issues such as domestic abuse or female genital mutilation. Politicians, even right-wing politicians use our language, they use feminist theory developed in the 1970s and 1980s; though they are probably unaware they are doing so. What has actually happened here is that radical feminist theory on male violence in particular, which was so contested in the Second Wave when it was first developed, has become mainstream, has, in many ways, been proved right all along. The journey to the mainstream, the insider drift, has of course not gone without hitch or drawback however, and we should remain alert to the way our language of liberation is too often turned on its head by the patriarchal status quo and used to further entrench our repression. Likewise, the fact that our terminology and theory is being used does not mean it is understood or acted upon and so there I add a note of caution.

While we still face many challenges, some of which are complex and hard to untangle, and while our movement is certainly not perfect, it is undeniably a profoundly successful, grounded, reflexive and forward thinking social movement. It is one of the oldest and most powerful justice movements. Feminism, and the political identity of feminist, is nothing to be ashamed of, quite the contrary. All of us can take action in our daily lives and further the revolution by just calling ourselves feminist, by discussing feminism regularly and by acting like it is the most normal thing in the world that one would of course be a feminist. So be proud of your feminism and shout it loudly from the rooftops. When people ask you why you are a feminist, ask them why they are not. Ask them why they disagree so strongly with the right to wear whatever clothes we like, the right to own property, to have a bank account, to get into university, to drive, to vote, to stand for political office, to travel alone, to have maternity leave, to have a safe and legal abortion if needed, to prosecute rapists and abusers. Many people think that these sorts of rights were just given to us by the state, that refuges and abuse helplines just fell out of the sky or grew on trees. Everything that we take advantage of today, everything that we see as basic are in fact rights that were hard won, and they were won for us by the feminists who have gone before; they were never freely given and they remain under threat. This is especially true in a climate of so-called austerity, where ideological right-wing cutbacks target essential services for the most vulnerable. This is a legacy we have to protect, not be embarrassed about nor turn away from. Your movement needs you now more than ever.

Violence was of course another area where activists wanted to see and make change. As I mentioned earlier, they were not naïve enough to think that one march or protest in their city was going to stop all rape or stop all domestic abuse. In fact, activists were not even sure that male violence would be wholly eradicated in a feminist future; but they hoped that such crimes would be drastically reduced and the societal response to them altered.

> I'd like to say no rape, but you know, like with murder, it probably would still happen, but it would be seen as the serious crime that it is and it would be seen that the perpetrator was to blame.
>
> (Christabel)

A feminist goal then, on the way to revolution, is to aim to prevent and reduce male violence against women of course, and also change the way it is treated when it does happen. Feminists want an end to victim-blaming, an issue which arose with so many of the activists I met. It was this issue that motivated them to march every year and why they personally were so committed to the continuation of RTN. We may not be able to end male violence in one night, or tomorrow, or next year or even in our lifetime. What we can do is ensure that all those affected by it have quick and transparent access to quality, local, women-only services run by the specialist services grounded in the WLM. We can try to influence policing and laws, so that women are believed when they report male violence, so that jurors, magistrates and judges are aware of how these crimes, often perpetrated over many years, come to affect and change the victims. We can support feminist organisations already in place to help women affected by violence and abuse, such as Women's Aid, Rape Crisis, Justice for Women and Women in Prison.

We can also challenge the reporting of male violence in the media, critiquing the sort of coverage which perpetuates those ideas of spatial provocation which I mentioned earlier in this book. If you see victim-blaming headlines in local papers focussing on the clothing of a rape victim, or the time she was out or whether she had been drinking for example, you can complain about that and you can write a public letter for the next issue. We can all point out that the only people to blame for rape are rapists themselves. You can also educate yourself on local and national crime statistics so you can challenge anti-feminist myths which try to suggest that most rapes are false reports or which grossly exaggerate the numbers of false reports. Incidentally, here in the UK, these are estimated to be no higher than for false reports of any other crime, they stand at around 2 per cent; in fact, they are significantly lower than false reports of crimes against property for example or car crime. Another immediate action we can take is to make sure that as many women as possible know about all the services and campaigns in place for survivors of male violence. I remember attending a survivor's breakfast once, in very formal surroundings in the Houses of Parliament. It was organised to launch some policy or manifesto, one in a long line which I have now forgotten; however, at this event, a brave survivor spoke, a man who had lost his sister to the man she married, to a husband and father who became fatally controlling, violent and abusive. I remember this survivor saying that before he was forced so brutally into this matter, into the issues of police responses, the lack of cultural belief, woman-blaming media reporting and the cutbacks of women's services, he had no idea that a whole movement of women existed to protect women affected by male violence and end these crimes. That is something we certainly can change.

We can make sure, right now, that every woman knows what services exist, and also knows that a global movement exists to make sure she never needs them. You can memorise the telephone help line numbers of national services for example, such as those run in the UK by Women's Aid and Rape Crisis, or you could order or print off wallet-sized cards with this information and carry them with you at all times. When friends or colleagues raise concerns for themselves or others, you can then make sure they access the right support quickly, rather than being passed from service to service and having to tell their story so many times. This really could be the difference between someone living with abuse for months or years, between someone surviving or thriving, between life and death. Make sure the organisation you work for, whatever area you are in, has a policy on domestic abuse and on what support it offers to employees affected, such as time off to attend housing or legal appointments, such as emergency loans or pay advances to move into temporary accommodation. Likewise, organisations and institutions also need policies on how to respond to employees who are perpetrators, to men who may represent a danger to women in the workplace or women they come into contact with through their work.

All these sorts of practical steps which activists identified were in pursuit of that much grander ultimate aim of feminism of course – dismantling patriarchy and ending the male supremacy which has brought us to the brink of planetary crisis. For many feminists, our movement is always about more than women and it is about way more than equality for women in our unequal world. Feminism is about anti-capitalism, it is about anti-racism and anti-imperialism, it is anti-militarisation and anti-war, it is for non-human animals and for the environment.

> Feminism is everything that patriarchy destroys. It's not just about gender and sex. All the violence, greed, the wars, nuclear weapons, poverty – all of that is linked to patriarchy and to a patriarchal world view. Feminism is beyond that.
>
> (Bronwyn)

It often seemed that whatever the revolutionary question, feminism was the answer. As Catherine said,

> feminism makes everyone a winner.
>
> (Catherine)

To win then, to get us to where we want to be, some activists felt it was time for a return to the Seven Demands, time for some sort of badge or sign-up pledge for feminists so that our movement can have clear meaning and clear direction. Mary felt that, while we may want to add to them in light of our changed environment, the Seven Demands could still stand as a useful benchmark, a useful beginning or basic wo-manifesto for feminism.

> I'm kind of fascinated by whether we do actually need a card-carrying feminist, you know, back to the Seven Demands. So, this is what it means to be a feminist, and if you don't agree with these, you're not a fucking feminist.
>
> (Mary)

Of course, there are contentious issues in there, not least the right to abortion on demand. This is another area of conflict within the Women's Movement globally, although it is one I have not touched on here, but some people may feel uncomfortable having to sign up to that demand. However, this is a good example of the difference between personal values for oneself and political goals for society. A woman could personally reject abortion and never seek one for herself; but she should surely not dictate bodily integrity or reproductive rights to another woman who may not share her values or may be put in a position, by violence or poverty, where she cannot share them. The right to safe, non-stigmatised and legal abortions is of course still another demand yet to be won. Organisations like Abortion Rights in the UK are working hard to protect what rights we do have and ensure access for others around the world; their details can also be found in the resources section at the back of this book. For those longer standing or more aware activists who knew of the Seven Demands, all these demands were seen as important personal as well as political goals. They were goals they wanted for their own lives as well as for the lives of others and they saw their activism individually and collectively as a way to speed up the securing of these demands. Perhaps they are as good a place to start as any. Perhaps in your feminist group, collective or CR meeting you could have a think about it more, you could add to and enrich this famous statement. Perhaps we could reinstate the tradition of National WLM Conferences, where we could put forward and interrogate such new ideas for times that are in so many ways changed, yet which in other ways remain so depressingly the same.

# Chapter 10

# Conclusion: The rally and after-party

In this last brief chapter, I will consider and reflect on the changes in the form and function of RTN over the decades, and think about any key lessons which may emerge for the WLM as a whole. I have looked at practical, political and theoretical changes between RTN of the past and today, differences in method and similarities in purpose and motivation. At the start of this book, I charted the emergence of RTN in the UK and its background in the Second Wave. I have presented the voices of feminists involved in this protest today, showcasing what it means to them and why it matters. I have also looked into some of the conflicts which affected their activism, feminist fault lines which also enriched their work nonetheless and resulted in the production of new theory and new standpoints. The rise and popularity of RTN shows that such fault lines can be bridged and that progressive and pragmatic praxis can result in the process.

There were of course many similarities between marchers of the current resurgence and RTN marchers who got involved when the protest was first founded. One of the saddest similarities was in the motivation to march due to feelings of risk. Women of all ages recounted certain tactics they used when out at night in public space. Even if they said they would never be stopped from going out or living their lives, they did so in spite of their fears or perhaps to spite their fears. Despite some of the older activists suggesting that maybe younger women have gained more freedom today, young participants themselves exhorted the urgency of RTN often based on their own or friend's experiences of sexual violence and threat in their home towns and cities.

On a more positive note, another thing that has stayed the same is the sense of empowerment, jubilation and solidarity which activists recounted experiencing on RTN marches. This was as true of the marches today as of the past, despite the changes activists noted in terms of the decline of NVDA for example. These positive experiences of solidarity contribute to what we can call a feminist collective identity, a class or group consciousness of shared identity and shared situation. In turn, this jubilance spills out beyond the stewarded boundaries of the march, it affects bystanders, it affects those watching the protest in the media. It provides an inspiring and attractive image to spectators, it recruits new people to the march and to the movement and it shows that feminism is not dead.

The biggest change in the marches is of course the inclusion of men. I have covered arguments raised both for and against this change and I have clearly positioned myself in favour of women-only marches and indeed women-only spaces, organisation and leadership. I suggest that the success and power of the women-only RTN marches of the past not be overlooked. Many of the contemporary activists I met felt that autonomous, though not usually separatist, women-only organising was a radical, relevant and progressive feature of the WLM of the past and they were concerned at its decline in the modern movement. However, this decline did not appear to be widely or strongly challenged in any organised way. Dedicated activist organisers voiced to me that they personally mourned the lack of women-only space, yet remained convinced that the only pragmatic route to ensure the popularity of feminism was to continue to widen the borders around it. The hostility they encountered to women-only space was stark and fierce, further discouraging them from organising in this way.

It is time then that we stood up for women-only space and resisted the narratives of different waves and theories that suggest women-only organising is somehow out of date or backward. There is some suggestion that this resistance is already happening. Often I noted that RTN marches which started out mixed, gradually shifted to women-only marches, as is the case in Leeds, the birthplace of RTN. It seemed that as activists became more experienced and more aware of feminist theory and history, they began to suspect that the hostility to women-only organising belies the potential power in that tactic. It was from women-only organising in 1970s activism and in CR groups that the vision for RTN first began of course. It was women-only action which then grew and built the original RTN marches, and this feature usually inspired rather than alienated supporters. It appears that it still can, as so many of the feminists I spoke to valued and spoke wistfully and emotionally about women-only space. Often this remains an aspiration though, and one I acknowledge is difficult to achieve in the current hostile climate.

The changes and conflicts in RTN are a microcosm of the changes and conflicts occurring in the broader WLM as a whole, as feminist fault lines bend and shift. Debates that have raged in public and private over the last 30 years and more, around power relationships between women, the inclusivity of the movement, the meaning of feminism and who it can speak for. These debates have also marched through the course of RTN from 1977 to the present day. The rocky route of RTN is therefore the same path that the movement as a whole has taken, and is still walking. The question is what direction it may take next and this largely depends on what destination is planned. In this book, I have attempted to show the continued variety, but also some of the agreement over definitions of feminism and the goals of this movement. Sometimes of course, these goals are marked by divergence of vision on the ideal feminist world.

These forks in the route occurred at the feminist fault lines I have covered. For example, some activists saw the ideal feminist future as one where prostitution and pornography may still exist in some way, but not in a capitalist form and where human beings of all sexes, genders, identities and physical appearance would be represented and share sexual exploration and enjoyment. For others, especially those defining themselves as radical feminists, institutions like pornography and prostitution were seen as simply incompatible with a feminist world. I spent many hours with the activists I interviewed, as they wrangled and wrestled with their thoughts around these, as yet theoretical, questions about a post-revolution feminist landscape. This was the case with activists regardless of their stated political identity, that is, regardless of whether they defined as socialist feminists or revolutionary feminists for example. Perhaps this was because one thread which united all of them was a socialist or broadly left-wing allegiance which made all of them suspicious of institutions and big business of any kind. What is clearly needed urgently here are spaces where these complex theoretical discussions can be had, and there was a hunger for that amongst the activists I met. Our sisters of the past wrote groundbreaking theory on these topics, but where is our grand theory of the day? Where can it emerge from and in what spaces can it be birthed, tended and sustained? This is the urgent challenge for the new resurgence of the movement and it depends on creating women's spaces and women's self-organisation, so that once again our theory can come from our own lived experiences, from the ground up.

Returning to the classic texts on these and other issues is also important, and this was another area where activists were hungry for knowledge and history. Wheels do not always have to be reinvented, though time and again that is what my digital recorder picked up, the sound of activists working through familiar tortured debates relayed alongside a distinct historical amnesia about how such questions may have been answered in the past. I am not saying that all the answers are there in the past, in your local friendly feminist archive, but I am saying that some of the answers may be there; certainly ideas to get us started so we can go forwards rather than backwards. So I would urge everyone new to feminism to go back to the classics, like those I have only briefly introduced in this book. Read the famous works, like Kate Millett, Susan Brownmiller, bell hooks, Andrea Dworkin and Audre Lorde. Get into feminist archives where you can, and actually return to the source, look through old copies of feminist magazines and journals and see for yourself if all the stories and myths are true. There are feminist archives in Leeds and Bristol and a feminist library in London. The Women's Library at the London School of Economics is also beginning to digitise many of its resources and some already are, for example, many issues of the radical feminist journal *Trouble and Strife* are now available online.

In conclusion, the activists of today are all attempting to navigate a new environment where some stubborn features remain all too similar – such as the fear of male violence as a motivator into feminist activism. Yet they do this within a context transformed by new methods of communication and new sites of exploitation in the internet; a context also transformed by the rise of queer and trans liberation movements, by the professionalisation of the women's sector, the pervasiveness of neoliberalism and by increasing state limitation on direct political action, particularly NVDA. The environment has also been transformed of course by the feminism that went before and by the rich legacy left by the Second Wave. Many of the younger women I meet acknowledge and speak emotionally of this debt. Activists today aim to learn from the mistakes of the past, while being all too aware of often overwhelming and deadening criticisms of the WLM; but they are also committed to learning from the successes, of which there were many. Today's activists have revived a global, powerful and symbolic tradition with RTN, which has resonated with a new generation of feminists and created marches larger than those of the past. In so doing, they march in the footsteps of the brave women who went before, mapping new routes in the process and I cannot wait to see what they do with the next 30 years of feminism.

# How to organise a Reclaim the Night march

First of all, it's good to point out what Reclaim the Night (RTN) is. It's traditionally a women's march to reclaim the streets after dark, a show of resistance and strength against sexual harassment and assault. It is to make the point that women do not have the right to use public space alone, or with female friends, especially at night, without being seen as 'fair game' for harassment and the threat or reality of sexual violence. We should not need chaperones (though that whole Mr Darcy scene is arguably a bit cool, as is Victorian clothing, but not the values). We should not need to have a man with us at all times to protect us from other men. This is also the reason why the marches are traditionally women-only; having men there dilutes our visible point. Our message has much more symbolism if we are women together. How many marches do you see through your town centre that are made up of just women? Exactly. So do think before ruling out your biggest unique selling point.

Anyway, the RTN marches first started in several cities in Britain in November 1977, when the Women's Liberation Movement (WLM) was last at its height, a period called the Second Wave. The idea for the marches was copied from co-ordinated midnight marches across West German cities earlier that same year in April 1977. The marches came to stand for women's protest against all forms of male violence against women, but particularly sexual violence. Today we march for the same reasons, except if anything, the situation is worse now than it was then. Then women were appalled that only 1 in 3 rapists were ever convicted; today that figure is around 1 in 20. It's important that as many women as possible take to the streets to say that this is not acceptable and to demand justice. We women make up the backbone of every social movement going, for peace, for the environment, for children's and animal rights, against war and racism; yet we don't specifically take up our own rights nearly often enough. And we have every right to. And we need to; now more than ever.

So, what ingredients do you need to start your own RTN march? First of all you take some fine chocolate, milk or dark will do, fair trade is best, vegan is better. And you eat that. Then you set to trying to find some political, savvy women with time on their hands. You need to find at least five or six of these women. This is the hard part. They can sometimes be stolen from other groups, though this won't enamour you to your local Stop the War or trade union branch, but hey, desperate times call for desperate measures. If you are a student, you may find the recruitment easier, though you will have to have at least 237 arguments about if, why, on what grounds and whether your march should be women-only or not, and what about men and whojamaflip's boyfriend, who is really, really lovely etc. Actually, you will probably have to have these arguments even if you are not a student. In fact, to be honest, if you are a woman working politically with other women on women's rights, you will need to have these arguments; that's why I said you would need to find women with time on their hands. Because we have to factor in justifying our own movement, as well as organising our own movement, it's a very good thing that we are all so talented and energetic. This is all before the organising even starts. Give up your day job.

Once you have found some women who you agree with on at least a most basic level, you need to set a date for your march. As soon as you have set a date, start immediately telling everyone and anyone, even without any other details; just get the date out in the ether, in real and cyber space. Usually the marches are around the 25th of November, to add an international flavour and mark the United Nations International Day for the Elimination of All Forms of Violence Against Women. Which, by the way, doesn't exactly roll of the tongue, so you may not want to put that in full on your flyers. But, be warned, it is cold in November, so you may want to hold your march in midsummer, or even relocate your protest to the South of France. Once you have set your date, and double-checked that it doesn't clash with the national RTN in England's capital (London), you need to plan a route.

It is good if the route can take in some public toilets. And, on a more serious note, it needs to end somewhere that women can get home safely from, as that's the whole point of the march after all – women's safety. So don't end it somewhere out in the sticks where there is no public transport, otherwise you will have to fork out for mini-buses etc. If you live in the sticks this will be a problem. Fundraise for mini-buses. As women don't get many chances to have the streets of their town or city closed down for their issues to be heard, you may as well pick a really central route. Aim high, go right for your town centre. Then you need to go and meet your friendly local police force (or agents of the state, depending on your political proclivities) who are there to facilitate your right to peaceful protest. Because we live in a democracy, remember? It is good to send the least anarchisty members of your group to meet the police, and don't call them 'filth' or 'pigs', at least not to their faces. The police that is. Give the police plenty of warning about your intentions; they will need to plan road closures and they may change your route slightly. Be flexible, but don't be pushed into side roads. It's polite to go to the police to ask for something called 'permission' to hold your protest, but really you just go and tell them what you are going to do. I'd let them know at least six months in advance. Yes, I can hear you saying: 'but that's nearly as long as it takes to grow a baby human' and you are right of course, but organising a RTN march is just about as difficult (can you tell I've never given birth?). In fact, here in London for the national march, we work on it all year (marching that is, not giving birth).

Now you have a route and police permission, you need to get publicity done and start snooping about for formal supporters. Unless you own your own printing press, publicity will require money. Usually you can get 1000 flyers done for between £50 and £70, and if you put the word out, you will usually find someone who knows a good printing firm. There are also good online ones that usually do next-day delivery. We all dream about finding the women's collective printing firm, so we can feel worthy about getting our fly-ers done there, but it ain't the 1970s any more sister, so don't worry if you can't find such a thing. Ask local activist groups who they use. Get flyers done as soon as possible, however you can. But – remember that it's good to have your supporters listed on the flyer, the bigger the organisations the better. So, you have a balancing act here – between getting your flyer done ASAP, and waiting to hear about formal support from large local organisa-tions. This is especially tricky if your group is not known to the mainstream political scene in your area. Big organisations like trade unions are going to be wary of taking a risk on you if they don't know you from Eve. This is because you are a liability until they know you. If they formally support your march and then you walk through your town centre smashing the windows of McShite 'restaurants' and supergluing the locks of porn shops (though you and I may well consider this good, clean family fun), they could get into trou-ble, and would be likely never to support you again. So, approach smaller groups first, build up a base and then go to bigger groups with this proof that people trust you enough to put their name under your event. Offer to speak at meetings to show them that feminists are normal people, or at least, can be when they want support from large organisations. Don't forget that it's actu-ally quite a big deal for a group to support you, so pat yourself on the back every time you get a new supporter, and don't be disheartened if you don't get big groups coming on board right at the beginning. These things take time.

Back to the flyers. I know it sounds obvious, but make sure you have the date, time and assembly location on your flyer. And a catchy piece of artwork too if you can get one. It's also worth bearing in mind that if your march is suc-cessful and you have more of them in the future, this artwork could become fixed in people's minds and become your 'brand'. So it's worth taking time to think of a good design. You may have some arty types in your group who could design something. We are all about the empowerment of women after all, and the means, in the WLM, are just as important as the ends (seeing as 'the ends' is like, full on revolution, and, similar to a base of good supporters, is going to take a bit of time).

Now the important bit is out of the way, you can focus on whether you are going to have an event after your march. 'What? Two events?' I hear you cry. Yes. If you have a rally after your march then you basically do have to organise two events. I know; it sucks. You don't have to though, and it will depend on how much money you can fundraise. But, as women will have come out in the cold and done some marching, it is nice to round off the evening with a few drinks and a splash of political speeches. So, you will need to find a venue for that. This venue will need to be either conveniently located at the end of your march route or you will have to plot your march route around an available and affordable venue. Sometimes people are tempted to hold a rally in a religious venue. Christianity for example is quite a successful organised religion and tends to own large venues called 'halls', which are not student residences but big spaces, usually in very central locations in almost all of our towns and cities, would you believe it. They are very seductive, but don't be tempted. You need to find a neutral venue which isn't going to offend potential marchers. And you also need to find somewhere which has disabled access, and it would be good if you could have food and drink there. Alcoholic beverages are good, generally, but the presence of a bar will potentially exclude strict Muslim or Methodist marchers, so you do have to think about that. Get used to the fact that organising any political event is a minefield – you are going to make mistakes, you will offend people and that is just the way it is. As long as you are generally pleasing more people than you are offending, it's a good idea just to carry on regardless (and write down your mistakes so you can learn from them next time). It's always better to do something rather than nothing after all.

Now to finding speakers for your rally. Try to get high-profile ones that represent large organisations if you can, like your local Women's Aid, your local Rape Crisis or a trade union. Remember that having a trade union speaker does not make you a corporate sell out; some people think they are overly bureaucratic and detached from 'ordinary people'. I know you were probably worrying about that. Trade unions represent millions of people however, and hundreds of thousands of women. So, having a speaker from one gives you the weight of all those people behind your event and also means you can get publicity to a very broad and diverse audience – the members of that union, who by the way are the 'ordinary' people you will bound to be asked whether your march reaches.

Once you have plans settled for your rally and entertainment, do another print run of flyers with that info highlighted. This is an attempt at attracting people to your march and is worth a try. You may also want to consider posters, and then flyposting them, only on buildings that you own of course. Note that I'm in no way suggesting anyone engage in criminal activities, remember, feminism says – always stay at home and do nothing.

You should definitely make some banners and encourage other people to do the same. It's great to look out across a march and see the breadth of support from all the different groups; it also looks good in the press, if you get any there. Which reminds me – do a press release! Send it to ALL your local press, including free papers for listings. Do this as soon as you set the date, assembly location and route. Throw in some sound bites, editor's notes and depressing stats about sexual violence in your area – unfortunately, these won't be difficult to find. The Fawcett Society or Rape Crisis websites have a good section on all UK police force conviction rates for rape in different areas for example, and this is useful to put in publicity. Keep everything as local as possible, as it's local press you are trying to attract. Get quotes from people, like the director of your local Rape Crisis or Women's Aid refuge. Think of someone in your group to be a press contact and put their full details on the release; identify who is happy to do press interviews. Get yourselves media trained up if you can. You may find a local activist resource centre or women's group that can offer this. Remember what I said about the means? This is another example. Organising a march is also about women learning new skills and gaining valuable experience for all areas of life. So share out jobs and try new things, like going on live television, it's great, though you do sometimes have to wear make-up.

And that's about it really. Sounds easy doesn't it? Well, women's groups have been doing just this all over the country, from Aberdeen to Devon. So, there are plenty of other people you can ask and learn from too. How about twinning with a nearby town that has already held a march? You could double your numbers as well as picking up tips and contacts. Basically, it is a lot of work organising an RTN, but it is worth it. I don't want to sound dramatic and worthy but let's get to the point: women are dying. Every day. The levels of male violence against women in this country and around the world are an outrage. Our conviction rate for rape and sexual violence is a national disgrace. Why are we not giving up our town halls and school gyms to women fleeing violence? Why are we not marching in the streets every single day to demand an end to the war being waged on our sex? Why is a woman raped or killed no longer news in our society? You can change this situation. Get together and make something happen because you can't rely on anyone else doing it. If not you, who? If not now, when? And all that jazz, etc. Anything is better than nothing.

Also, finally, remember: if you put your head above the parapet, you will get flack and you will work like a person that works very hard for very little reward, kind of like a woman. But even all this hard and thankless work can never be as bad as the atrocities that too many of our sisters resist and survive on a daily basis. If you have the time and freedom to do more than survive, then you should use it.

# *Get active! Useful websites*

Abortion Rights UK http://www.abortionrights.org.uk/

Aldermaston Women's Peace Camp http://www.aldermaston.net/

APMP www.antipornmen.org (discussion and campaigns by men against porn)

Black Cultural Archives http://www.bcaheritage.org.uk/ (includes an archive on the Black Women's Movement)

British Union for the Abolition of Vivisection http://www.buav.org/

Broken Rainbow http://www.brokenrainbow.org.uk/ (support for LGBT people affected by domestic abuse)

Campaign for Nuclear Disarmament http://www.cnduk.org/

CATW www.catwinternational.org (Coalition Against Trafficking in Women)

CGVR http://www.bristol.ac.uk/sps/research/centres/genderviolence/ (Centre for Gender & Violence Research, University of Bristol)

CSC http://www.cuba-solidarity.org.uk/ (Cuba Solidarity Campaign, UK)

CWASU http://www.cwasu.org/ (Child & Woman Abuse Studies Unit, London Metropolitan University)

Daughters of Eve http://www.dofeve.org/ (campaigns & raises awareness to protect girls at risk of FGM)

Disability Rights UK http://disabilityrightsuk.org/

Emma Humphreys Memorial Prize http://emmahumphreys.org/

End Demand UK www.enddemand.uk (campaign for Nordic policy on prostitution)

EVAW http://www.endviolenceagainstwomen.org.uk/ (End Violence Against Women Coalition)

False Economy http://falseeconomy.org.uk/ (fighting against cuts)

Fawcett Society www.fawcettsociety.org.uk

Feminism in London http://www.feminisminlondon.co.uk/

Feminist Archive http://www.feministarchivenorth.org.uk/ (Leeds and Bristol)

Feminist Library London http://feministlibrary.co.uk/

Freedom Project UK http://www.moretodogstrust.org.uk/freedom-project/freedom-project (temporary foster care for dogs & cats when owners flee domestic abuse)

FWSA http://fwsablog.org.uk/ (Feminist & Women's Studies Association)

IKWRO http://ikwro.org.uk/ (campaigns on so-called honour crimes & forced marriage)

Justice for Women http://www.justiceforwomen.org.uk/

Karma Nirvana http://www.karmanirvana.org.uk/ (campaign/support for those affected by forced marriage/'honour' crimes)

KONP http://www.keepournhspublic.com/index.php (stopping privatisation of the National Health Service in the UK)

London Reclaim the Night www.reclaimthenight.org

MALE www.mensadviceline.org.uk (support for men affected by domestic abuse)

Men Can Stop Rape www.mencanstoprape.org

Million Women Rise http://www.millionwomenrise.com/ (annual march against VAWG on IWD London)

NAAR http://www.naar.org.uk/ (National Assembly Against Racism, UK)

No More Page 3 http://nomorepage3.org/

NSPCC UK http://www.nspcc.org.uk/ (National Society for the Prevention of Cruelty to Children)

Object www.object.org.uk (campaign against sex object culture)

OFN London http://www.olderfeminist.org.uk/ (Older Feminist Network)

OLN London http://www.olderlesbiannetwork.btck.co.uk/ (Older Lesbian Network)

One25 http://www.one25.org.uk/ (working with women in prostitution)

Prostitution Education & Research www.prostitutionresearch.com

PSC http://www.palestinecampaign.org/ (Palestine Solidarity Campaign)

Rape Crisis UK www.rapecrisis.org.uk

Respect www.respect.uk.net (advice and services for male perpetrators of domestic abuse)

Southall Black Sisters http://www.southallblacksisters.org.uk/ (campaigns against VAWG in BME communities)

Stonewall http://www.stonewall.org.uk/ (campaign for lesbian, gay & bisexual equality)

Survivors UK www.survivorsuk.org (support for male victims of rape and sexual abuse)

SWAN http://www.socialworkfuture.org/ (Social Worker Action Network)

UK Feminista www.ukfeminista.org

Vegan Society UK http://www.vegansociety.com/

Vegetarian Society UK https://www.vegsoc.org/

WAMT www.wamt.org (Women and Manual Trades)

WEA http://www.wea.org.uk/ (Worker's Educational Association)

White Ribbon UK www.whiteribboncampaign.co.uk (men against violence against women)

WILPF http://www.wilpfinternational.org/

WISH http://www.womenatwish.org.uk/ (voice for women's mental health)

Women's Aid UK www.womensaid.org.uk

Women in Prison http://www.womeninprison.org.uk/

50/50 Campaign UK http://www.5050parliament.co.uk/ (campaigning for equal representation of women)

# Bibliography

Allen Katie (2010) 'Equal Pay for Women Not Likely Till 2067, Says Research', *The Guardian*, 19th August, http://www.theguardian.com/uk/2010/aug/19/equal-pay-women-2057 (Accessed 7th September 2010).

Amina Mama (1989) *The Hidden Struggle: Statutory and Voluntary Sector Responses to Violence Against Black Women in the Home*. London: London Race and Housing Research Unit.

Annan Kofi (1999) 'Remarks of Secretary-General Kofi Annan to the Interagency Videoconference for a World Free of Violence Against Women', *United Nations: Press Release*, http://www.un.org/News/Press/docs/1999/19990308.sgsm6919.html (Accessed 19th August 2012).

Appignanesi Lisa, Holmes Rachel & Orbach Susie (eds.) (2013) *Fifty Shades of Feminism*. London: Virago.

Aronson Pamela (2003) 'Feminists or "Postfeminists"? Young Women's Attitudes Toward Feminism and Gender Relations', *Gender & Society*, 17(6), pp. 903–922 [Online].

Arora Kim (2013) 'Bus Gigs Seek to Reclaim the Night', *The Times of India*, 5th February, http://articles.timesofindia.indiatimes.com/2013-02-05/delhi/36763916_1_public-transport-night-bus-routes (Accessed 6th May 2013).

Bader-Zaar Birgitta (2007) 'Women's Suffrage Demonstrations, 1906–14', in Reiss Matthias (ed.) *The Street as Stage: Protest Marches and Public Rallies Since the Nineteenth Century*. Oxford: Oxford University Press, pp. 105–124.

Bagguley Paul (2002) 'Contemporary British Feminism: A Social Movement in Abeyance?' *Social Movement Studies*, 1(2), pp. 169–185 [Online].

Bagilhole B. (1997) *Equal Opportunities and Social Policy*. London: Longman.

Baker Joanne (2008) 'The Ideology of Choice. Overstating Progress and Hiding Injustice in the Lives of Young Women: Findings From a Study in North Queensland, Australia', *Women's Studies International Forum*, 31, pp. 53–64 [Online].

Banks Olive (1986) *Faces of Feminism*. Oxford: Blackwell.

Banyard Kat (2010) *The Equality Illusion*. London: Faber & Faber.

Banyard Victoria L., Plante Elizabethe G. & Moynihan Mary M. (2004) 'Bystander Education: Bringing a Broader Community Perspective to Sexual Violence Prevention', *Journal of Community Psychology*, 32(1), pp. 61–79 [Online].

Bashkevin Sylvia (1996) 'Tough Times in Review: The British Women's Movement During the Thatcher Years', *Comparative Political Studies*, 28(4), pp. 525–552.

Baumgardner Jennifer & Richards Amy (2000) *Manifesta: Young Women, Feminism and the Future*. New York: Farrar, Straus & Giroux.

BCS, British Crime Survey 2009/10. London: Home Office, http://rds. homeoffice.gov.uk/rds (Accessed 17th June 2011).

Beauvoir de Simone (2009) *The Second Sex*. London: Jonathon Cape.

Beckett Andy (2010) *When the Lights Went Out: Britain in the Seventies*. London: Faber & Faber.

Belden Jack (1970) *China Shakes the World*. New York: Monthly Review Press.

Bell Diane & Klein Renate (eds.) (1996) *Radically Speaking: Feminism Reclaimed*. Melbourne: Spinifex.

Belsize Lane Women's Group (1978) 'Nine Years Together: A History of a Women's Liberation Group', *Spare Rib*, 69(April), pp. 41–46.

Benjamin Harry (1966) *The Transsexual Phenomenon*. New York: Warner Books.

Bhavnani Kum-Kum & Coulson Margaret (2005) 'Transforming Socialist-Feminism: The Challenge of Racism', *Feminist Review*, (80), pp. 87–97.

Bianchini Franco (1995) 'Night Cultures, Night Economies', *Planning Practice & Research*, 10(2), pp. 121–126 [Online].

Bidisha (2010) 'Women's Mass Awakening', *The Guardian, Comment Is Free*, 4th August 2010, http://www.theguardian.com/commentisfree/2010/aug/04/women-mass-awakening (Accessed 8th August 2010).

Bindel Julie (1999) 'Never Give Up', in Walter Natasha (ed.) *On the Move: Feminism for a New Generation*. London: Virago, pp. 68–85.

Bindel Julie (2009) 'The Operation That Can Ruin Your Life', *Standpoint*, November, http://standpointmag.co.uk/the-operation-that-can-ruin-your-life-features-november-09-julie-bindel-transsexuals (Accessed 24th June 2012).

Bindel Julie (2010a) 'Legalising Prostitution Is Not the Answer', *The Guardian*, 2nd July, http://www.guardian.co.uk/commentisfree/2010/jul/02/prostitution-legalise-criminalise-swedish-law (Accessed 6th July 2010).

Bindel Julie (2010b) 'Why Men Use Prostitutes', *The Guardian*, 15th January.

Bindel Julie (2012) 'On Why Paying for Sex Is Wrong', *The Agitator, Things Unseen*, http://www.thefifthcolumn.co.uk/the-agitator/julie-bindel-on-why-paying-for-sex-is-wrong/ (Accessed 27th September 2014).

Bindel Julie (2013) 'An Unlikely Union', *Gaze – A Modern Review*, (1).

Bindel Julie (2014) *Straight Expectations*. London: Guardian Books.

Black Lawrence, Pemberton Hugh & Thane Pat (eds.) (2013) *Reassessing 1970s Britain*. Manchester: Manchester University Press.

Bland Lucy (1995) *Banishing the Beast: English Feminism and Sexual Morality, 1885–1914*. London: Penguin.

Bolourian Lily (2012) 'Lena Dunham Racism: How Caitlin Moran Exemplifies the Problem of Feminist Privilege', *PolicyMic*, http://www.policymic.com/articles/17824/lena-dunham-racism-how-caitlin-moran-exemplifies-the-problem-of-feminist-privilege (Accessed 3rd May 2013).

Bolt Christine (1993) *The Women's Movements in the United States and Britain From the 1790s to the 1920s*. London: Harvester Wheatsheaf.

Bookchin Murray (1974) *Post-Scarcity Anarchism*. London: Wildwood House.

Bornstein Kate (1995) *Gender Outlaw*. New York: Vintage.

Bouchier David (1983) *The Feminist Challenge: The Movement for Women's Liberation in Britain and the USA*. London: Macmillan.

Bourdieu Pierre (1986) 'The Forms of Capital', in G. Richardson John (ed.) *Handbook of Theory and Research for the Sociology of Education*. New York: Greenword, pp. 241–258.

Bourke Joanna (2007) *Rape: A History From 1860 to the Present*. London: Virago.

Boyle Karen (ed.) (2010) *Everyday Pornography*. Oxon: Routledge.

Braithwaite Anne (2002) 'The Personal, the Political, Third Wave and Postfeminisms', *Feminist Theory*, 3(3), pp. 335–344.

Brison Susan (2011) 'An Open Letter From Black Women to SlutWalk Organisers', *Huffington Post*, *The Blog*, 27th September, http://www. huffingtonpost.com/susan-brison/slutwalk-black-women_b_980215.html (Accessed 8th May 2012).

Brooks Libby (2011) 'Grooming and Our Ignoble Tradition of Racialising Crime', *The Guardian*, *Comment Is Free*, 7th January, http://www.the guardian.com/commentisfree/2011/jan/07/grooming-racialising-crime-tradition (Accessed 9th January 2011).

Brown Jennifer, Horvath Miranda, Kelly Liz & Westmarland Nicole (2010) *Has Anything Changed? Results of a Comparative Study (1977–2010) on Opinions on Rape*. London: Government Equalities Office.

Brownmiller Susan (1975) *Against Our Will*. London: Penguin.

Brownmiller Susan (1999) *In Our Time: Memoir of a Revolution*. New York: The Dial Press.

Bryan Beverley, Dadzie Stella & Scafe Suzanne (eds.) (1985) *The Heart of the Race: Black Women's Lives in Britain*. London: Virago.

Budgeon Shelley (2011) *Third Wave Feminism and the Politics of Gender in Late Modernity*. Basingstoke: Palgrave Macmillan.

Buechler Steven M. (2000) *Social Movements in Advanced Capitalism*. New York: Oxford University Press.

Bulbeck Chilla & Harris Anita (2007) 'Feminism, Youth Politics, and Generational Change', in Anita Harris (ed.) *Next Wave Cultures: Feminism, Subcultures, Activism*. London: Routledge, pp. 221–243.

Bundesministerium für Familie, Senioren, Frauen & Jugend (2007) 'Report by the Federal Government on the Impact of the Act Regulating the Legal Situation of Prostitutes (Prostitution Act)' (German).

Butler Judith (1990) *Gender Trouble*. London: Routledge.

Butler Judith (1993) *Bodies That Matter*. London: Routledge.

Butler Judith (2004) *Undoing Gender*. London: Routledge

Butler Judith (2014) Interview with Cristan Williams, 'Gender Performance: The TransAdvocate Interviews Judith Butler', in *The Transadvocate* (blog), www.transadvocate.com (Accessed 27th August 2014).

Butler Patrick (2011) 'Domestic Violence: Women's Charities Face 100% Funding Cuts', *The Guardian*, CutsBlog, 25th January, http:// www.theguardian.com/society/patrick-butler-cuts-blog/2011/jan/25/ domestic-violence-charities-face-100-cuts (Accessed 2nd August 2013).

Byrne Paul (1996) 'The Politics of the Women's Movement', in Lovenduski Joni & Norris Pippa (eds.) *Women in Politics*. Oxford: Oxford University Press, pp. 57–72.

Caine Barbara (1997) *English Feminism 1780–1980*. Oxford: Oxford University Press.

Califia Patrick (1997) *Sex Changes: The Politics of Transgenderism*. San Francisco: Cleiss Press.

Cameron Deborah & Scanlon Joan (eds.) (2009) *The Trouble & Strife Reader*. London: Bloomsbury Academic.

Campbell Beatrix (1980) 'A Feminist Sexual Politics: Now You See It, Now You Don't', *Feminist Review*, 5, pp. 1–18 [Online].

Campbell Delilah (2013) 'Who Owns Gender?' *Trouble & Strife*, http://www.troubleandstrife.org/new-articles/who-owns-gender/ (Accessed 6th June 2013).

Carby Hazel V. (1982) 'White Woman Listen! Black Feminism and the Boundaries of Sisterhood', in Centre for Contemporary Cultural Studies (eds.) *The Empire Strikes Back: Race and Racism in 70s Britain*. London: Hutchinson & Co, pp. 211–235.

Chan Beatrice (2004) *Reclaim the Night*, Paper Presented at Social Movements in Action Conference, University of New South Wales.

CMI, Chartered Management Institute, *The Ambitious Women's Toolkit*, http://www.managers.org.uk/glassceiling (Accessed 6th April 2011).

Cochrane Kira (2010) 'Feminism Isn't Finished', *The Guardian*, 24th July, http://www.theguardian.com/lifeandstyle/2010/jul/24/feminism-not-finished-not-uncool (Accessed 24th July 2010).

Cochrane Kira (2013) 'No More Page 3 Campaigner Lucy-Anne Holmes on Her Battle With the Sun', *The Guardian*, *The Women's Blog*, 10th March, http://www.theguardian.com/lifeandstyle/the-womens-blog-with-jane-martinson/2013/aug/23/online-activism-page-3-campaign (Accessed 19th April 2013).

Cockburn Cynthia (2007) *From Where We Stand: War, Women's Activism and Feminist Analysis*. London: Zed Books.

Cockburn Cynthia (2013) 'Beyond the Fragments: I'm a Socialist Feminist. Can I be a Radical Feminist Too?' *Open Democracy*, 17th May, http://www.opendemocracy.net/5050/cynthia-cockburn/%E2%80%9Cbeyond-fragments%E2%80%9D-i%E2%80%99m-socialist-feminist-can-i-be-radical-feminist-too (Accessed 20th May 2013).

Condon Stephanie, Leiber Marylene & Maillochon Florence (2007) 'Feeling Unsafe in Public Places: Understanding Women's Fears', *Revue francaise de Sociologie*, 48, pp. 101–128.

Connell R.W. (1995) *Masculinities*. Oakland: University of California Press.

Connell R.W. (2009) *Gender*. Cambridge: Polity Press.

Coole Diana (2010) 'Threads and Plaits or an Unfinished Project? Feminism(s) Through the Twentieth Century', *Journal of Political Ideologies*, 5(1), pp. 35–54 [Online].

Coote Anna & Cambell Beatrix (1987) *Sweet Freedom*. Oxford: Picador.

Correspondent (2013) 'People Throng Markets, Bus Stops to "Reclaim the Night"', *Hindustan Times*, 1st January, http://www.hindustantimes.com/India-news/NewDelhi/People-throng-markets-bus-stops-to-reclaim-the-night/Article1-983393.aspx (Accessed 12th January 2013).

Cosslett Rhiannon Lucy & Baxter Holly (2012) 'In Defence of Caitlin Moran and Populist Feminism', *New Statesman, Blogs*, 22nd October, http://www.newstatesman.com/lifestyle/2012/10/defence-caitlin-moran-and-populist-feminism (Accessed 9th November 2012).

Cox Cherise (1990) 'Anything Less Is Not Feminism: Racial Difference and the WMWM', *Law and Critique*, 1(2), pp. 237–248.

Crenshaw Kimberle (1989) 'Demarginalising the Intersection of Race and Sex: A Black Feminist Critique of Antidiscrimination Doctrine, Feminist Theory, and Antiracist Politics', *University of Chicago Legal Forum*, 14, pp. 538–554.

Crenshaw Kimberle (1991) 'Mapping the Margins: Intersectionality, Identity Politics, and Violence Against Women of Colour', *Stanford Law Review*, 43(6), pp. 1241–1299.

Croson Rachel (2001) 'Sex, Lies and Feminism', *Off Our Backs*, June, pp. 6–9.

Crossley Nick (2002) *Making Sense of Social Movements*. Buckingham: Open University Press.

Crow Barbara A. (2000) *Radical Feminism: A Documentary Reader*. London: New York University Press.

Daly Mary (1993) *Outercourse: The Be-Dazzling Voyage*. London: The Women's Press.

Davis Angela Y. (1982) *Women, Race and Class*. London: The Women's Press.

Davis Kathy (2007) *How Feminism Travels Across Borders: The Making of 'Our Bodies, Ourselves'*. London: Duke University Press.

Davis Kathy (2008) 'Intersectionality as Buzzword: A Sociology of Science Perspective on What Makes a Successful Feminist Theory', *Feminist Theory*, 9(1), pp. 67–85 [Online].

Davis Petra (2013) 'Trans People and the Current Feminist Movement', *New Statesman, Blogs*, 18th January, http://www.newstatesman.com/lifestyle/2013/01/trans-people-and-current-feminist-movement (Accessed 20th January 2013).

Davy Zowie (2014) 'Deepti Kapoor; Sheila Jeffreys; Over-sharing Online', *Woman's Hour*, BBC Radio 4, 7th August.

Dean Jonathan (2009) 'Who's Afraid of Third Wave Feminism?' *International Feminist Journal of Politics*, 11(3), pp. 334–352 [Online].

Dean Jonathan (2010) *Rethinking Contemporary Feminist Politics*. Basingstoke: Palgrave Macmillan.

DeKeseredy Walter S., Schwartz Martin D. & Alvi Shahid (2000) 'The Role of Profeminist Men in Dealing With Woman Abuse on the Canadian College Campus', *Violence Against Women*, 6(9), pp. 918–935 [Online].

Della Porta, D. & Diani Maria (1999) *Social Movements: An Introduction*. Oxford: Blackwell.

Dixon Janet (1988) 'Separatism: A Look Back at Anger', in Cant Bob & Hemmings Susan (eds.) *Radical Records: Thirty Years of Lesbian and Gay History*. London: Routledge, pp. 69–85.

Dodd Vikram (2012) 'Police up to 28 Times More Likely to Stop and Search Black People – Study', *The Guardian*, 12th June, p. 10.

Dougan Patrice and Fletcher Hamish (2014) 'Aukland bar, stripclub hit with liquor bans' *New Zealand Herald*, 22nd May [Online] http://www.nzherald.co.nz/business/news/article.cfm?c_id=3&objectid=11259680    (Accessed 19ᵗʰ July 2014)

Duggan Lisa (2004) *The Twilight of Equality?* Boston: Beacon.

Duncan Lauren E. (1999) 'Motivation for Collective Action: Group Consciousness as Mediator of Personality, Life Experiences and Women's Rights Activism', *Political Psychology*, 20(3), (September), pp. 611–635 [Online].

Dworkin Andrea (1981) *Pornography: Men Possessing Women*. London: The Women's Press.

Dworkin Andrea (1983) *Right-Wing Women*. London: The Women's Press.

ECP (2014) 'What We Campaign For' [Online] http://prostitutescollective.net/2010/03/28/recommendations-for-changes-in-prostitution-law-and-policy-2/ (Accessed 18th April 2014)

Elgot Jessica (2012) 'Jill Meagher: Death Sparks Melbourne "Reclaim the Night" Protest Over Women's Safety', *The Huffington Post UK*, 28th September,    http://www.huffingtonpost.co.uk/2012/09/28/jill-meagher-death-reclaim-the-night-melbourne_n_1922248.html    (Accessed    14th December 2012).

Elliott Cath (2009) 'The Great IUSW Con', *Too Much to Say for Myself* (blog),    http://toomuchtosayformyself.com/2009/01/09/the-great-iusw-con/ (Accessed 20th January 2014).

Emmott Chloe (2013) 'Young Women Are Not Failing Feminism, We Are Its Lifeblood', *Huffington Post*, 17th June, http://www.huffingtonpost.co.uk/chloe-emmott/young-women-are-not-failing-feminism_b_3454711.html (Accessed 22nd June 2013).

Engels Friedrich [1887] (1993) *The Condition of the English Working Class*. Oxford: Oxford University Press.

England Kim V.L. (1994) 'Getting Personal: Reflexivity, Positionality, and Feminist Research', *The Professional Geographer*, 46(1), pp. 80–89 [Online].

Epstein Barbara (2003) 'The Decline of the Women's Movement', in Goodwin Jeff & Jasper James M. (eds.) *The Social Movements Reader: Cases and Concepts*. Oxford: Blackwell, pp. 328–335.

Erickson Bailee (2010) 'Every Woman Needs Courage: Feminist Periodicals in 1970s West Germany', *Preteritus: A Graduate History Journal*, 2 [Online].

Eschle Catherine & Maiguashca Bice (2010) *Making Feminist Sense of the Global Justice Movement*. Plymouth: Little Brown.

Evans Elizabeth (2015) *The Politics of Third Wave Feminisms: Neoliberalism, Intersectionality and the State in Britain and the US*. Basingstoke: Palgrave.

EVAW – End Violence Against Women Coalition (2007) *Making the Grade? The Third Annual Independent Analysis of UK Government Initiatives on Violence Against Women*. London: EVAW.

EVAW – End Violence Against Women Coalition (2011) *A Different World Is Possible: A Call for Long-Term and Targeted Action to Prevent Violence Against Women and Girls*. London: EVAW.

EVAW – End Violence Against Women Coalition (2013) *Deeds or Words: An Analysis of Westminster Government Action to Prevent Violence Against Women and Girls*. London: EVAW.

Exeter RTN www.exeterrtn.wordpress.com (Accessed 8th June 2013).

FAC – Feminist Anthology Collective (ed.) (1981) *No Turning Back: Writings From the Women's Liberation Movement, 1975–1980*. London: The Women's Press.

Faderman Lillian (1991) *Odd Girls and Twilight Lovers: A History of Lesbian Life in Twentieth-Century America*. New York: Columbia University Press.

Fairweather Eileen (1979) 'Leeds: Curfew on Men', *Spare Rib*, (83), June; reprinted in Rowe, M. (1982) Spare Rib Reader, Harmondsworth: Penguin, pp. 441–442

Faludi Susan (1992) *Backlash*. London: Chatto & Windus.

Farley Melissa , Cotton ann, Lynne Jacqueline, Zumbeck Sybille, Spiwak Frida, Reyes Maria E., Alvarez Dinorah and Sezgin Ufuk (2003) 'Prostitution and Trafficking in Nine Countries: An Update on Violence and Posttraumatic Stress Disorder', *Journal of Trauma Practice*, 2(3–4), pp. 33–74.

Feinberg Lesley (1993) *Stone Butch Blues*. Ann Arbor: Firebrand Books.

Feinberg Lesley (1996) *Transgender Warriors*. Boston: Beacon Press.

Feminist Archive North (FAN Chronology), http://www.feministarchivenorth.org.uk/ (Accessed 22nd July 2013).

Ferguson Michaele L. (2010) 'Choice Feminism and the Fear of Politics', *Symposium*, 8(1), pp. 247–253 [Online].

Firestone Shulamith [1970] (1993) *The Dialectic of Sex: The Case for Feminist Revolution*. New York: Quill.

Freedman Estelle B. (2002) *No Turning Back: The History of Feminism and the Future of Women*. New York: Ballantine Books.

Freeman Jo (1973) 'The Tyranny of Structurelessness', *Ms Magazine*, Volume 9, pp. 76–89.

Freeman Jo (1975) *The Politics of Women's Liberation*. New York: David McKay Company Inc.

Freeman Jo (2003) 'The Women's Movement', in Goodwin Jeff & Jasper James M. (eds.) *The Social Movements Reader: Cases and Concepts*. Oxford: Blackwell, pp. 22–31.

Friedan Betty (1963) The Feminine Mystique. New York: WW Norton

Friedman Susan Stanford (1995) 'Making History: Reflections on Feminism Narrative, and Desire', in Elam Diane & Wiegman Robyn (eds.) *Feminism Beside Itself*. London: Routledge, pp. 11–55.

Frye Marilyn (1983) *The Politics of Reality: Essays in Feminist Theory*. Berkely: Crossing Press.

Gamson Joshua (1995) 'Must Identity Movements Self-Destruct? A Queer Dilemma', *Social Problems*, 42(3), pp. 390–407 [Online].

Gamson William A. (1992) 'The Social Psychology of Collective Action', in D. Morris Aldon & Mueller Carol McClurg (eds.) *Frontiers in Social Movement Theory*. New Haven: Yale University Press, pp. 53–76.

Gangoli Geetanjali (2007) *Indian Feminisms: Campaigns Against Violence and Multiple Patriarchies*. Surrey: Ashgate.

Gardiner Judith Kegan (ed.) (2002) *Masculinity Studies and Feminist Theory*. New York: Columbia University Press.

Gelb Joyce (1986) 'Movement Strategies: Inside or Outside the "System" ', in Dahlerup Drude (ed.) *The New Women's Movement: Feminism and Political Power in Europe and the USA*. London: Sage, pp. 103–122.

Gentleman Amelia (2011) 'Women's Refuge Chief Returns OBE in Protest Over Cuts', *The Guardian*, 15th February, http://www.theguardian.com/society/2011/feb/15/women-refuge-chief-protest-cuts (Accessed 16th February 2011).

G Helen (2012) 'Update: Trans Inclusion and Reclaim the Night London', *The F Word*, 24th October 2012, http://www.thefword.org.uk/blog/2012/10/update_trans_inclusion_rtn (Accessed 25th October 2012).

Gibson Anne (2012) 'High rise brothel comes step closer' *The New Zealand Herald*. 17th January [Online] http://www.nzherald.co.nz/business/news/article.cfm?c_id=3&objectid=10779186 (Accessed 20th March 2014)

Gilbert David (2007) 'Geographies of Protest Marches', in Reiss Matthias (ed.) *The Street as Stage: Protest Marches and Public Rallies Since the Nineteenth Century*. Oxford: Oxford University Press, pp. 41–48.

Gill Rosalind C. (2007) 'Critical Respect: The Difficulties and Dilemmas of Agency and "Choice" for Feminism: A Reply to Duits and van Zoonen', *European Journal of Women's Studies*, 14(1), pp. 69–80 [Online].

Goodwin Jeff & Jasper James M. (eds.) (2003) *The Social Movements Reader: Cases and Concepts*. Oxford: Blackwell.

Green Adam Isaiah (2013) ' "Erotic Capital" and the Power of Desirability: Why "Honey Money" Is a Bad Collective Strategy for Remedying Gender Inequality', *Sexualities*, 16(1/2), pp. 137–158 [Online].

Green Eli R. (2006) 'Debating Trans Inclusion in the Feminist Movement', *Journal of Lesbian Studies*, 10(1–2), pp. 231–248 [Online].

Green Victoria (1976) 'Their Primary Purpose Is to Help Raped Women Regain Their Strength as Individuals: Rape Crisis Centre Opens', *Spare Rib*, 46(May), pp. 17–18.

Greer Germaine (2006) *The Female Eunuch*. London: Harper.

Griffin Gabrielle (ed.) (1995a) *Feminist Activism in the 1990s*. London: Taylor & Francis.

Griffin Gabrielle (1995b) 'Introduction', in Griffin Gabrielle (ed.) *Feminist Activism in the 1990s*. London: Taylor & Francis, pp. 1–10.

Griffith D.W. (1915) The Birth of a Nation. (silent film) Producer D.W. Griffith; Distributer Epoch Producing Company, United States of America

Grinyer Anne (2002) 'The Anonymity of Research Participants: Assumptions, Ethics and Practicalities', *Social Research Update*, Sociology at Surrey, 36(Spring) [Online].

Grover Chris & Soothill Keith (1996) 'Ethnicity, the Search for Rapists and the Press', *Ethnic and Racial Studies*, 19(3), pp. 567–584.

Gunew Sneja (ed.) (1991) *A Reader in Feminist Knowledge*. London: Routledge.

Gupta Rahila (2013) '50 Billion Shades of Feminism', *Trouble & Strife*, 6th July, http://www.troubleandstrife.org/2013/07/50-billion-shades-of-feminism/ (Accessed 7th July 2013).

Hague Gill, Mullender Audrey & Aris Rosemary (2003) *Is Anyone Listening? Accountability and Women Survivors of Domestic Violence*. London: Routledge.

Halberstam Judith (1998) *Female Masculinity*. Durham: Duke University Press.

Hall Jenny (1977) 'How Can We Organise Against Rape?' *Spare Rib*, 61(August), pp. 19–21.

Hall Ruth (1977) 'When Rape, Like Charity, Begins at Home', *The Guardian*, 1st August, p. 14.

Hamer Emily (1995) *Britannia's Glory: A History of Twentieth-Century Lesbians*. London: Continuum.

Hamer Emily (1996) *Britannia's Glory*. London: Cassell.

Hanisch Carol ([undated] 2000) 'The Personal Is Political', in A. Crow Barbara (ed.) *Radical Feminism: A Documentary Reader*. London: New York University Press, pp. 113–117.

Hanmer Jalna (1981) 'Male Violence and the Social Control of Women', in Feminist Anthology Collective (eds.) *No Turning Back: Writings From the Women's Liberation Movement, 1975–1980*. London: Women's Press, pp. 190–195.

Hanmer Jalna & Maynard Mary (eds.) (1987) *Women, Violence and Social Control*. Basingstoke: MacMillan.

Hanmer Jalna, Lunn Cathy, Jeffreys Sheila and McNeill Sandra (1977) 'Sex Class – Why Is It Important to Call Women a Class?' Scarlet Woman, Issue 5, p. 8.

Hansen Susan B. (1997) 'Talking About Politics: Gender and Contextual Effects on Political Proselytizing', *The Journal of Politics*, 59(1), (February), pp. 73–103 [Online].

Haraway Donna J. (1991) *Simians, Cyborgs, and Women: The Reinvention of Nature*. London: Free Association Books.

Harding Sandra (1991) *Whose Science? Whose Knowledge?* Milton Keynes: Open University Press.

Harne Lynne & Radford Jill (2008) *Tackling Domestic Violence: Theories, Policies and Practice*. Buckingham: Open University Press.

Harris Anita (ed.) (2007) *Next Wave Cultures: Feminism, Subcultures, Activism*. London: Routledge.

Hawthorne Susan (1991) 'In Defence of Seperatism', in Gunew Sneja (ed.) *A Reader in Feminist Knowledge*. London: Routledge, pp. 312–318.

Healey Emma (1996) *Lesbian Sex Wars*. London: Virago.

Hearn Jeff (1998) *The Violence of Men*. California: Sage.

Hemmings Clare (2011) *Why Stories Matter: The Political Grammar of Feminist Theory*. London: Duke University Press.

Henry Astrid (2004) *Not My Mother's Sister: Generational Conflict and Third-Wave Feminism*. Indiana: Indiana University Press.

Hernon Ian (2006) *Riot!: Civil Insurrection From Peterloo to the Present Day*. London: Pluto Press.

Hesford Victoria (2005) 'Feminism and Its Ghosts: The Spectre of the Feminist-as-Lesbian', *Feminist Theory*, 6(3), pp. 227–250 [Online].

Hester Marianne (1990) 'The Dynamics of Male Domination Using the Witch Craze in 16th and 17th Century England as a Case Study', *Women's Studies International Forum*, 13(1–2), pp. 9–19 [Online].

Hester Marianne (1992) *Lewd Women & Wicked Witches*. London: Routledge.

Hester Marianne, Kelly Liz & Radford Jill (eds.) (1996) *Women, Violence and Male Power: Feminist Activism, Research and Practice*. Buckingham: Open University Press.

Heyes Cressida J. (2003) 'Feminist Solidarity After Queer Theory: The Case of Transgender', *Signs*, 28(4), pp. 1093–1120 [Online].

Heywood Leslie L. (ed.) (2005) *The Women's Movement Today: An Encyclopedia of Third-Wave Feminism*. Connecticut: Greenwood Press.

Hilton Emily (2013) 'Is "Lad Culture" Causing a Surge in Student Feminist Societies?' *The Guardian Online*, 8th May, http://www.theguardian.com/education/2013/may/08/lad-culture-student-feminism (Accessed 9th May 2013).

Hinton William (1966) *Fanshen: A Documentary of Revolution in a Chinese Village*. New York: Monthly Review Press.

History of Feminism Network (2011) http://historyfeminism.wordpress.com/ (Accessed 4th May 2011).

Hoagland Sarah L. & Penelope Julia (eds.) (1988) *For Lesbians Only: A Separatist Anthology*. London: Onlywomen Press.

Hobson Janell (2011) 'Should Black Women Oppose the SlutWalk?' *Ms*, 27th September, http://msmagazine.com/blog/2011/09/27/should-black-women-oppose-the-slutwalk/ (Accessed 4th February 2012).

Holloway Wendy (1984) ' "I Just Wanted to Kill a Woman" Why? The Ripper and Male Sexuality', in Kanter Hannah, Lefanu Sarah, Shah Shaila and Spedding Carole (eds.) *Sweeping Statements*. London: The Women's Press, pp. 14–23.

Holmgren Linn E. & Hearn Jeff (2009) 'Framing "Men in Feminism": Theoretical Locations, Local Contexts and Practical Passings in Men's Gender-Conscious Positionings on Gender Equality and Feminism', *Journal of Gender Studies*, 18(4), pp. 403–418.

Home Office (HO) (2010) *Call to End Violence Against Women and Girls*. HM Government. London: Home Office.

Home Office (HO) (2004) *Paying the Price: A consultation paper on prostitution*. HM Government. London: Home Office.

hooks bell (1986) 'Sisterhood: Political Solidarity Between Women', *Feminist Review*, 23, pp. 125–127.

hooks bell (2000) *Feminism Is for Everybody*. Cambridge, MA: South End Press.

hooks bell (2004) *The Will to Change: Men, Masculinity and Love*. New York: Washington Square Press.

Horvath Miranda A.H. & Brown Jennifer (eds.) (2009) *Rape: Challenging Contemporary Thinking*. Oxford: Willan Publishing.

Hudson Kate (2005) *CND – Now More Than Ever: The Story of a Peace Movement*. London: Vision Paperbacks.

Huxley Aldous (1984) *Brave New World Revisited*. London: Chatto & Windus.

Inglehart Ronald (1977) 'Changing Values in Post-Industrial Societies', in Goodwin Jeff & Jasper James M. (eds.) *The Social Movements Reader: Cases and Concepts*. Oxford: Blackwell, pp. 64–71.

Jasper Lee (2011) 'Deaths in Police Custody Cut Deep in the Psyche of Black Britons', *The Guardian, Comment Is Free*, 15th December, http://www.theguardian.com/commentisfree/2011/dec/15/deaths-in-custody-black-britons-ipcc (Accessed 23rd May 2012).

Jeffreys Sheila (1977) 'Revolutionary Feminism', *Spare Rib*, 58(May), p. 12.

Jeffreys Sheila (2012) 'Let Us Be Free to Debate Transgenderism Without Being Accused of "Hate Speech"', *The Guardian, Comment Is Free*, 29th May, http://www.theguardian.com/commentisfree/2012/may/29/transgenderism-hate-speech (Accessed 1st June 2012).

Jeffreys Sheila (2014) *Gender Hurts*. London: Routledge.

Jeffreys Sheila, McNeill Sandra & Rhodes Dusty (1985) 'Introduction', in Rhodes Dusty & McNeill Sandra (eds.) *Women Against Violence Against Women*. London: Onlywomen Press, pp. 6–8.

Jones Beverley & Brown Judith ([1968] 2000) 'Toward a Female Liberation Movement', in A. Crow Barbara (ed.) *Radical Feminism: A Documentary Reader*. London: New York University Press, pp. 17–57.

Kanter Hannah, Lefanu Sarah, Shah Shaila and Spedding Carole (eds.) (1984) *Sweeping Statements: Writings From the Women's Liberation Movement*. London: The Women's Press

Kappeler Susanne (1986) *The Pornography of Representation*. Cambridge: Polity Press.

Kaveney Roz (1999) 'Talking Transgender Politics', in More Kate & Whittle Stephen (eds.) *Reclaiming Genders*. London: Cassell, pp. 146–158.

Kaveney Roz (2013) 'Julie Burchill Has Ended up Bullying the Trans Community', *The Guardian, Comment Is Free*, 13th January, http://www.theguardian.com/commentisfree/2013/jan/13/julie-birchill-bullying-trans-community (Accessed 14th January 2013).

Kelly Liz (2000) 'Wars Against Women: Sexual Violence, Sexual Politics and the Militarised State', in Jacobs Susie, Jacobson Ruth & Marchbank Jennifer. (eds.) *States of Conflict: Gender, Violence and Resistance*. London: Zed Books, pp. 45–66.

Kelly Liz (2013) 'Changing It Up: Sexual Violence Three Decades On', in Appignanesi Lisa, Holmes Rachel & Orbach Susie (eds.) *Fifty Shades of Feminism*. London: Virago, pp. 133–137.

Kendall Mikki (2013) '#SolidarityIsForWhiteWomen: Women of Colour's Issue With Digital Feminism', *The Guardian, Comment Is Free*, 14th August, http://www.theguardian.com/commentisfree/2013/aug/14/solidarityisforwhitewomen-hashtag-feminism (Accessed 15th August 2013).

Kessler Susanne (1990) 'The Medical Construction of Gender: Case Management of Intersexed Infants', *Signs*, 16(1), pp. 3–26.

Kinser Amber E. (2004) 'Negotiating Spaces for/Through Third Wave Feminism', *National Women's Studies Association Journal*, 16(3), pp. 124–153 [Online].

Koopmans Ruud (2004) 'Protest in Time and Space: The Evolution of Waves of Contention', in A. Snow David, A. Soule Sarah & Kriesi Hanspeter (eds.) (2007) *The Blackwell Companion to Social Movements*. Oxford: Blackwell Publishing, pp. 19–47.

Lallo Michael (2012) 'Thousands March to Reclaim the Night', *The Age*, 20th October, http://www.theage.com.au/victoria/thousands-march-to-reclaim-the-night-20121020-27yln.html (Accessed 12th February 2013).

Law John (2004) *After Method: Mess in Social Science Research*. London: Routledge.

Lees Paris (2013) 'An Open Letter to Suzanne Moore', *DIVA Online*, 13th January, http://www.divamag.co.uk/category/comment/an-open-letter-to-suzanne-moore.aspx (Accessed 24th January 2013).

Lees Paris (2014) 'The Trans vs Radical Feminist Twitter War Is Making Me Sick', *Vice*, 20th August [Online].

Lefler Jordan (2011) *I Can Has Thesis?: A Linguistic Analysis of LOLSPEAK*. Unpublished MA Thesis, Louisiana State University, http://etd.lsu.edu/docs/available/etd-11112011-100404/unrestricted/Lefler_thesis.pdf (Accessed 3rd May 2012).

Lerner Gerda (1986) *The Creation of Patriarchy*. New York: Oxford University Press.

Levine Phillippa (1987) *Victorian Feminism 1850–1900*. London: Hutchinson.

LFN – London Feminist Network, www.londonfeministnetwork.org.uk (Accessed 8th June 2010).

Lister Ruth (1997) 'Citizenship: Towards a Feminist Synthesis', *Feminist Review*, 57(Autumn), pp. 28–48 [Online].

Long Julia (2012) *Anti-Porn: The Resurgence of Anti-Pornography Feminism*. London: Zed Press.

LRCC – London Rape Crisis Centre (1984) *Sexual Violence*. London: The Women's Press.

Mackay Finn (2013) 'Arguing Against the Industry of Prostitution – Beyond the Abolitionist Versus Sex-Worker Binary', *Feminist & Women's Studies Association* (blog) 16th June. http://fwsablog.org.uk/2013/06/16/arguing-against-the-industry-of-prostitution-beyond-the-abolitionist-versus-sex-worker-binary/ (Accessed 18th November 2014).

Mackay Finn (2014) 'Mapping the Routes: An Exploration of Charges of Racism Made Against the 1970s UK Reclaim the Night Marches', *Women's Studies International Forum*, 44, pp. 46–54 [Online].

Maiguashca Bice (2006) 'Making Feminist Sense of the "Anti-Globalisation Movement": Some Reflections on Methodology and Method', *Global Society*, 20(2), pp. 115–136.

Malik Kenan (1995) 'Too Many Killings to Ignore', *The Independent*, 17th December, http://www.independent.co.uk/voices/too-many-killings-to-ignore-1526160.html (Accessed 21st June 2013).

Marhia Natasha (2008) *Just Representation? Press Reporting and the Reality of Rape*. London: Lilith Project, Eaves.

Marinucci Mimi (2010) *Feminism Is Queer: The Intimate Connection Between Queer and Feminist Theory*. London: Zed Press.

Marychild-Claire Roxanne (1981) 'The Personal Is Political', *Revolutionary and Radical Feminist Newsletter*, 8(Autumn), pp. 17–19.

Marx Ferree M. & McClurg Mueller C. (2007) 'Feminism and the Women's Movement: A Global Perspective', in A. Snow David, A. Soule Sarah &

Hanspeter Kriesi (eds.) *Blackwell Companion to Social Movements*. Oxford: Blackwell Publishing, pp. 576–607.

Marx Karl & Engels Friedrich [1848] (2002) *The Communist Manifesto: Introduction by Gareth Stedman Jones*. London: Penguin Books.

May Theresa (2010). *Speech to 36th Annual Women's Aid National Conference*, 16th July, http://www.womensaid.org.uk/page.asp?section=0001000100150008000400002&sectionTitle=Theresa+May%27s+Speech (Accessed 2nd September 2010).

McCabe Jess (2009) 'Sexually Assaulted During Reclaim the Night London', *The F Word*, 22nd November, http://www.thefword.org.uk/blog/2009/11/sexually_assaul (Accessed 25th November 2009).

McCabe Jess (2013) 'Is There Another Way to Talk About Porn?' *Southbank Centre Blog*, http://blog.southbankcentre.co.uk/2013/03/11/is-there-another-way-to-talk-about-porn/ (Accessed 11th March 2013).

McIntosh Mary (1993) 'Queer Theory and the War of the Sexes', in Bristow Joseph (ed.) *Activating Theory*. London: Lawrence & Wishart, pp. 30–52.

McKay George (1998) *DiY Culture: Party and Protest in Nineties Britain*. London: Verso.

McRobbie Angela (2008) 'Postfeminist Passions', *The Guardian, Comment Is Free*, 25th March, http://www.theguardian.com/commentisfree/2008/mar/25/gender (Accessed 9th June 2013).

McRobbie Angela (2009) *The Aftermath of Feminism: Gender, Culture & Social Change*. Sage: London.

McSmith Andy (2010) *No Such Thing as Society: A History of Britain in the 1980s*. London: Constable.

Medew Julia (2011) 'Prostitute to Sue Brothel Over Gun', *The Age*, Victoria, 13th July, http://www.theage.com.au/victoria/prostitute-to-sue-brothel-over-gun-20110712-1hc7n.html (Accessed 10th September 2014).

Meehan Elizabeth (1990) 'British Feminism From the 1960s to the 1980s', in L. Smith Harold (ed.) *British Feminism in the 20th Century*. Massachusetts: University of Massachusetts Press, pp. 189–207.

Meisner Maurice (1999) *Mao's China and After: A History of the People's Republic* (3rd Ed). New York: Free Press.

Melucci Alberto (1980) 'The New Social Movements: A Theoretical Approach', *Social Science Information*, 19, pp. 199–226.

Melucci Alberto (1988) 'Getting Involved: Identity and Mobilisation in Social Movements', *Research in Social Movements, Conflicts and Change*, 1, pp. 329–348.

Melucci Alberto (1989) *Nomads of the Present: Social Movements and Individual Needs in Contemporary Society*. London: Hutchinson.

Mendes Kaitlynn (2011) *Feminism in the News*. Basingstoke: Palgrave Macmillan.

Merrick Jane (2013) ' "Keep the Bare Boobs out of the Sun": Is Page 3 About to Move Upmarket?' *The Independent*, 21st July, http://www.independent.co.uk/news/uk/politics/keep-the-bare-boobs-out-of-the-sun-is-page-3-about-to-move-upmarket-8723138.html (Accessed 25th July 2013).

Mesure Susie (2009) 'The March of the New Feminists', *The Independent*, 29th November, http://www.independent.co.uk/news/uk/home-news/the-march-of-the-new-feminists-1830514.html (Accessed 6th January 2011).

Mies Maria & Shiva Vandana (1993) *Ecofeminism*. London: Zed.

Miles Matthew B. & Huberman Michael A. (1994) *Qualitative Data Analysis: An Expanded Sourcebook*. London: Sage.

Mill John S. (1869) 'The Subjection of Women', in M. Robson John (ed.) (1984) *J.S. Mill, Collected Works, xxi, Essays on Equality, Law and Education*. Toronto: University of Toronto Press, pp. 261–340.

Millett Kate [1969] (1972) *Sexual Politics*. London: Abacus.

Mirza Heidi S. (ed.) (1997) *Black British Feminism*. London: Routledge.

Mitchell Juliet (1966) 'Women: The Longest Revolution', *New Left Review*, 40, pp. 11–37.

Moore Suzanne (2013a) 'Seeing Red: The Power of Female Anger', *The New Statesman, Blogs*, 8th January, http://www.newstatesman.com/politics/2013/01/seeing-red-power-female-anger (Accessed 8th January 2013).

Moore Suzanne (2013b) 'I Don't Care If You Were Born a Woman or Became One', *The Guardian, Comment Is Free*, 9th January, http://www.theguardian.com/commentisfree/2013/jan/09/dont-care-if-born-woman (Accessed 9th January 2013).

Morgan Robin (ed.) (1970) *Sisterhood Is Powerful*. New York: Random House

Mott Rebecca (2009) Speech to Feminism in London Conference, http://www.feminisminlondon.org.uk/feminism-in-london-2009/speeches/rebecca-motts-speech/. (Accessed 18th November 2014).

Mueller Carol (1994) 'Conflict Networks and the Origins of Women's Liberation', in Lorana Enrique, Johnston Hank & R. Gusfield Joseph (eds.) *New Social Movements: From Ideology to Identity*. Philadelphia: Temple University Press, pp. 234–236.

Mullen Michael Ann (1977) 'Why Socialist Feminism? Gatherings in Paris and Amsterdam', *Spare Rib*, 61(August), pp. 26–28.

Mulvey Laura (1989) *Visual and Other Pleasures*. Basingstoke: MacMillan.

MWR – Million Women Rise (2013) www.millionwomenrise.com (Accessed 14th July 2013).

Nataf Zachary I. (1996) *Lesbians Talk Transgender*. London: Scarlett Press.

'Newsnight', Interview with Jack Straw, BBC2, Screened 7th January 2011.

No More Page 3 Campaign www.nomorepage3.org (Accessed 23rd June 2013).

Norma Caroline (2011) 'Brothel Safety a Dangerous Myth', *Brisbane Times*, 15th July, http://www.brisbanetimes.com.au/opinion/society-and-culture/brothel-safety-a-dangerous-myth-20110714-1hfwh.html (Accessed 10th September 2014).

Norris Pippa (2002) *Democratic Phoenix: Reinventing Political Activism*. Cambridge: Cambridge University Press.

Norris Pippa, Lovenduski Joni & Campbell Rosie (2004) *Gender and Political Participation*. London: The Electoral Commission.

NZ Press Association, NZPA (2010) 'Brothel-Keepers Jailed for Rape', *TVNZ OneNews*, 8th January, http://tvnz.co.nz/national-news/brothel-keepers-jailed-rape-3326080 (Accessed 27th September 2014).

NZ Press Association, NZPA (2011) 'NZ a Destination for Illegal Prostitution – Report', Stuff.co.nz, 3rd July, http://www.stuff.co.nz/national/5225830/ NZ-a-destination-for-illegal-prostitution-report (Accessed 27th September 2014).

Olson Mancur (1965) *The Logic of Collective Action*. Cambridge, MA: Harvard University Press.

OP Onlywomen Press (eds.) (1981) *Love Your Enemy? The Debate Between Heterosexual Feminism and Political Lesbianism*. London: Onlywomen Press.

Orr Catherine M. (1997) 'Charting the Currents of the Third Wave', *Hypatia*, 12(3), (Summer), pp. 29–45 [Online].

O'Sullivan Sue (1982) 'Passionate Beginnings: Ideological Politics 1969–72', *Feminist Review*, 11, pp. 70–86 [Online].

O'Sullivan Sue (1996) *I Used to Be Nice: Sexual Affairs, Sexual Politics*. London: Continuum International Publishing.

O'Toole Emer (2013) 'Delhi Gang-Rape: Look Westward in Disgust', *The Guardian, Comment Is Free*, 1st January, http://www.theguardian. com/commentisfree/2013/jan/01/delhi-rape-damini (Accessed 8th January 2013).

Pain Rachel H. (1997) 'Social Geographies of Women's Fear of Crime', *Transactions of the Institute of British Geographies*, New Series, 22(2), pp. 231–244 [Online].

Parliament.co.uk (2013)*Frequently Asked Questions, How Many Female MPs are There?* http://www.parliament.uk/about/faqs/house-of-commons-faqs/ members-faq-page2/ (Accessed 6th April 2013).

Pateman Carole (1989) *The Disorder of Women: Democracy, Feminism and Political Theory*. Cambridge: Polity Press.

Peacock Louisa (2010) 'Smallest Gender Pay Gap on Record "Deceiving" CIPD Warns', *The Telegraph*, 9th December, http://www.telegraph.co. uk/finance/jobs/8189893/Smallest-gender-pay-gap-on-record-deceiving-CIPD-warns.html (Accessed 12th May 2012).

Pearson Allison (2013) 'Oxford Grooming Gang: We Will Regret Ignoring Asian Thugs Who Target White Girls', *The Telegraph*, 15th May, http://www.telegraph.co.uk/news/uknews/crime/10060570/Oxford-grooming-gang-We-will-regret-ignoring-Asian-thugs-who-target-white-girls. html (Accessed 18th May 2013).

Penny Laurie (2012) 'Lena Dunham, Caitlin Moran and the Problem of Unexamined Privilege', *The New Statesman, Blogs*, 9th October, http: //www.newstatesman.com/laurie-penny/2012/10/lena-dunham-caitlin-moran-and-problem-unexamined-privilege (Accessed 10th October 2012).

Polletta Francesca & Jasper James M. (2001) 'Collective Identity and Social Movements', *Annual Review of Sociology*, 27, pp. 283–305 [Online].

Porteous Debbie (2011) 'Under-Age Sex Worker Claims Spur Concern', *Otago Daily Times*, 4th March, http://www.odt.co.nz/news/dunedin/150243/under-age-sex-worker-claims-spur-concern (Accessed 7th September 2014).

Pugh Martin (2000) *Women and the Women's Movement in Britain, 1914–1999*. London: Macmillan.

Puwar Nirmal (2004) 'Thinking About Making a Difference', *BJPIR*, 6, pp. 65–80 [Online].

Radford Jill (1994) 'History of Women's Liberation Movements in Britain: A Reflective Personal History', in Griffin Gabrielle et al. (eds.) *Stirring It: Challenges for Feminism*. London: Taylor & Francis, pp. 40–58.

Rahm Tanja, Viola Alice, Christensen Christina, Malmberg Lita, Christensen Pia and Poulsen Odile. (2013) 'Exited Women: Prostitution Is Violent and Unfree', *Pass the Flaming Sword* (blog), https://passtheflamingsword.word press.com/2013/05/04/exited-women-prostitution-is-violent-and-unfree/ (Accessed 2nd August 2014).

Raphael Samuel History Centre (RSHC) http://www.raphael-samuel.org.uk/ about/raphael-samuel (Accessed 3rd September 2013).

Raymond Janice (1979) *The Transsexual Empire*. New York: Teacher's College Press.

Reclaim the Night www.reclaimthenight.org [online] (Accessed 18th August 2011).

Redfern Catherine & Aune Kristin (2010) *Reclaiming the F Word: The New Feminist Movement*. London: Zed Books.

Redfern Catherine & Aune Kristin (2013) *Reclaiming the F Word: Feminism Today* (Revised Ed). London: Zed Books.

Rees Jeska (2010) 'A Look Back at Anger: The Women's Liberation Movement in 1978', *Women's History Review*, 19(3), pp. 337–356 [Online].

Regeringskansliet 'Prostitution & Trafficking in Women' Policy Report, (Swedish) Ministry of Industry, Employment & Communications, July 2004.

Reger Jo (2002) 'More Than One Feminism: Organisational Structure and the Construction of Collective Identity', in S. Meyer David, Whittier Nancy & Robnett Belinda (eds.) *Social Movements: Identity, Culture and the State*. Oxford: Oxford University Press, pp. 171–184.

Rehman Yasmin, Kelly Liz & Siddiqui Hannana (eds.) (2013) *Moving in the Shadows: Violence in the Lives of Minority Women and Children*. Surrey: Ashgate.

Reid Sue (2010) 'Asian Gangs, Schoolgirls and a Sinister Taboo: As Nine Men Are Jailed for Grooming up to 100 for Sex, the Disturbing New Trend Few Dare Talk About', *Daily Mail*, 27th November, http://www.dailymail. co.uk/news/article-1333537/Nine-men-Derby-jailed-grooming-100-sex. html (Accessed 28th November 2010).

Reiss Matthias (ed.) (2007) *The Street as Stage: Protest Marches and Public Rallies Since the Nineteenth Century*. Oxford: Oxford University Press.

Reuters (2010) 'Stricter Brothel Rules Sought in Amsterdam', *TVNS OneNews*, 20th January, http://tvnz.co.nz/world-news/stricter-brothel-rules-sought-in-amsterdam-3335121 (Accessed 10th September 2014).

rhodes dusty & McNeill Sandra (eds.) (1985) *Women Against Violence Against Women*. London: Onlywomen Press.

Ribbeck Michael (2012) 'Lap-dancing Chain Spearmint Rhino Plans to Open Club in Bristol', *The Bristol Post Online*, 1st November, http://

www.thisisbristol.co.uk/Lap-dancing-chain-Spearmint-Rhino-plans-open-club/story-17208273-detail/story.html#axzz2dqPXHJyu (Accessed 18th December 2012).

Rich Adrienne (1980) 'Compulsory Heterosexuality and Lesbian Existence', *Signs*, 5(4), pp. 631–660 [Online].

Rich Emma (2005) 'Young Women, Feminist Identities and Neo-Liberalism', *Women's Studies International Forum*, 28, pp. 495–508 [Online].

Riddel Carol (1996) 'Divided Sisterhood', in Ekins Richard & King Dave (eds.) *Blending Genders*. London: Routledge, pp. 171–190.

Riordan Ellen (2001) 'Commodified Agents and Empowered Girls: Consuming and Producing Feminism', *Journal of Communication Enquiry*, 25(3), pp. 279–297.

Robnett Belinda (2002) 'External Political Change, Collective Identities, and Participation in Social Movement Organisations', in S. Meyer David, Whittier Nancy & Robnett Belinda (eds.) *Social Movements: Identity, Culture and the State*. Oxford: Oxford University Press, pp. 266–285.

Romanowicz Emma (2011) 'Shocked by City's Response to March', *Yorkshire Evening Post*, Letters to the Editor, 8th December. [Online] http://www.york shireeveningpost.co.uk/news/letters/letter-shocked-by-city-s-response-to-march-1-4040917 (Accessed 5th February 2014)

Roscoe Will (1994) 'How to Become a Berdache: Toward a Unified Analysis of Gender Diversity', in Herdt Gilbert (ed.) *Third Sex; Third Gender*. New York: Zone Books, pp. 329–372.

Roseneil Sasha (1995) *Disarming Patriarchy: Feminism and Political Action at Greenham*. Buckingham: Open University Press.

Rowbotham Sheila (1972) 'The Beginnings of Women's Liberation in Britain', in Wandor Michellene (ed.) *The Body Politic: Writings From the Women's Liberation Movement in Britain, 1969–72*. London: Stage One, pp. 91–102.

Rowbotham Sheila (1989) *The Past Is Before Us: Feminism in Action Since the 1960s*. London: Pandora.

Rowbotham Sheila (1992) *Women in Movement: Feminism and Social Action*. London: Routledge.

Rowbotham Sheila (1997) *A Century of Women: The History of Women in Britain and the United States*. London: Viking.

Rowbotham Sheila, Segal Lynne & Wainwright Hilary (2013) *Beyond the Fragments* (New Ed). Powys: Merlin Press.

Rowland Robyn & Klein Renate (1996) 'Radical Feminism: History, Politics, Action', in Bell Diane & Klein Renate (eds.) *Radically Speaking: Feminism Reclaimed*. London: Zed Books, pp. 9–37.

RTN Reclaim the Night (2011) www.reclaimthenight.org (Accessed 18th August 2011).

RTN Leeds (2013) http://reclaimthenightleeds.wordpress.com/ (Accessed 12th September 2013).

Rubin Gayle (1984) 'Thinking Sex: Notes for a Radical Theory of the Politics of Sexuality', in Vance Carole (ed.) *Pleasure and Danger*. New York: Routledge, pp. 267–319.

Rudolfsdottir Annadis G. & Jolliffe Rachel (2008) ' "I Don't Think People Really Talk About It That Much": Young Women Discuss Feminism', *Feminism & Psychology*, 18(2), pp. 268–274 [Online].

Rupp Leila J. & Taylor Verta (1999) 'Forging Feminist Identity in an International Movement: A Collective Identity Approach to Twentieth-Century Feminism', *Signs*, 24(2), pp. 363–386 [Online].

Russell Diana E.H. & Van de Ven Nicole (1976) *The Proceedings of the International Tribunal on Crimes Against Women*. California: Les Femmes.

Ryan Barbara (1992) *Feminism and the Women's Movement: Dynamics of Change in Social Movement Ideology and Activism*. London: Routledge.

Sanday Peggy Reeves (1996) 'Rape-Prone Versus Rape-Free Campus Cultures', *Violence Against Women*, 2(2), pp. 191–208 [Online].

Sandell Marie (2012) *The Rise of Women's International Activism: Identity and Sisterhood Between the World Wars*. London: I.B. Tauris.

Scarman Leslie George (1981) *The Brixton Disorders 10–12 April 1981: Report of an Inquiry*. London: HMSO.

Sebestyen Amanda (1977) 'Rape Rally Wrangle', *Spare Rib*, 62(September), pp. 27–28.

Sebestyen Amanda (ed.) (1988) *68, 78, 88: From Women's Liberation to Feminism*. Bridport: Prism Press.

Sebestyen Amanda (2009) *Forty Years of Women's Liberation*, Conference Presentation. London: The Women's Library, 17th October.

Segal Lynne (1987) *Is the Future Female? Troubled Thoughts on Contemporary Feminism*. London: Virago.

Segal Lynne (1989) 'Slow Change or No Change? Feminism, Socialism and the Problem of Men', *Feminist Review*, 31(Spring), pp. 5–21 [Online].

Segal Lynne (2005) *Why Feminism? Gender, Psychology, Politics*. Cambridge: Polity Press.

Segal Lynne (2013) 'Jam Today: Feminist Impacts and Transformations in the 1970s', in Black Lawrence, Pemberton Hugh & Thane Pat (eds.) *Reassessing 1970s Britain*. Manchester: Manchester University Press, pp. 149–166.

Setch Eve (2002) 'The Face of Metropolitan Feminism: The London Women's Liberation Workshop, 1969–79', *Twentieth Century British History*, 13(2), pp. 171–190 [Online].

Seven Revolutionary Feminists (1981) 'Why I'm a Revolutionary Feminist', *WIRES*, 9, pp. 5–8.

Shapiro Judith (1991) 'Transsexualism: Reflections on the Persistence of Gender and the Mutability of Sex', in Epstein Judith & Straub Kristina (eds.) *Body Guards*. London: Routledge, pp. 248–279.

Shiva Vandana (1989) *Staying Alive*. London: Zed Press.

Short Clare (1991) *Dear Clare: This Is What Women Feel About Page 3*. London: Radius.

Silbert Mimi & Pines Ayala (1982) 'Victimization of Street Prostitutes', *Victimology: An International Journal*, 7, pp. 122–133.

Smelser Neil (1962) *Theory of Collective Behaviour*. London: Routledge.

Smith Harold L. (ed.) (1990) *British Feminism in the 20th Century*. Massachusetts: University of Massachusetts Press.

Smyth Ailbhe (1995) 'Haystacks in My Mind or How to Stay SAFE (Sane, Angry and Feminist) in the 1990s', in Griffin Gabrielle (ed.) *Feminist Activism in the 1990s*. London: Taylor & Francis, pp. 192–206.

Snow David A., Soule Sarah A. & Kriesi Hanspeter (eds.) (2007) *The Blackwell Companion to Social Movements*. Oxford: Blackwell Publishing.

Soho Sixteen (1981) 'The Soho Sixteen & Reclaim the Night', in Feminist Anthology Collective (eds.) *No Turning Back: Writings From the Women's Liberation Movement, 1975–1980*. London: The Women's Press, pp. 221–223.

Solnit Rebecca (2000) *Wanderlust: A History of Walking*. London: Viking Penguin.

Solomons Mark (2011) 'Slowing Economy and Competition From Illegal Outlets Closing Brothels in Queensland', *The Courier Mail*, 30th September. [Online] http://www.theaustralian.com.au/news/hard-times-for-brothel-proprietors/story-e6frg6n6-1226152278163?nk= eee35d6e62fe2021a959fb1ef9949c0a (Accessed 11th January 2013)

SPC, Special Committee on Pornography and Prostitution (1985), Pornography and Prostitution in Canada 350.

Spivak Gayatri C. (1993) 'An Interview With Gayatri Chakravorty Spivak', in Danius Sara, Jonsson Stefan & Spivak Gayatri Chakravorty (eds.) *Boundary*, 20(2), (Summer), pp. 24–50.

Spivak Gayatri Chakravorty (2008) *Outside in the Teaching Machine*. London: Routledge.

SR
   *Spare Rib*, May 1976, Issue 46.
   *Spare Rib*, May 1977, Issue 58.
   *Spare Rib*, August 1977, Issue 61.
   *Spare Rib*, September 1977, Issue 62.
   *Spare Rib*, November 1977, Issue 64.
   *Spare Rib*, January 1978, Issue 66.
   *Spare Rib*, May 1978, Issue 70.

Stanko Elizabeth A. (1985) *Intimate Intrusions: Women's Experience of Male Violence*. London: Routledge.

Stanko Elizabeth A. (1990) *Everyday Violence: How Women and Men Experience Sexual and Physical Danger*. London: Pandora.

Stanko Elizabeth A. (1995) 'Challenging the Problem of Men's Individual Violence', in Newburn Tim & Stanko Elizabeth A. (eds.) *Just Boys Doing Business? Men, Masculinities and Crime*. London: Routledge, pp. 32–46.

Stanley Liz & Wise Sue (1983) *Breaking Out*. London: Routledge.

Startmeoff (2013) 'Shit We Don't Play: Class v. Gender', www.startmeoff.wordpress.com (Accessed 3rd April 2013).

Stone Sandy (1991) 'The Empire Strikes Back: A Posttranssexual Manifesto', in Epstein Julia & Straub Kristina (eds.) *Body Guards*. London: Routledge, pp. 280–304.

Strijbosch Margreet (2006) 'Legalised Prostitution: A Dying Trade', *Radio Netherlands Worldwide*, 31st October, http://www.rnw.nl/english/article/legalised-prostitution-dying-trade (Accessed 9th August 2014).

Stryker Susan (2008) *Transgender History*. Berkeley: Avalon Publishing.

Summerscale Kate (2012) *The Queen of Whale Quay*. London: Fourth Estate.

Sutton Jo & Hanmer Jalna (1984) 'The Early Days of Women's Aid', *Trouble and Strife*, 4, pp. 55–60.

Swan Jonathan (2012) 'Reclaim the Night to Bring 1000 out in Force', *Sydney Morning Herald*, 27th October, http://www.smh.com.au/national/reclaim-the-night-to-bring-1000-out-in-force-20121026-28az3.html        (Accessed 19th June 2013).

Sweeney Belinda (2004) 'Trans-Ending Women's Rights: The Politics of Trans-Inclusion in the Age of Gender', *Women's Studies International Forum*, 27, pp. 75–88 [Online].

Sweney Mark (2008) 'WI to Check Local Papers' Sex Ads', *The Guardian Online*, 25th November, http://www.theguardian.com/media/2008/nov/25/wi-local-papers-sex-ads (Accessed 15th December 2008).

Swift Carolyn F. & Ryan-Finn Kimberly (1995) 'Perpetrator Prevention: Stopping the Development of Sexually Abusive Behaviour', in F. Swift Carolyn (ed.) *Sexual Assault and Abuse: Sociocultural Context of Prevention*. New York: Haworth Press, pp. 13–44.

Tang Nain Gemma (1991) 'Black Women, Sexism and Racism: Black or Antiracist Feminism?' *Feminist Review*, 37(Spring), pp. 1–22 [Online].

Tarrow Sidney G. (2011) *Power in Movement: Social Movements and Contentious Politics* (3rd Ed). Cambridge: Cambridge University Press.

Taylor Verta (1989) 'Social Movement Continuity: The Women's Movement in Abeyance', *American Sociological Review*, 54(5), pp. 761–765.

Taylor Verta (1989b) 'Sisterhood, Solidarity and Modern Feminism' (Review Essay), *Gender & Society*, 3(2), pp. 277–286 [Online].

TBTN *Take Back the Night*, Online Archive, Launched 2001, http://www.takebackthenight.org/history.html (Accessed 7th December 2010).

Thane Pat (2013) 'Women and the 1970s: Towards Liberation?' in Black Lawrence, Pemberton Hugh & Thane Pat (eds.) *Reassessing 1970s Britain*. Manchester: Manchester University Press, pp. 167–186.

Thiara Ravi K. & Gill Aisha K. (eds.) (2010) *Violence Against Women in South Asian Communities: Issues for Policy and Practice*. London: Jessica Kingsley.

Thomas Colin J. & Bromley Rosemary D.F. (2000) 'City-Centre Revitalisation: Problems of Fragmentation and Fear in the Evening and Night-Time City', *Urban Studies*, 37(1403) [Online].

Tilly Charles (1978) *From Mobilisation to Revolution*. Massachusetts: Addison Wesley.

Topping Alexandra (2012) 'Feminists Hail Explosion in New Grassroots Groups', *The Guardian*, 9th April [Online].

Toynbee Polly (1977) 'Reclaim the Night', *The Guardian*, 14th November 1977, in Cohrane Kira (ed.) (2010) *Women of the Revolution: Forty Years of Feminism*. London: Guardian Books, pp. 49–55.

UK Feminista www.ukfeminista.org.uk (Accessed 12th June 2013).

Valentine Gill (1992) 'Images of Danger: Women's Sources of Information About the Spatial Distribution of Male Violence', *Area*, 24(1), pp. 22–29 [Online].

Van Aelst Peter & Walgrave Stefaan (2001) 'Who Is That Wo(man) in the Street? From the Normalisation of Protest to the Normalisation of the Protestor', *European Journal of Political Research*, 39, pp. 461–468 [Online].

Venkatesh M.R. (Undated) 'Chennai's Tryst With "Reclaim the Night"' *Deccan Herald Online*, http://www.deccanherald.com/content/40616/chennais-tryst-reclaim-night.html (Accessed 2nd May 2013).

Verloo Mieke (2005) 'Displacement and Empowerment: Reflections on the Council of Europe Approach to Gender Mainstreaming and Gender Equality', *Social Politics*, 12(3), pp. 344–366.

Wages for Housework (W4H) See: Crossroads Women's Centre, http://www.crossroadswomen.net/Crossroads%20Women%20what%20we%20do.htm (Accessed 22nd August 2013).

Walby Sylvia (1990) *Theorizing Patriarchy*. Oxford: Blackwell.

Walby Sylvia (2011) *The Future of Feminism*. Cambridge: Polity Press.

Walby Sylvia & Allen Jonathan (2004) *Domestic Violence, Sexual Assault and Stalking: Findings From the British Crime Survey*, Home Office Research Study 276. London: Home Office.

Walby Sylvia, Hay Alex & Soothill Keith (1983) 'The Social Construction of Rape', *Theory, Culture & Society*, 2(1), pp. 86–98.

Walker Rebecca (1995a) *To Be Real: Telling the Truth and Changing the Face of Feminism*. New York: Doubleday.

Walker Rebecca (1995b) 'Becoming the Third Wave', *Ms*, January–February, pp. 39–41.

Wall Derek (1999) *Earth First! and the Anti-Roads Movement: Radical Environmentalism and Comparative Social Movements*. London: Routledge.

Walter Natasha (2010) *Living Dolls: The Return of Sexism*. London: Virago.

Wandor Michelene (ed.) (1990) *Once a Feminist: Stories From a Generation*. London: Virago.

Weekes John (2013) 'Beyer: We Were Naïve Liberalising Prostitution', *The New Zealand Herald*, 7th April, http://www.nzherald.co.nz/nz/news/article.cfm?c_id=1&objectid=10875922 (Accessed 27th September 2014).

Weir Angela & Wilson Elizabeth (1984) 'The British Women's Movement', *New Left Review*, 148, pp. 74–103 [Online].

Weisberg Kelly D. (1985) *Children of the Night: A Study of Adolescent Prostitution*. Lexington, MA: Lexington Books.

Westmarland Nicole & Gangoli Geetanjali (eds.) (2011) *International Approaches to Rape*. Bristol: Policy Press.

Wheelwright Julie (1989) *Amazons and Military Maids*. London: Pandora.

Whelehan Imelda (2000) *Overloaded: Popular Culture and the Future of Feminism*. London: The Women's Press.

Whitbread Helena (2010) *The Secret Diaries of Miss Ann Lister*. New York: Hachette.

Whittier Nancy (1995) *Feminist Generations: The Persistence of the Radical Women's Movement*. Philadelphia: Temple University Press.

Whittier Nancy (2002) 'Meaning and Structure in Social Movements', in Meyer David S., Whittier Nancy & Robnett Belinda (2002) (eds.) *Social*

*Movements: Identity, Culture and the State*. Oxford: Oxford University Press, pp. 289–309.

Whittier Nancy (2003) 'Sustaining Commitment Among Radical Feminists', in Goodwin Jeff & Jasper James M. (eds.) *The Social Movements Reader: Cases and Concepts*. Oxford: Blackwell, pp. 103–116.

Whittle Stephen (2000) *The Transgender Debate*. Reading: Garnet.

Wieviorka Michel (2010) 'After New Social Movements', *Social Movement Studies*, 4(1), pp. 1–19 [Online].

*WIRES*, July 1977, Issue 36.

*WIRES*, September 1977, Issue 38.

*WIRES*, October 1977, Issue 40.

*WIRES*, November 1977, Issue 41.

*WIRES*, December 1977, Issue 42.

*WIRES*, January 1978, Issue 43.

*WIRES*, March 1978, Issue 47.

*WIRES*, Winter 1981, Issue 9.

Withers Deborah M. (2012) 'Women's Liberation, Relationships and the "Vicinity of Trauma"', *Oral History*, (Spring), pp. 79–88 [Online].

Wittig Monique (1992) *The Straight Mind and Other Essays*. New York: Harvester Wheatsheaf.

Woodward Kath & Woodward Sophie (2009) *Why Feminism Matters: Feminism Lost and Found*. Hampshire: Palgrave.

York Jessica, Leonard Diana, Liensol Corine, Chester Gail, Warrick Jane, Sebestyen Amanda, Henderson Rob and Pachachi Reema (1991) 'We Are the Feminists That Women Have Warned Us About', in Gunew Sneja (ed.) *A Reader in Feminist Knowledge*. London: Routledge, pp. 308–311.

Young Antonia (2001) *Women Who Become Men: Albanian Sworn Virgins*. London: Bloomsbury.

Younge Gary (2013) 'Open Season on Black Boys After a Verdict Like This', *The Guardian, Comment Is Free*, 14th July, http://www.theguardian.com/commentisfree/2013/jul/14/open-season-black-boys-verdict (Accessed 14th July 2013).

Yuval-Davis Nira (2006) 'Intersectionality and Feminist Politics', *European Journal of Women's Studies*, 13(3), pp. 193–209.

# Index

Printed and bound by CPI Group (UK) Ltd, Croydon, CR0 4YY